Head Start

in

Action

Head Start
in
Action

CLARA M. D. RILEY
Institute of Therapeutic Psychology
Formerly with Pepperdine College

FRANCES M. J. EPPS, Director
Delta Sigma Theta's Head Start
Formerly with Los Angeles City Schools

Parker Publishing Company, Inc.
West Nyack, N. Y.

dedicated to

dynamic

deltas

To the women of Delta Sigma Theta Sorority, Inc., whose public spirit and humane conscience made this Head Start Project, as well as other Projects throughout the country, possible.

foreword

Operation Head Start may prove to be one of the most effective mental health programs ever undertaken in the United States. Its objectives of bringing therapeutic educational experiences to poverty-stricken youngsters in their early formative years, and of utilizing support services—social, medical, nutritional, and psychological—to strengthen family life and provide a spirit of hope through education, concern, and opportunity—these goals are basic to the mental health of our nation.

That struggle is an inherent part of any growth process is sensitively portrayed by the authors, who in this book, *Head Start in Action,* have shared with us the frustrations and heartaches, as well as the rewards and joys, of dealing with governmental bureaucracy, alienated peoples, and communicating with cross-cultural communities.

The humanist and the skeptic alike will be grateful to the authors for their painstaking care and foresight in keeping adequate records so that the results of Head Start could be evaluated in an objective way. Growth toward school readiness, acceptance by the parents of the Head Start program, and the importance of securing competent teachers are well substantiated as cardinal principles.

Perhaps one of the reasons for the comparative success of Head Start is its focus upon the whole child—not only his physical, mental, emotional, and social self, but also the child as a part of his family, his community, and as a potential contributing citizen of these United States.

Head Start in Action is more than a record of one successful program; in its sensitive portrayal of the confrontation of a group of well-meaning individuals with the despair of poverty on one hand and government bureaucracy on the other, it is a contribution of inestimable value.

Professionals from the fields of psychology, speech, nutrition, social welfare, medicine, public health, communications, government, and public relations will profit from seeing the principles which they espouse being put into practice in the culture of poverty. The comprehensive bibliographies are of great value to the professional unused to working with the poor.

When the history of the War on Poverty is written, I am confident that one of the most successful battles will be known as Operation Head Start. I predict this book will become known as one of the most complete and exciting records of this great achievement.

I am pleased to have been associated with one of the writers, Clara Riley, and I commend the work of both authors.

Everett L. Shostrom
Institute of Therapeutic Psychology
Santa Ana, California

preface

HEAD START, a total preschool program for children of low income families, was conceived as a preventive measure to help eradicate poverty in the United States. Although federally funded, programs were organized and administered at the local level.

HEAD START IN ACTION tells the story of one of the first of these summer programs which was granted to Delta Sigma Theta, Inc., a nonprofit service organization, to serve 300 children in the heart of south central Los Angeles. Our book has four aspects that offer a unique contribution: First, an overview of what Head Start is; second, a detailed section on setting up a program; third, the program as it worked in actual practice; and fourth, the promise that Head Start offers as indicated by research.

Section I, *PROCEDURES,* details the legal, physical, and personnel requisites for establishing a program. We found particularly valuable the census data which gave us a background for understanding the people and the neighborhood in which we were to work.

Section II, *PROGRAM,* recounts the opening and operation of the session proper. Since a program emanates from the people who staff it, the chapters in this section are written from the point of view of the professionals—the teacher, nurse, pediatrician, social worker, language specialist, child development specialist, and coordinator. Specialists from the various disciplines contributed to parent education. Internally, the chapters give an account of our program, an evaluation or summary and implications for future programs.

Section III, *PROMISE,* is original research based on this Head Start project. It includes (1) an evaluation of the children's growth, (2) the development of a quick screening test, (3) teacher effectiveness and student growth, (4) a report of parents' attitudes and (5) the design for a model follow-up.

Of particular significance to workers new in the field of early childhood education or working with poverty groups are the Selected Bibliography and Film Guide in the Appendix.

acknowledgments

Grateful acknowledgment is made to the following individuals for their professional contributions:

Glyndon Riley, Ph.D., Director of the Speech and Hearing Clinic at Pepperdine College for his contributions to the chapter, "The Speech and Hearing Specialist."

Juanita Goodman, M.S.W., Social Worker for Los Angeles County, for her collaboration on the Chapter, "Social Worker."

Elizabeth McBroom, M.S.W., Professor of Social Work at the University of Southern California for her thesis on the disadvantaged child.

Dorothy Jenkins, M.Ed., Public Health Nurse for the Los Angeles City Schools, for her collaboration in Medical Services.

Milton Arnold, M.D., President of the Los Angeles County Academy of Pediatrics and Chairman for Project Head Start for his donation of medical services and ideas for all medical support services.

Helen M. Beard, Ph.D., Assistant Professor of Home Economics, California State College at Los Angeles, for making available the results of the research from her doctoral dissertation, "The Effects of Operation Head Start on School Readiness."

Rosalee Blau, M.A., National Consultant on Project Head Start and Director of Ocean Park Children's Center, Santa Monica, California, for her contribution to Parent Education and her ideas on standards for the teacher.

Jewel Graham, M.A., Home Economist, formerly with the Extension Service and presently a Homemaking Teacher for the Los Angeles City Schools for her contribution to Parent Education.

Mary Kramer, M.S., Assistant Professor of Home Economics, California State College at Los Angeles, and Dr. Dorothy Baker, Associate Professor of Home Economics, California State College at Long Beach, for their critical appraisal of the material concerning Nutrition.

Dr. Edward Zigler, Professor of Child Development and Psychology of Yale University, for his encouragement and permission to reproduce the Psychological Screening Procedure.

The entire staff, the children, and the families involved in Operation

Head Start, and whose participation made our program a reality.

The President and Congress of the United States, whose vision and courage made possible the legislation and funding of Operation Head Start as part of the War on Poverty.

To Lady Bird Johnson for her inspiration and sense of urgency in facilitating and avidly supporting Head Start Projects.

introduction

OPERATION HEAD START—AN OVERVIEW

Head Start is a unique, bold, and broadly conceived program designed to cope with one area of poverty. Poverty in itself is no new phenomenon; it has been with us in some form since the beginnings of recorded history. Nor are programs which are planned to alleviate poverty and its causes a particularly new innovation, having evolved through the concepts of neighbor-help-neighbor in agrarian societies, the almshouses of old, the "Lady Bountiful" concept of handing out preplanned aid deemed best for the poor, to the current concept of "do-it-yourself."

HOW HEAD START ATTACKS POVERTY

In the latter class, we find Head Start, which is a grass-roots movement by community groups (although financed by the federal government) to alleviate poverty through increasing educational opportunities for children. The unique feature, in this instance, is the involvement of the people themselves in the planning and execution of preschool programs and the development of latent leadership abilities among the people for whom the programs are designed. The latter aim is extremely significant as it holds substantial promise of a sustaining impetus to do something about the existing problems of poverty.

Head Start has captured the hearts and the imaginations of those persons concerned with the welfare of children and their development. It truly provides the proving ground for the oft-voiced concept, which has tended too often to be mere lip service, of dealing with the "whole child." Through Head Start, teachers, doctors, psychologists, social workers, and families are planning and concerting their efforts in a "package" for the true concern and development of the "whole child." For the first time, substantial numbers of children from economically and culturally disadvantaged homes have the opportunity to participate in a well-rounded program of preschool experiences. For the first time, the means are available not only to uncover the problems existent among children of limited opportunities, but to follow-through to alleviate them.

By helping children . . .

Head Start has contributed to the lives of the *children* whom it has served in a most significant way. This four-pronged approach of (1) Health and Nutrition, (2) Welfare, (3) Educational Readiness Activities, and (4) Parent Education, netted phenomenal changes in a short eight-week period. Generally, it has wrought elevation of health awareness and standards of healthful living, provided a more perceptive sense of give-and-take, increased verbal facility and articulation, fostered a friendly recognition of authority figures, developed an augmented sense of self-worth, and brought about a general widening of the purview of the child's world.

By including parents . . .

Parents' contributions to the Project in observations, planning, and participating in volunteer services have reaped harvests in terms of self-improvement. Through improved communication with the local school and agencies seeking to serve their children, and through increased understanding of their children and of their own parental roles, they were able to develop pride and motivation toward a new sense of responsibility.

By challenging the neighborhood . . .

The *neighborhood* accepted Head Start programs because its needs and its feelings were intricately woven into the plans for the program. Through the efforts of Neighborhood Adult Participation Agencies, (NAPA), much was achieved which becomes the permanent property of the neighborhood. Associating with professionals as co-workers bolstered the pride of neighborhood leaders in their own abilities to tackle their problems and to do something about them. Being part and parcel of the neighborhood, these neighborhood leaders were extremely perceptive of the needs of their neighborhoods and proved to be a valuable resource in helping us focus programs in the right direction.

By training youth . . .

The *Neighborhood Youth Corps* figured prominently in Head Start as program aides to custodial services, food services, clerical staff, gardeners, and other job designations. Most participants were unskilled, untrained school drop-outs. In redirecting and utilizing the services and the talents of these young people, Head Start, in many instances, provided the first meaningful work experience that these young people had enjoyed. Since they were mostly residents of the areas in which Head Start programs were in operation, this corps of 16- to 21-year-olds had a contribution to make in terms of community awareness and understanding. Having found acceptance in Head Start, even in view of their limited capabilities and often-misguided values, the aspirational levels for many were raised to the extent of a desire to seek further education, or to find satisfaction in a paid job. We do not intend to imply that miracles were wrought in one eight-week period, but we believe that the seeds of hope were planted. The finale can be written only when continual utilization of this pool of manpower is made a reality, and continuing recognition of their worth as individuals is accepted.

By employing professional teachers . . .

The *teachers* in Delta Sigma Theta Sorority's Head Start were all highly trained and experienced professionals, credentialed by the state. Naturally, they brought with them knowledge of early childhood education, child growth and development, and a wide range of skills and methodology.

Over-shadowing, by far, what these teachers brought to the Project was what they took away. Topping the list was an increased perceptiveness of the influences which contribute to the life of "Johnny Who Can't Read," and a heightened sense of their own leadership, through the role-image which they supply. They took back to their classrooms new understandings of the chasms separating the disadvantaged child from his more advantaged middle-class peer. They returned to their regular classrooms in the fall with renewed dedication, determined to serve the children with a new recognition of their worth, aware of the hopes entrusted to them for a better way of life.

By joining with the public schools . . .

Implications were inherent in Head Start evaluations which pointed toward the *school's* increased effectiveness in alleviating poverty through education. Programs at all levels geared to the TIME, the PLACE, the NEED, and the PEOPLE, should shape the focus of curriculum changes. As a result of Head Start experiences, an entirely different product will come to grade schools. Will the schools be ready to receive them? Only if they become fully cognizant of the true impact which continued and long term preschool programs will have on children's school readiness, and take a long hard look at the kindergarten curriculum and that of all the grades to follow. Nothing could be more disappointing than to have unleashed the floods of curiosity, interest and acceptance in young minds and then have them meet inadequate challenge or variety of experience in kindergarten.

Articulation between Head Start and kindergarten strikingly presents itself as a need deserving of consideration.

In programs of higher education, sensitivity training, adeptness in human relations, and reshaping attitudes must necessarily receive emphasis. Once these children, these people of limited educational, cultural, and economic opportunity, are imbued with their own worth, reflect a positive self-image possess the necessary leadership, skills and attitudes to function in twentieth century U.S.A., we will begin to see poverty diminishing.

WHAT WE DID THROUGH THE PROGRAM

Delta Sigma Theta's Head Start program served 300 children organized into 20 classes of 15 children each. Enough adults served in the program to provide a ratio of one adult to every five children. Staffing each room with a third person, a volunteer, (for there were no funds for hiring) was not easily achieved. While we had many wonderful participating and visiting parents, we did not get sufficient numbers on a continuing basis for firm scheduling. But, through the use of friends of various staff members, young neighborhood residents, and junior and senior high school volunteers, the desired ratio was usually achieved.

Providing health services . . .

All 300 children in the project were checked first by two full-time nurses. Before the doctor's examination, hemoglobin and urinalysis tests were made, TB tests were administered, and height, weight and vision were measured. Every child was given a complete physical examination by a physician. Afterwards parents were invited for conferences with the doctor regarding their children's health needs. In instances where parents did not come, medical social workers went into the homes to acquaint the parents with the doctor's findings. Through an agreement with the County Health Department in the neighborhood, the children were taken by volunteers to that office for their inoculations.

Securing psychological services . .

Through services from a local college, children were given psychological tests and special studies were made of their needs. These findings were helpful in both the placement of the children within groups, and in the development of programs that best met their particular needs. We had the services of a visiting child development consultant four days a week. She, in turn, enlisted the services of a teacher of special education who dealt further with several cases of neurologically handicapped children who were discovered. The consultant also recruited a speech pathologist and a team of speech therapists who tested each child for speech and worked on a weekly schedule of speech therapy and correction. Audiometry tests were administered by the same team.

Providing nutrition . . .

The *nutritional* aspects of the children's health were a primary concern. Each child was provided with a nutrition snack, consisting of milk, crackers, small sandwiches or fruit, on an informal basis upon arrival in the morning. This snack served as breakfast for many of the children. At noon, just before the AM sessions departed, and the PM sessions were arriving, all children were served a complete, hot, and nutritious lunch. Despite the 28 cent ceiling set in the budget, the children had an adequate balance of delicious and nutritious lunches.

Teaching the children . . .

Many enriching educational activities were provided in the classrooms, with the emphasis being on development of oral language and a positive self-image.

Puzzles, games, flannel board stories, books, music, art, rhythmic activities, listening posts and activities, opportunities for talk, talk, talk, visits by local policemen and firemen, are but a few of the ways we sought to implement the educational development of the children in Delta's Head Start. A balance of indoor and outdoor· activities was maintained, with sufficient wheel toys, climbing apparatus, play equipment, outdoor games, and other activities to bring a balance to the activities of the day. All activities emphatically fostered socialization and communication skills.

Implementing social welfare services . . .

Cognizant of the pull of environmental forces in the development of the child, Head Start wisely conceived of social workers, teachers, parents and home, working together for the welfare of the child. We had the part-time services of fourteen fully trained social workers and two full-time social work aides. They went into every home, seeking family information which could assist them in being of service to families and children. Contacts were made with existing service agencies which were already working with our families and attempts were made to work together.

Accounts were established with neighborhood merchants for the purchase of used or low-cost clothing and shoes for the children, to ensure that they would have the necessary clothing to wear to school. Social workers and aides picked up the children from home and took them to the store to shop for them. Late in the program another valuable service of the Neighborhood Adult Participation Program—a Clothes Closet—was made available to us. We were then able to go there and select clothing at no cost for children who needed them.

The social workers initiated a family night program at one of the local parks where a Question and Answer Forum helped families with their problems by providing them with the proper referral service. In the final stages of the Project, these same workers were able to report glowing and laudatory comments from the parents and the community concerning the values of Head Start to their children and to themselves.

Involving parents . . .

Parental involvement as a feature of Head Start programs was not easily secured. The manifold problems of survival often made parent participation difficult, if not impossible. Summer programs did not demand parent participation but suggested it as being desirable. While classroom and program involvement on the part of parents was not at a level that we desired, the planned Parent Education classes and workshops held once a week met with overwhelming success. Bus transportation for parents as well as children was provided on these days, which made attendance possible for a larger number of parents.

Meetings were held with the nurse, psychologist, and speech analyst in interpreting child growth and development as they related to the activities of the preschool program. Parents received these discussions enthusiastically and often got to the heart of their own problems with their children.

Other significant and well-attended meetings featured a home economist who worked with parents in planning low cost yet nutritious meals for their children. Sample menus and recipes were provided. Parents, with the help of the nutritionist, prepared sample meals and ate them with their children.

To evidence our concern for the play aspect of children's lives, we held a workshop in creative experiences for children. Parents were taught how to make homemade toys and playthings at no cost through the use of common things around the house. A teacher from a local college who was a part of preservice education conducted this session for us.

Taking trips . . .

Trips were made into the community to the neighborhood library, science center, museum, and health department. A complete family outing was arranged to Griffith Park Children's Zoo; bag lunches and bus transportation were provided for all and the Merry-Go-Round was rented for the exclusive use of Head Start children during the afternoon.

Some 500 persons participated along with the children in a Community Carnival held all day on a Saturday. The tykes and their parents got a taste of riding on the amusement rides as many times as their legs could hold up at no charge. Popcorn and cotton candy, games of chance, and all of those activities in the carnival world so exciting to children were a part of the day's festivities.

Some of our problems . . .

If these remarks appear glowing, it is by no means meant to imply that all was smooth sailing. The problems were many—checks that were held up in Washington with a payroll due and less than $2,000.00 in the bank; an office that would compete with Barnum and Bailey's Circus in atmosphere because of the numerous people coming and going; confusion and noise due to cramped quarters; schedules that did not mesh; activities which were curtailed mid-stream due to a doctor's visit, nurse's call, or something similar, despite planned appointments; shortages of dishes and silverware at lunch time; scorching sun in the lunch area and a quick attempt to change location before serving; government forms, forms, forms *ad infinitum*—these were only a few. But none of us regret the work it took as we reflect on the happy expressions of the children as they headed for home on the last day of Head Start with traces of ten giant birthday cakes on their faces, having had a "Happy Unbirthday" for every child. Each child clutched a book—a gift to remind him of a summer of new and exciting experiences. Everything became worthwhile when we considered the warm appreciation of the parents, the children's test scores which showed a growth in mental age of years and months in a six-week span, the improved speech on the part of the children, the discovery of health problems which may result in the saving of lives, and the increased social, emotional, and academic readiness of our children.

POSTSCRIPT

We are concerned about the future of Head Start programs. There is no question of the need; there is no question of the values; these have been proven. Will the spirit continue to manifest itself in continued national support? We found no one who could associate with Head Start in any way without feeling moved by the program and impelled to continue in some way to identify with it. It is this spirit which we hope will impel Congress to fund Head Start programs on a year-round basis throughout the nation so that all of America's boys and girls may be given the chance for equality of opportunity.

Delta Sigma Theta held an Evaluation Conference several weeks after the close of the summer program, at which time all of the workers on the project, selected visitors, and representatives of colleges and universities came together. We evaluated the summer program in terms of improving future Head Start programs and keeping them on a year-round basis.

table of contents

toms ∴ A model follow-up proposal based on the research
results ∴ Staffing of other professionals . Professional consultants on a part-time basis ∴ Summary

APPENDICES

Section I

PROCEDURES

1

securing the program

Opening the program

Forms went out to the printers, signs were made, classrooms set up, registration kits prepared, and we assured ourselves that every detail had been anticipated for the opening day of Head Start.

Satisfied in the thought that all was in readiness, we flung open the doors to Delta Sigma Theta's Head Start Project early on opening day. At the appointed hour, not even one registrant was waiting. The anticipated deluge did not materialize; it scarcely was a trickle. As the minutes developed into hours, our first real fears assailed us. Where had we been remiss in preplanning procedures? Had we not sent notices to the press and the P.T.A.? Did we not have signs all about announcing the opening of the program? Hadn't our speakers been effective in their church announcements? Where were these 300 children whom we were committed to serve?

The first children to arrive were a small group of ten who had been previously enrolled in a local church nursery program. They came accompanied by their teachers who tried to complete their registration papers and enroll them in Head Start. But there were too many gaps in their knowledge of the children's birth dates and family backgrounds, which were a necessary part of registration forms. Finally, the teachers either took the papers along with them to fill out at the homes of the children, or waited until the parents came to pick them up from the all-day church school.

At the end of our first full day of registration, we had less than 40 children. The second and third days came and went in the same manner, with only a few additional registrants. It became evident that we were in trouble unless we could somehow reach the people and the hundreds of potential kindergarteners whom we knew, by virtue of census data as well as observation, to be residing in the community. After a hasty conference with all personnel, Operation Crusade for Head Start Recruitment

3

was initiated. The Crusade gained momentum by the end of the first week as every teacher, teacher aide, social work aide, and other workers on the Project took to the sidewalks and rang every doorbell, seeking the preschool children. Incredulous, we discovered that the news about Head Start programs had *not* reached the people. Stranger yet to us was the necessity for some real salesmanship to convince the people of the true nature of the program . . . that it was available at no charge, and that enrolling their children could bring only benefits to them.

How poverty prevents school attendance

As we canvassed the blocks, we found many instances of home conditions and physical needs which prevented school attendance, such as lack of shoes or sweaters or other clothes good enough to wear to school—"I don't want her laughed at." In every way, we committed ourselves to getting these children into school—taking the registration papers to the homes, arranging transportation, giving direct assistance to families in dire need of clothing and shoes, or providing them with the necessary referral sources which could supply them. Once some of these immediate and absorbing problems were worked out with the homes, and we began to be trusted, the families seemed very willing and eager, in most instances, to have their children enrolled. (We are using the term *families* instead of *parents* because over half of our children were cared for either by only one parent or by some other relative, such as aunt or grandmother.)

Proving birth dates a problem

Birth certificates or other adequate verification of birth proved a deterrent to registration in many cases. It was surprising to discover the large number of children whose parents possessed no acceptable verification of children's ages. We acquainted these homes with the procedures for securing a valid birth certificate or affidavit to facilitate their child's enrollment in school. We see this service as being a valuable one rendered through Head Start. Lack of proof of age would have presented the same obstacle at the time of registration for kindergarten in the fall and might have delayed, or even prevented, a child's getting into school.

One aide on the project, who had spent a lifetime in doing political volunteer work, had knowledge of the Neighborhood Adult Participation Project (NAPP), another anti-poverty program functioning in our neighborhood. This contact proved to be the missing ingredient in our hasty and frantic recruitment of children, for NAPP had already canvassed the immediate neighborhood. They were able to turn over waiting lists from local schools which could not, at that point, accommodate sufficient numbers; they provided the names and addresses of homes with preschool children desiring to get into the program. More valuable yet, they provided the necessary "foot service" in walking out the blocks and helping to get children enrolled in our program.

Finally, through these combined efforts, we met our goal of 300 children. With this accomplished, we began to reflect on the beginnings of it all, how we became involved in this Head Start fever.

When we decided to apply for Head Start

A feverish excitement characterized Head Start from that moment in the spring when the local president of Delta, Mrs. Harriett Williams, read the letter of appeal from our national president, Dr. Geraldine P. Woods, urging locals to apply for Head Start programs.

The feeling was, "Here is a real service to be performed, one which provides a true challenge." An enthusiastic committee spent hours in outlining proposals and programs, planning, tossing ideas back and forth until we came up with a satisfactory proposal, and a totally unrealistic budget. (This we were to discover much later.) We went ahead with preplanning, even without official approval and funding, always with the thought that Head Start would be a reality. In a sense, this gave *us* a head start on site selection, procurement of staff, and the multiplicity of other considerations which preceded the actual beginnings of the program.

We drew up a list of "to do's" which included:

1. Selecting a site.
2. Surveying the facilities, and listing of physical needs.
3. Making supply orders and requisitions of needs.
4. Securing welfare license; health and fire department permits.
5. Seeking insurance, workmen's compensation and Social Security permits.
6. Planning publicity releases to radio, television, and the local paper.
7. Enlisting volunteers from the sorority, colleges and churches.
8. Arranging for a special in-service training program at U.C.L.A.
9. Establishing recruitment and canvassing procedures through school contacts, churches, and local stores.
10. Developing curriculum and program by working with the teachers.
11. Securing library books and services from the local public library.
12. Contacting Goodwill Industries, Salvation Army, and used supply and toy stores for purchase of consumable and non-consumable supplies and equipment.
13. Scheduling planned talks in churches and community to share our plans.
14. Requesting Neighborhood Youth Corps participation from the local Office of Economic Opportunity.
15. Interviewing and selecting staff.
16. Procuring surplus foods and milk from the government.

17. Contacting doctors and laboratories for medical services.
18. Arranging with Toy Loan for use of toys.

Through weeks of waiting amid local problems, the planning went on.

The red tape that preceded the grant

This section details the steps in formulating the proposal from its inception until the time that the grant was officially received. We are including this information because we had no idea at that time of the formalities associated with having a Head Start and as time went on we were often overwhelmed.

Meeting with Officials from Governor's Office

The Governor's Office was very helpful once we made contact. This initial contact with a representative of the Governor's Office proved fruitful in terms of guidelines which were to shape the proposal. The meeting took place early in April, at which time the representative announced that the deadline for submission of the proposal was April 15! He suggested that we include specifics in writing the proposal, which proved most helpful to us in formulating the final proposal. Those were:

1. The proposal must be submitted through the "Umbrella" or Community Action Agency. This was, at the time, the Youth Opportunities Board. (How soon could we get an appointment?)
2. The proposal should be clear and free of journalistic jargon. (This seemed simple enough.)
3. The plan should be developed in essay, not outline form. (Who could write it?)
4. Due consideration should be given to planning the budget so that all areas were covered and figures were in line with "going rates." (How were we to find out what "going rates" were?)

A series of working meetings preceded the formulation of a satisfactory proposal, the next step along the road to securing a Head Start grant. The Coordinator (the term for the director at that time) found it practicable to delegate portions of the proposal to specialists in the various categories for development of the several facets of the program. *Social workers* developed a plan for working with the home in relating the needs of the child, and in practical implementation of fulfilling the needs of the child and his family. A *school nurse* and a public health nurse developed specifics for the health component. The aims and scope of the educational activities which were designed to aid school readiness represented the pooled thinking of a group of *teachers*. In several subsequent sessions, all ideas were mulled and merged into what we considered to be a reasonable proposal.

Meeting with Community Action Agency

Guidelines submitted by the county schools were helpful in arriving at the next step, the Youth Opportunities Board (YOB). A conference was held with the Program Planning Specialist for Head Start Programs to review the proposal. This meeting turned out to be primarily a job of selling YOB on the ability of our agency by presenting proof of it's qualifications and capabilities to perform. What they wanted to know was, "Who are the Deltas?" Did we have the manpower and leadership to perform adequately? Were we a non-profit organization with a reputation for fiscal responsibility? Could we rewrite the proposal including the answers to these questions?

Submitting the Proposal

After more committee meetings to incorporate the suggestions of YOB, we came to the final step of submitting the proposal. Then came the long restless wait for a hearing. At the hearing our proposal was accepted by the Community Agency for screening along with all other proposals, leaving us relieved but feeling somewhat anonymous. The local community agency submitted the "package" of proposals to Washington, and our long wait for federal approval began.

In the meantime, the days stretched into weeks, and the weeks into months, before we were assured that a grant was imminent. How did we find out that we were approved? Not by the telegram we expected but through a newspaper release announcing acceptance of the proposals for the entire county. Listed down among the fine print was our name, Delta Sigma Theta. Disappointingly, the announced budget was $10,000 less than the requested budget. We had to meet immediately to re-evaluate the requested budget in terms of what items were defensible and which were expendable, as well as to ferret out any unrealistic budget items in the waiting interim. These activities kept us too busy to worry while we waited for the call which finally came requesting us to appear for a budget hearing. (We would like to say that all of us—from Coordinator to committees, were working full time in other jobs all during the preparatory time.)

The Budget Hearing

It was small solace to find that all sponsors of pending proposals were also waiting to be heard. The time came and went as each agency presented "its story" in turn. When our appointment came, we discovered that fears which accompanied meeting a "Budget Man from Washington" were unfounded. The hearing was relaxed and easy as we were asked to explain the need for money in the various areas. We learned the lesson well that a realistic approach, founded on research into the community and facilities, going rates for services, accurate presentation of contracted services and costs, and realistic per diem costs, are the best defense to offer a "Budget Man from Washington." A revised budget was developed in the course of the hearing which netted us restitution of the curtailed $10,000 as well as an additional sum which "The Man" thought would more realistically represent the amount which it would take to do effectively the job we had set forth.

Understanding the community

Head Start was now a possibility—at least there was the money to do the job. But what about the myriad details which we must consider before opening day?

Getting Acquainted with the Neighborhood

Confirmation and interpretation of 1960 census data clearly delineated nine major areas of poverty in Los Angeles County. These areas had large populations (75,000 to 100,000 persons), with one-fourth or more of the families having incomes below $4,000. They were mapped as *target areas,* to be given priority in the war on poverty. Our poverty area was in the south central area—the heart of the city! If we were to adequately serve our target area, we felt we needed to find out more about it. We visited the County Department of Community Services to find out essential facts which would describe our area and help us understand its essential quality.

A Look at the Central City

We were appalled to read there of the *extent* of poverty, unemployment and ignorance: "In 1960 . . . over 40 per cent of the families had incomes below $4,000 level. This rate is more than twice that of the county as a whole. Unemployment rates among males over 14 ranged upwards from 9 per cent to almost 30 per cent. The county rate was 5.7 per cent.

"About 50 per cent of the total Negro population and 25 per cent of the people with Spanish surnames in the county lived within the seven central areas. To put it a different way, about 70 per cent of all residents of these areas were either Negro or Mexican-American and the proportion was growing steadily. . . .

"Problems of poor health, low educational attainment, unemployment, crime, dependency, and delinquency are greatly intensified here."

Census Tract Data: Extent of Poverty

Delta Sigma Theta's Head Start was located in the section of Los Angeles County designated as *Avalon.* The Avalon area was comprised of 13 census tracts covering 3.4 square miles. Negroes predominated in the area and were living largely in poverty—the poverty extent running from 40 to 58 per cent from tract to tract.

Income

Five census tracts showed median incomes below the $4,000 level set for poverty. In all cases, the median income for the area was considerably lower than the county median of $7,046. Population and income levels as provided to us by the Census Bureau are shown in Table I.

A prevalence of all the concomitant indices of poverty were apparent— low median education, high percentage of unskilled labor, high percentage of deterioration and dilapidation of housing, and high mobility rates.

We found the educational level of a community to be an accurate predictor of the income of its inhabitants. A low level of education is indicative of the number of semi-skilled and unskilled workers found. Table II reveals the disproportionately high percentage of unskilled and semi-skilled labor in the Avalon Area. In some census tracts it ran as high as 91.6 per cent. By contrast, the average for the county as a whole was 59.5 per cent. This was the community, these were the people we were committed to serve.

Housing and Mobility

Table III shows the age and condition of housing and degrees of mobility in the Avalon Area. The percentages of renter-occupied houses ranged from 56.8 per cent to 75.9 per cent. The average for the city was 50.3 percent and for the county, 42.6 per cent. This percentage is a further indication of the non-permanency of the roots of these families of poverty.

All of these factors we considered as contributory to the meager backgrounds, inadequate social intellectual growth, and the insecurity and doubts of self-worth of the children we wished to enroll in Project Head Start.

Percentage of Children

The children were there waiting for us. Table IV shows the percentage of preschoolers in the total population, by census tracts. Thousands of little children growing up without opportunity.

Mobility

Oddly, while there was considerable mobility of population in the area, it was still below the two-year mobility averages for the City and County of Los Angeles. It was also low when compared with national averages which show a 17 per cent mobility in one year. However, of this 17 per cent of families who move nationally, 12 per cent move within the county, and 3 per cent move to another state. Most of the in-county moves are attributed to class mobility, with relatively free mobility from class to class.

Conversely, the mobility in our area did not represent a change for the better. Those of us who teach have noted in the cumulative records of children in elementary schools in the area that large numbers of children change schools as many as ten or more times between kindergarten and sixth grade. *All of these moves seem to follow a rotating cycle of neighboring schools within the same poverty area.* Their mobility is primarily horizontal with no improvement in housing or socio-economic status. This pattern strongly suggests that the range of their boundaries have been predetermined by their limited financial means. They move, therefore, from one low-cost housing area to another, strangled within the boundaries of poverty.

What we came to understand about mobility

The deleterious effects of repeated family moves on the stability of children and their school readiness cannot be underestimated. In his book, *Love and Conflict,* Gibson Winter draws a striking analogy between the roots of a plant and the effects of mobility on children. He states that a plant which is properly planted, nurtured, and allowed to remain in one spot develops strong, steady roots which go deeper and deeper into the ground fostering anchorage and leverage. On the other hand, the plant that is constantly uprooted and replanted produces many short roots which penetrate only the upper layers of the soil. Plants of this nature cannot withstand the vicissitudes of nature.

Similarly, children who are uprooted lack a sense of security and belongingness which are basic to their acceptance of formalized education, rules for orderly conduct of life, and a sense of "community."

Table I

POPULATION AND INCOME LEVELS OF AVALON AREA

Census Tract	Size	Density	1965 Population	Total # Families	# Families Earning Under $4000	% Poverty	Median Income
2281	0.36	10,789	3884	973	560	57.5	$3603
2282	0.29	17,490	5072	1286	594	46.1	4203
2283	0.33	16,076	5305	1292	638	49.3	4060
2284	0.29	19,634	5694	1286	595	46.2	4265
2285	0.17	17,512	2977	728	291	39.9	4575
2286	0.20	14,990	2998	713	295	41.3	4701
2287	0.30	19,597	5879	1350	671	49.7	4022
2288	0.31	12,539	3887	861	476	55.2	3608
2289	0.20	14,845	2969	654	361	55.1	3500
2291	0.19	14,642	2782	693	379	54.6	3622
2292	0.16	17,988	2878	702	377	53.7	3842
2293	0.18	17,272	3109	830	343	41.3	4436
2294	0.43	12,121	5212	1183	568	48.0	4156
County Average						19.1%	$7046

Table II

EDUCATIONAL LEVEL OF MAJORITY RACES

Avalon Area

Census Tract	Median Education	% Negro	Median Negro Education	% Mexican-American	Median Mexican-American Education	% Unskilled & Semi-skilled Labor	% Skilled Labor
2281	8.4	87.4	8.4	8.7	—	85.1	11.1
2282	9.0	98.9	9.1	0.4	—	85.9	8.4
2283	9.0	96.9	9.0	0.9	—	86.7	8.7
2284	8.7	90.1	8.8	3.7	—	87.6	8.4
2285	8.9	96.2	9.0	2.3	—	79.9	12.5
2286	9.2	97.5	9.2	0.2	—	81.5	7.9
2287	9.0	96.4	9.1	0.9	—	86.6	7.5
2288	9.3	97.3	9.3	1.9	—	84.8	10.5
2289	8.9	89.0	9.4	9.5	—	91.6	5.6
2291	9.5	97.6	9.7	0.8	—	84.1	10.6
2292	9.9	97.8	9.9	—	—	90.1	7.5
2293	8.7	93.2	8.7	2.0	—	82.2	7.9
2294	9.1	94.5	9.2	1.9	—	85.0	8.1
County Average						59.5%	14.9%

Table III

HOUSING AND MOBILITY PATTERN, AVALON, 1960

Census Tract	% Renter Occupancy	% Deterioration & Dilap- idated	# Single Dwellings	Total Dwellings	2-yr. Mobility	% Divorced & Separated	% Male Unemployed in 1960
2281	65.0	32.8	1028	1325	37.6%	15.3	18.2
2282	66.0	18.7	1664	1898	35.9%	19.8	8.6
2283	67.6	26.0	1257	1931	37.7%	19.6	11.0
2284	72.8	17.7	1374	2072	38.7%	20.1	11.9
2285	66.3	18.0	833	1199	32.1%	20.7	16.0
2286	69.3	24.1	698	1222	37.0%	21.3	11.0
2287	66.0	29.9	1577	2052	37.0%	19.6	12.8
2288	64.4	21.7	665	1070	36.9%	17.6	15.1
2289	75.9	17.2	547	793	34.2%	19.3	12.2
2291	56.8	33.0	900	937	37.3%	13.5	9.9
2292	68.3	22.8	884	1084	30.7%	18.9	15.1
2293	70.9	2.1	997	1244	24.1%	15.1	6.6
2294	64.0	11.7	1489	1930	33.2%	18.3	9.4
L.A. City Average	50.3	8.8			42.4%	8.5	6.7
(non-white)						13.5	
L.A. County Average	42.6	7.9			41.5%	7.1	5.7
(non-white)						12.3	

Table IV

PERCENTAGE OF AVALON FOUR AND FIVE YEAR OLDS IN TOTAL POPULATION

Census Tract	Total Population	Number of 4 & 5 year olds	Percentage of total Population
2281	3884	212	5.2
2282	5072	193	3.8
2283	5305	240	4.6
2284	5694	231	4.0
2285	2977	105	3.5
2286	2998	100	3.4
2287	5879	258	3.9
2288	3887	230	6.0
2289	2969	236	7.7
2291	2782	139	4.8
2292	2878	125	4.4
2293	2109	128	4.1
2294	5212	257	4.8
Total		2454	

2

furnishing the facility

Social welfare requirements

Fortunately for us, Head Start occurred during summer months when the buildings which we selected had only limited use. We were able to effect a contractual arrangement for the rental of three buildings; two of which were adjacent on the same lot, with the third approximately three-fourths of a block down the street.

With the grant awarded, and a very desirable program site contracted for, we felt that the major obstacles were out of the way. As steps in the licensing procedure for the facility were undertaken we soon discovered that the end was not imminent. We had labored under the impression that a building already licensed for school purposes would be adequate for the operation of a preschool program. We learned that the California State Department of Social Welfare, like most states and counties, had definite rules and regulations for the licensing and operation of preschool and nursery programs. Licenses are issued for a specific place and to a specific person or corporation. Thus, even though the buildings which we were to occupy had been previously licensed for nursery school purposes, we, as the seeking parties, had to request a new license. Licenses were not transferable!

More legal technicalities

A letter from the Chief Licensing Section of the Department of Social Welfare jolted us into realizing how much remained to be done.

Fingerprint cards were required of the director. All persons who were to work in the program directly with the children needed chest X-rays or had to submit proof of a recent X-ray. A detailed application form for operation of the program, including diagrams of the building and yard design, were requested. As soon as these requirements were accomplished, we sought an early appointment and interview with the agency representative of the Social Welfare Department. They specifically requested that the Coordinator or someone *responsible* for the program be present to discuss details on program.

The interview

At the interview with the representative of the State Department of Social Welfare we were queried about our overall plans for the program, phasing-in procedures, and scheduling, description and diagram of physical plant and arrangements (we had to produce a diagram of the building floor plan), educational standards for teachers, financial management plans, our intent to adhere to regulations of Safety and Building Codes in regard to the degree of occupancy, and adult/pupil ratio for the program. California State Department of Social Welfare approval required one adult for every ten children; Head Start guidelines specified one to five.

The Fire Marshall

Compliance with these suggestions still did not clear the way for immediate licensing. A license could not be issued until there was a clearance by the State Fire Marshall and the County Health Department of our intentions to operate a nursery program. Some counties require business licenses, though this was not necessary for the County of Los Angeles.

We strongly urge that persons seeking licenses to operate Head Start programs find out through their County and State Welfare Departments the procedures applicable to their particular states well in advance of plans for opening the facilities, as it is most disconcerting to find out piecemeal as we did.

In complying with the fire inspection requirement, we faced disappointment. Inspection by the State Fire Marshall permitted occupancy of the site by only 230 children. With our O.E.O. contract specifying that we serve 300 children, this obstacle seemed an insurmountable setback at this stage. The only solution seemed to be to reorganize and schedule double sessions—150 children in AM classes and 150 children in PM classes.

Lastly, the use of the parking lots as an auxiliary play area to meet the standard of 75 square feet per child was permissible only if temporary fencing or barriers were erected to block all entrances. The supervision ratio when the parking lot area was used as a play area was specifically noted as one adult for every five children.

Finally, the license was approved with certain conditions. Only those children who had met preadmission health requirements could share facilities with the existing nursery program in one of the three buildings which we were to occupy. The number of children whom we could house in the shared facility was dependent upon the number of children being served in the existing program. The total number was not to exceed the licensed capacity of 230. There had to be a guarantee that the Head Start program was to be conducted in such a manner that it would not interfere with the existing program (i.e., free from noise during nap time, scheduling to prevent crowding, and so forth).

Survey of physical facilities

Although the plant selected was new and modern in its design, a survey of physical facilities netted a lengthy list of things to do, items to purchase, and adjustments to be made in adapting the equipment and materials to a preschool program. The classrooms all had adequate floor space to accommodate the requirement of 35 square feet per child. Housed in them was considerable furniture such as desks, side armchairs, and tables that were either too large or too small and had no function in our program. No rugs or mats were available for rest or quiet activities. Play materials in sufficient variety and quantity were lacking, as well as items for food service. There were no scales or cots for the health office. There was insufficient office equipment, and a shortage of storage areas for children's belongings, supplies, and materials.

On the positive side, the building met nursery school building requirements in some ways. The rooms were light and airy, as the windows were at a height and of a size which allowed maximum light, sunshine and ventilation. The indoor play space was large enough to accommodate all of the children and the variety of interest centers peculiar to such a program. Space was sufficient to permit scheduling of different types of play activities at the same time and yet remain free of interference from other areas. Two rooms were over-sized, lending themselves to either one group or two groups, depending on the nature of their activities. An accordion-type wall made it possible to separate the room into two parts, thus accommodating two groups simultaneously.

Toilet, drinking and handwashing facilities were conveniently located for easy access from both indoor and outdoor areas. There were toilets and basins in sufficient numbers to satisfy the requirements for the proper height and size for the preschool children. The kitchen was modernly equipped with stainless steel sinks and space for ample refrigeration and storage.

Legal considerations

We point out here, as a matter of procedural interest, other considerations which were necessary before the path was cleared for operation: (1) arrangements for Social Security through the Department of Internal Revenue, (2) workmen's compensation and insurance through private agencies, and (3) a comprehensive liability policy to cover all areas of the project's operation. We found that having a good, trusted insurance agent who could handle all areas of insurance was a tremendous asset, for he saved us money, time, and the bother of all the details which were rather foreign to us.

Supplies and equipment

It has been pointed out that, since our three buildings were designed for school purposes, the minimal basic requirements were there as a beginning point, so we did not have many of the problems encountered by many other programs which were housed in store fronts, churches, or basements. However, many adaptations and improvisations were necessary to make the classrooms functional.

Most of the rooms were equipped with armchair type desks, numerous small square tables measuring approximately 18 square inches, and chairs and tables adjusted to a height for elementary school age children. Some rooms had no bulletin boards, storage closets or permanent bookshelves. The creativity and ingenuity of the teachers was tested in their ability to bring into shape an effective and functional environment in the *one brief weekend* between the closing session of the regular day school and the opening of our program.

Tables and chairs

Much of the excess furniture was removed and stored in an extra class-room in order to leave ample open floor space. Tables and chairs were adjusted to the necessary height for the age group. Tables of the right size for centers of interest, display and work areas in each classroom were devised through assembling clusters of four of the small 18-inch tables. Additional used chairs of ten-inch height were purchased at a school supply house at considerable savings from what the new price would have been. In one classroom, mothers contributed trading stamps to purchase a child-size bridge set of table and folding chairs to supplement what was available.

Floor mats

Old rugs and blankets from home, covered with rubber sheeting or plastic became floor mats and rest pads. Another effective sitting device was the "Sit-Upon," a square mat woven from strips of newspaper and shellacked. A full double spread of newspaper was folded lengthwise into strips of approximately three inches. Fourteen of these strips were used, placing seven in each direction and woven firmly together. Every other edge was tucked from alternating sides, and painted or shellacked. The shellac served to strengthen the mat and thus lengthen its life. Bright colors of spray paints enhanced their attractiveness. Resourceful teachers made the rounds of carpet and rug firms and secured scraps and samples of carpeting to use as mats also.

Storage

Necessity dictated that storage be handled in many inventive ways by various teachers. Large numbers of adult-size folding chairs were available. Rows of these served as room dividers in some large classrooms and doubled as storage "LOCKERS" for the children's wraps and belongings. Each chair was labeled with the children's names on colored strips of paper. As the program developed, the chairs served also as a place for the children's finished paintings, clay, individual plants, or whatever was to be taken home with them at the end of the day.

Several old wooden-type folding *screens* were found in someone's garage. These screens were used to corner off certain sections of the room for STORAGE behind them. The fronts of the screens made desirable BULLETIN BOARDS for grouping children's art work or display of teacher material. One teacher brightened the atmosphere of her room through the application of discarded strips of wallpaper to the panels of the folding screens.

Bricks standing on end with *planks* across them made effective BOOK-SHELVES and STORAGE UNITS. Apple and orange crates stacked in clusters and secured with plastic string to keep them from toppling, doubled for storage in one situation, or, separated, for outdoor building activities in another.

Peg boards with hooks provided hanging places for children's clothing, painting aprons, "dress up" clothing for dramatic activities, or for drying paintings.

The *second-hand furniture stores* of the neighborhood were the favorite haunts of some teachers as they ferreted out many useful items which could be converted to STORAGE at small cost. An old-fashioned cane-back chair uncovered in one of the "hunts" into second hand stores became the delight of one classroom. It was brightly redecorated and became the "BIRTHDAY CHAIR," to be occupied by a child on his birthday. A can of spray paint and some brightly colored knobs did wonders in transforming old bookcases, dresser bases, dressing tables and mirrors to cheery, functional pieces.

The play house

A room which was already equipped with a professionally made play house corner—constructed so as to be collapsible and adjustable in size, with swinging door, shutters, and all the trimmings—was the envy of all. A bit of ingenuity and resourcefulness, coupled with an odd assortment of boxes, packing crates, and scrap lumber provided the other rooms with equally effective, and certainly no less enjoyable, play houses for the children's use.

A large refrigerator crate, when painted and cut out, became a house itself, or alternately a closet for clothing in the playhouse, a puppet theater, or a children's stage. Various sizes of *packing boxes* were painted white, doors cut out, and burners painted on for stoves, or knobs glued on for refrigerators. Wooden *Coca-Cola* boxes with their pigeon holes served effectively as storage units for kitchen utensils and "food" in the play house. A most ingenious *sink* (sans water) was created through the use of two boxes, one large and one small. A hole was cut in the top of the larger box and the smaller box was recessed into the opening. A bit of doweling for handles and a discarded piece of rubber hosing was added for a final touch of authenticity.

One play house was formed with a series of *orange crates* with the open ends facing inside, in a corner of the room. Strips of heavy corrugated paper were stapled tautly around the framework of boxes enclosing the corner. The exposed insides of the crates were then conveniently employed as storage units for the play house equipment.

Free and inexpensive materials . . .

The following items were free or inexpensive to obtain and proved to be very effective in the program. In improvising with such common items we were able to save precious budget dollars for other items:

Bulletin board, easel, or paint-drying rack—Large pieces of chipboard (24" x 36") hinged teepee fashion.
Drums—Coffee cans with plastic tops; plastic bleach containers.
Dramatic play toys—Scraps of lumber sanded for safety with a notch here and there.
Saw horses for construction—Lumber scraps.
T.V. Screens—Boxes with the front cut out for picture, and rollers top and bottom to roll the pictures.
Indoor garden—In the base of a barrel-like rim from a packing crate.

And so, from lumber scraps, second-hand stores, storage rooms and attics came the raw material which, coupled with the inventiveness and enthusiasm of a group of dedicated teachers, became the basis for the children's activities.

Our reference book for classroom furnishings

A useful reference book which was helpful in furnishing the facilities was *Good Schools for Young Children* by Sarah Lou Hammond, et al. (1964).

Toys and equipment

How to acquire these toys and equipment in sufficient quantity for 20 classrooms presented a problem. There was limited budget consideration for toys and no provision for large outdoor playground items and equipment of a permanent nature.

Delta Sigma Theta Sorority held a toy shower for its members and friends. Each person attending donated a toy. Through this means many new toys, as well as old, usable toys, were secured. Repairing old, usable toys not only added to the stock of necessary materials for the program, but also provided work experience for Neighborhood Youth Corp participants in the program as well as an opportunity for parent involvement.

Another resource uncovered in our explorations was the County Toy Loan Service of Los Angeles County. This organization lends toys to qualified organizations in much the same way as a library. Our request to them for a loan of wheel toys for the duration of the program was answered with three tricycles, three sidewalk autos, three wagons, one scooter, one rocking horse and an assortment of twenty small manipulative toys.

The only major company to answer the appeal of Head Start was Mattel, the manufacturers of a national toy line. Their donation of large wagons, bicycles, trucks, dolls, puppets, puzzles, and games was the largest single donation and greatly appreciated.

Flannel board figures, inlaid puzzles, accessory material for dramatic representation and playhouse activities, play housekeeping units, educational toys, art supplies, balls, records and other audio-visual aids were purchased through the budget allotted for these items. Solid floor blocks and hollow outdoor blocks were rented for the duration of the program from School Days Equipment Company.

So it was we became beggars that we might better serve our children. We ransacked second-hand stores, gave toy showers, repaired donated items, borrowed from Toy Loan and solicited from toy manufacturing companies, rented large equipment, and bought what we could not beg or borrow. A major contribution to the preparation and utilization of sufficient and suitable equipment was the ingenuity of the professional teaching staff. Once again we were reminded that PEOPLE are the most important ingredients in preparing a program.

Medical supplies

First aid kits and medical supplies were purchased immediately, for the safety of the children is always a first consideration in any program. Standard first aid kits were equipped for office use and for transportation purposes to be taken on field trips.

Clinical thermometers, tongue depressors, rolls of sterile paper for use on examining tables, cotton, gauze, and petroleum jelly constituted other medical supplies needed.

Laboratory Materials were supplied by Bio-Science Laboratories, the lab we subcontracted with to do our lab work. Kits came fully prepared with bottles prelabeled for urinalysis and hemoglobin. P.B.D. Tine Tests for tuberculosis also came in kits in units for individual use.

An Eye Chart was already in our possession, having been previously purchased for use in a remedial reading program.

Dental Supplies were brought along by the dentist, Doctor Fields. He donated all the materials necessary as well as his time. His generosity was typical of the support we received from the medical profession.

Clerical supplies

Enormous quantities of ditto and mimeograph supplies were consumed during the program. Every notice, every bulletin, required a minimum of approximately 300 sheets of paper. We found that we had not adequately planned for the amounts of clerical supplies that we would need for a government-funded program. It became necessary to set up a complete office with provisions for ditto, mimeograph, record keeping, and book-keeping services.

It is well to plan amply for these supplies in budgets. A beginning shopping list should include:

1. Letterhead bond paper
2. Onionskin paper
3. Mimeograph and ditto bond in 8½ x 11, 8½ x 13, and 8½ x 14
4. Dry mimeograph stencils
5. Duplicator carbon
6. Office pencils and pens
7. Felt tip markers
8. Staplers and staples
9. Paper clips
10. File folders of differing cuts and sizes
11. Dater stamps
12. Envelopes
13. Manila envelopes
14. Cross-cut manila envelopes for identification files
15. Typewriter ribbons
16. Rulers
17. Rubber bands

No funds were available for the purchase of *office equipment;* consequently, typewriters, ditto and mimeograph machines were rented. In future programs which may operate over a longer period of time it would appear to us to be more economical to rent with an option to buy as rental fees easily exceed the purchase price in a few months.

Food supplies and equipment

The provision of an adequate nutritional program was anticipated as one of the biggest problems in our Head Start operation. Our experience with elementary school cafeteria price lists and practices had pointed up the inadequacy of even a 35¢ charge then allotted for student lunches. A large number of local elementary school cafeterias were either operating at a deficit or were forced to ease opeartions for failure to be self-sustaining. Here we were being asked to provide a hot lunch *and* a nutritional snack daily at a total cost of 28¢.

A Surplus Food contact with the local State Department of Surplus Commodities was a bonanza! An initial telephone call, with subsequent written follow-up, established our program needs and eligibility to receive surplus commodities.

Surplus commodities with a fair value of approximately $200.00 were consigned to our Project. We were responsible for payment of shipping charges of $24.75 and for picking up the commodities at the freight depot. For this we rented a truck for $20.00.

These items of cheddar cheese, butter, bulgur, cornmeal, flour, rice, rolled wheat, lard, dry packaged milk, dry pinto beans, and dry split peas, meant considerable relief for our food budget. In the hands of a skilled cook, many innovative and nutritious menus were developed through combining these goods with other purchased items. (It is assumed that most states have comparable agencies which may provide surplus foods. California residents may apply through the State of California, State Educational Agency for Surplus Property, 721 Capitol Mall, Sacramento, California 95814).

Our *Milk Program* expense was lessened by securing milk from the School Lunch Program through the State Department of Education. We signed a simple agreement stipulating the dates of the program, the number of days on which milk would be served, the number of programs included in the report, and an agreement to meet all the terms and conditions of the Special Milk Program. Milk was purchased through local distributors, and then a claim for reimbursement, at the rate of 2¢ per one-half pint of milk, was filed each calendar month. Although the federal government financed surplus foods and milk rebates, the procedure was handled through the state government.

3

choosing people to work in head start

Importance

Planning, organizing, selecting physical facilities, and even implementing programs are somewhat dimmed in significance when compared with the selection of persons to work with the preschool children. This is one of the areas of greatest concern, for the persons responsible for planning experiences for children overshadow all other considerations in determining the product which the preschool will produce. A child's initial experiences in the environs of a school setting can easily shape his attitudes toward school throughout his entire life. Their complete social, emotional, physical and intellectual growth are at stake. We may consider, therefore, the persons who work with the child at this stage as, indeed, the navigators and pilots who will chart and steer the course of this primary school experience.

Recruitment

Applications for all positions were made available at regular meetings of the sponsoring agency and neighborhood churches and clubs. Weekly speakers at churches brought information about the program's needs for certain job classifications. Announcements regarding job opportunities were given to the State Department of Employment and placed in local newspapers. A local junior high school was announced as the location of the first inverviews.

Our first glimpse of the public's responsiveness to the call of Head Start came as those of us who would be interviewing approached the site. The hours designated for interviews were 10 AM to 1 PM. Upon arrival at 9:30 there were already lines of people waiting at the gates to be admitted for interviews. This sight was encouraging for those of us who had no precedent in these matters. Indeed, it was surprising to find people of so many ages, races and occupational groups anxious to work with our Head Start.

Three teams of two interviewers each set up interviewing quarters in separate rooms. A member of the sponsoring agency acting as receptionist passed out application blanks and showed interviewees into the rooms. Many of the applicants were referrals from the State Department of Employment. They brought along cards from this agency for return, indicating the action taken and the reasons for it. Alas, we needed a secretary even before we started.

We set a second interview date to take place on the program site. Through this means we hoped to achieve greater utilization of the residents of the immediate neighborhood in the program. We were rewarded by receiving larger numbers of church and community referrals. Again there was an overflow crowd and the announced hours had to be extended to interview all persons present.

Standards for selection of personnel

Initially there were no guidelines, specific qualifications or uniform standards for the selection of personnel to operate the programs. Each separate agency, therefore, developed its own criteria. Our agency used as its guide in the selection of teachers the standards set forth in the book, *Good Schools for Young Children* (Hammond, 1964). Guidelines and descriptions of other job classifications evolved from our thinking of what we thought the job would entail and excerpts from City School and Civil Service Job Descriptions. Their qualifications were further shaped by Social Welfare Personnel Requirements as set forth in the Welfare and Institutions Code of the State of California.

Social welfare personnel requirements

Welfare and institutions codes of all states prescribe some qualifications to be met by personnel working in nursery and preschool programs. The rules applying to California were:

1. Section 1633 of the Welfare and Institutions Code requires that a criminal record clearance be made and a full criminal record report be secured by the coordinator.
2. Form C11-7 with accompanying fingerprints are required of the coordinator or director of a program.
3. DN-141. All persons having direct contact with children must be of suitable age and temperament to work with children. These persons must have the following qualifications.
   a. They must be mature, responsible adults.

    b. They must have the qualities of warmth and friendliness.

    c. They must have the ability to understand and accept individual differences in children and in all persons with whom they will be working.

4. DN-148-1. Staff Health—A complete physical examination by a licensed physician shall be required of *each staff member* (including the director, teachers, parent participants, cooks, etc.) prior to beginning of work.

This examination must include the verification of freedom from tuberculosis required by W. & I.C. Sec. 1632. (By law, the school must also have on file reports showing that each employee has had the required test or X-ray within the last twelve months, and is free from tuberculosis.)

The physcian's report shall be in writing and shall be kept on file in the offlce.

These considerations and the personnel's willingness and ability to comply with them were prerequisite to the hiring of personnel.

Qualifications which were sought in each applicant regardless of job title were (1) his interest in seeking the job, (2) experience with young children, and (3) attitudes in working with families living in poverty.

Surprisingly, answers to the questions, "How did you hear about Head Start" and, "Why do you feel that you would like working in this program" revealed much about the candidate's attitudes. It was easy to discern the person to whom it was "just another job that he had been sent on by the State Employment Service." Equally obvious was the chronic job seeker who always set his standards and his expectancy slightly higher than the job so as not to qualify. Falling into this category was the apparent alcoholic who possessed a *bona fide* college degree and who sought no less than a teaching position, though he well knew that personal qualifications would disqualify him for this particular job. The majority, however, were sincere, interested persons who had read of Head Start and its goals and were there in the hope of being employed in the program to help children of disadvantaged homes bridge the gap which would give them a head start in their school readiness.

Standards for teachers

In our teachers we sought a Bachelor's Degree from an accredited institution, a valid California teaching credential, and experience in kindergarten or early primary grades. In addition, we felt that the qualities of warmth, ingenuity and tolerance would be helpful to those responsible for the implementation of the program. From a large pool of applicants we made the final selection of 20 teachers whom we felt fitted these requirements. There was no dearth of applicants.

Teacher assistants

We particularly sought indications of resourcefulness and sensitiveness in the teacher assistant because of the role which she was to occupy in the child's life. In the area of professional preparation we sought (1) some background in early childhood education, (2) at least a junior college education, and (3) evident interest in and personality for working with young children. A final selection of 20 teacher assistants was made. As the program progressed they proved to be some of our most valuable workers. Their youth and vitality made them exceedingly adaptable to the demands of the program and the needs of the young children. Many of them were close enough in age and background to be able to identify with the children. Our children sought them out and found in them true friends. Their values in interpreting the feel of the neighborhood and the mores, attitudes and beliefs of its people cannot be overstated.

One striking example of an excellent assistant teacher was "Miss Lucy." Lucy Harris was a nursery school teacher in the church's established program, a member of the community church and a resident. She was personally responsible for enrolling more children in the program than any other single worker through her door-to-door contacts, her cheerfulness in enticing the children to want to enroll and her warmth and attitude in meeting parents and convincing them of the values of Head Start. Miss Lucy was "bus driver" and "bus teacher." Each daily trip into the community for a pick-up of children netted us additional enrollees or inquiries about enrollment as the result of Miss Lucy's influence.

An exemplary teacher aide was Mary Beth Crossland, whose enthusiasm, spirit and genuine desire to work in the program (perceived at the time of interviewing) proved to be of great value. Although she had just graduated from high school, she possessed the intuition to be in the needed place at the right time, the versatility to adapt to the current need, and sufficient maturity and judgment to see many of the socially maladjusted children in the program through some of their most trying moments. (Note the case of Ramon in the chapter entitled "The Child Development Specialist.")

These are merely two examples which we cite from many teacher assistants who were "naturals with young children."

We hired two male aides to satisfy the need for a "male figure" in the lives of Head Start children. The male figure is noticeably lacking in many homes of poverty, thereby depriving these children of the strength and security to be gained from the father role. Future programs must recognize the need for the male in the program and seek to include larger numbers of men in all of its aspects, particularly teachers and assistants or aides having direct contact with the children.

Social workers and social work aides

The delicate and varied roles to be performed by social workers in Head Start dictated the type of professionals necessary for the job. The majority of the families of children enrolled in Head Start were relief recipients who had experienced contacts in the past with social workers within the traditional framework of public agency operations. Too often, social workers were identified with investigation, punitive, or paternal roles. We sensed the need for experienced, knowledgeable and skilled human relations specialists who would attempt to refocus existent attitudes.

Two such skilled workers were drawn from the reservoir of talented professionals who comprise the sponsoring agency. Both were graduates in social work and possessed experience in both public and private social work agencies. These experiences guaranteed the necessary acquaintances with community resources and practices. They had immediate knowledge of services received by families, eligibility for other services and a proper referral for the needed family and child welfare services.

Two recent graduates in social work, schooled in professional preparation but lacking in work experience, were hired as social worker aides. They were able, under the direction of the trained professional worker, to assume many of the responsibilities in service to families and children. It is possible that sensitive persons with less formal education may be employed in this role. However, it is exceedingly important that they possess discretion, sensitivity and maturity of judgment in view of the delicacy of the social worker role.

An additional team of volunteer social workers came in later in the program to facilitate the taking of family histories and to assist in interpreting medical and other problems.

Medical workers

Based on our knowledge of the functions of the elementary school nurse, we established guides for the selection of a nurse and a medical assistant. We sought and hired a full-time nurse, Dorothy Jenkins, a person who despite *our* ignorance of what her role was to become at the time of the interview, possessed all the desirable qualifications for Head Start nurse. She was a Registered Public Health Nurse with experience in elementary schools. She possessed strong organizational and managerial skills which stood her in good stead when she discovered that she had to do a solo in general management and setting up of the total medical program. Her knowledge of educational objectives and know-how in educational practices made it easy for her to work with teachers and children in acquainting them with medical procedures. The public health aspect of her training enabled her to work with other medical professionals, teachers, parents and community. Competence in these areas was truly an asset in recruiting all of the professionals and services necessary in the implementation of a total health program for our Head Start boys and girls.

Willie Haas, a human dynamo of a nurse, was hired on an hourly basis to assist the regular nurse at the peak of operations. This nursing partnership during the first two weeks of the program made it possible to perform all of the initial health examinations, laboratory work and physical examinations necessary for each child.

A competent medical assistant, Margaret Love, was hired to assist the nurses in record keeping and history taking. Special qualifications for this job were (1) knowledge of medical terminology, (2) knowledge of medical procedures, and (3) strong clinical skills for the setting up and maintenance of medical records. Later in the program, when a record keeper was authorized by the federal government for the program, this person qualified for the job. She assumed the responsibility for the transference of health data to government forms and the coordination of information from all reporting forms including social welfare and medical records. (We found it slightly amusing to first hire a necessary person and then *later* have the government send out a similar job description).

Kitchen staff

A nutrition staff of five was selected to perform the full chore of providing food services for all the children. Our need for a skilled cafeteria manager who would be able to make the most of existing facilities, supervise a team of workers and get the best by way of nutritional quality foods for our 28¢ per day allotment was apparent. We selected the cafeteria manager of a local junior high school who had qualified under city school requirements for cafeteria managers. She possessed considerable experience and skill in quantity cooking and managerial compentencies.

Two mature women experienced in nursery schools and food services for young children were hired as nutritional aides. Their patience, responsibility and knowledge of the eating habits and consumption by the young child were invaluable contributions. Two other aides selected from the Neighborhood Youth Corps completed the nutritional staff.

Custodial staff

The ability to understand young children was also a requirement in our selection of the custodial workers. All persons in the preschool program affect the children's total development. Equal care needed to be exercised, therefore, in the selection of custodial personnel. We set forth the following qualifications for the selection of a custodian: (1) knowledge of school plant maintenance, (2) possession of simple repair and mechanical skills, (3) possessing the ability to supervise and direct a staff of workers, (4) knowledgeable in health and sanitation requirements for school operations, (5) possessing the ability to work with other personnel, and (6) love and understanding of young children.

Our final selection as head custodian was a young man with custodial experience in a large office building. The budget provided for one assistant custodian; two aides from NYC augmented the custodial team.

Our custodial operations ranked among the weaker phases of our program and cut heavily into administrative time. We have applauded youthful enthusiasm and the ability to identify with children in the program as laudable qualifications. This proved to be true in many aspects of the program's operations but the immaturity and inexperience of our custodial staff seriously affected their performance of the routines which were inherent in this program. The organizational structure necessitated double sessions, staggered and overlapping lunch periods, quick changes in furniture and locations to accomodate medical teams or staff meetings. The demands of 20 teaching teams and 300 children, three separate buildings, outdoor play areas, wheel toy maintenance, and minor plant repairs, was a complex and demanding job.

The night time maintenance of empty office buildings is a great contrast to the maintenance of three fully occupied classroom buildings which accommodate an activity program from water play to art activities. These children's activities, a normal part of the preschool routine, would provide a challenge to any custodian, but they were especially frustrating to one oriented to a static office routine.

With the knowledge that we have gained from this initial program experience it would seem that a sound investment in the smooth, safe and healthful maintenance of the school plant would be to retain a qualified, experienced and mature custodial staff and willingly pay the cost in dollars.

Neighborhood Youth Corps

Title 1-B of the Economic Opportunity Act established a work training program for unemployed men and women aged 16 through 21 from low income families. The purpose of the program was to make it possible for them to remain in school, or to return to school if they had already left the classroom, by earning their way at a regular job. This program was called the Neighborhood Youth Corps.

Los Angeles County had an established Neighborhood Youth Corps program which was functioning under the local Youth Opportunities Board. The young people in this program were faced with unemployment and idleness during the summer months. In an effort to circumvent this situation NYC enrollees were incorporated in Head Start programs as cafeteria aides, clerical aides, custodial aides, teacher aides and program aides.

Application had to be made to become a participating agency in the Neighborhood Youth Corps program. We had to provide on-the-job supervision of the enrollees and keep the required time and attendance records.

It was not our responsibility to pay these youths or to participate in recruiting procedures for them, but our request for ten Neighborhood Youth Corps enrollees was granted. The office of NYC set up appointments for screening of the youth and left the final selection to the sponsoring agency. A very successful job of prescreening was done, obviously, as most of the applicants were successfully placed in various jobs on the program and performed their routines remarkably well. They worked for a total of four hours a day for five days a week, or 20 hours a week. Two males out of the total helped our strongly unbalanced male-female ratio of employees.

Volunteers

From the neighborhood—A preplanning meeting with community, church and club groups did not yield a sizeable volunteer corps. This deficit was one of the discordant notes of the entire program. No provision had been made for a paid person to maintain the ratio of adults to children and we had counted on staffing one of the positions from among volunteers. This lack of foresight led to a serious staffing problem. As the program developed and people became more aware of the true nature of it, volunteers from the neighborhood and church began to drift in. A few parents accompanied their children to school and remained as classroom aides. A serious deterrent to their effectiveness in the initial phases was their lack of regularity and attendance. We were unable, therefore, to schedule them for specific jobs or times for their performances.

From the extended community—Increased publicity about Head Start, including two telecasts about our program and spot radio announcements hourly throughout the day, soon attracted volunteers from areas farther removed from the immediate neighborhood. A few teachers volunteered to serve a few hours a week, and students from local colleges and universities, usually on the recommendation of their teachers, began to volunteer in specialized areas of the program. Pepperdine College students devoted many hours to the program as speech specialists, program aides and in administering individual and group tests to the children. One city school systems, heard of our Head Start program through news media retired principal, having chalked up over 42 years as an educator in the and came weekly to assist in the classroom program and in administering government tests.

From sponsors—The sponsoring agency circulated among its membership a volunteer sign-up card. The card, in check sheet form, specified designated areas of service and hours and days of availability for volunteer work. In filing these cards in an index file by category of service we became aware of the fact that most of the services offered were for transportation and trips or the donation of goods, still leaving us short of volunteers for classroom functions.

4

getting under way

Registration day procedures

On registration day a series of tables labeled appropriately for the activities which were to take place were set up in the patio. These tables were labeled:

1. Information
2. Forms here
3. Fill out forms here
4. Assistance with filling out forms
5. Checking forms
6. Room assignments
7. Preregistered children's room assignments
8. Nurse's station

Aides were placed at each station to provide the designated service and assist parents in registration procedures.

Kits of registration forms had been preassembled in manila envelopes, cut lengthwise with an extended tab. Included in the kit were: enrollment form, health history form, emergency information cards, parent consent slips for trips, parent consent slips for medical services, and a form indicating parent preference for transportation to and from school. At the station where forms were checked, the child's name was placed immediately on the tab of the kit with a large black felt marker, and served as that child's record file for the duration of the project.

Necessity for name tags

As children received their room assignments their names and that room number were marked with a felt marker on name tags made of large construction paper squares. The name tag was to serve as a permanent identification for the child throughout the program. This device proved an invaluable aid with little children. Many could not tell you their names beyond a first name or nickname, (or refused to talk at all!) and "Room 10 AM" (Room 10, morning session) had no significance at all to them.

The nurse's station, on opening day was approximately a block away from the setting for registration in another building. It was necessary to appoint relays of monitors to take the children and their parents from the registration area down to the nurse's station. Later in the program, the registration operation was moved to the same building as the nurse's station.

The nurses and medical assistant took this opportunity to review the health history form with the parents, secure as much family data as possible, and check with the parents and secure signatures on the health consent forms. During slack periods, they were able to complete the initial health screening—weighing, measuring, conducting eye examinations and initial cursory health examinations to assure that the children were free of disease.

At this stage of the program, the nursing station did more good than any other single feature in establishing rapport with the families of the children and winning their confidence.

Classroom contacts were established as children were released from the nurse's station and escorted by the monitor, or directed when with a parent, to the assigned room. Both in-service training and social welfare manuals had impressed us with the desirability for an effective intake policy. Among the procedures recommended was a staggered intake so that children would enter the program a few at a time. Such a procedure assures the child of a better first impression and adjustment to the school setting. Due to limited numbers of newcomers at a given time, the teacher was able to individualize her program, meet and know each child as an individual, and gradually orient him to the areas within the school environs in which he was to function.

This gradual intake came about in a natural way for us as a result of the slow registration. Children were absorbed into classes a few at a time as they enrolled.

Initial adjustments

Thus, teachers were able to meet each child at the door, to personally acquaint him with the classroom, to allow him the freedom of exploration, and to permit the warmth and friendliness which one can achieve in a one-to-one relationship. Children were given a sense of belonging and security through being immediately given a designated spot complete with name tag for their own personal belongings. All activities were of an informal, unstructured nature in the beginning, with ample time for the child to explore, experiment, and discover.

As additional children came, the attention was focused on the new arrivals who were recipients of the same type of individualized welcome. The assistants were capable of supervising small groups by this time, and the first arrivals had made the adjustment to the classroom environment. Therefore, the teacher was freed to meet and work with new arrivals and their parents.

Welcoming the parents

Some valuable contacts with parents were established at this time. Transportation arrangements and the manner of recruitment limited the number of parents accompanying their children. However, those who came enjoyed the opportunity to see at first hand what the program was like. In time, they felt the confidence to become an integral part of the program and to participate in its activities.

Transporting the children

The need for transporting large numbers of children had not entered our thinking as we planned to get the program under way. It was expected that the children would come from a geographic area which would make walking feasible. Volunteers for transportation were expected to be used for trips and medical visits. Due to the difficulty, pointed out in "Opening the Program," in getting sufficient enrollment for which the program had been set up, it became necessary to extend our area of recruitment. We found ourselves, as a result, faced with the need for some means of transporting large numbers of children efficiently. The safety factor and the risks involved in numerous volunteers' cars posed a problem at this point, and we seriously doubted the effectiveness of such modes of transportation.

Teachers as bus drivers

We used a directory of the addresses of all enrollees to pinpoint clusters of children's residences. Lists were made up on this basis, and the teachers consented to pick up small groups of children who were in their customary transportation route. We rented a nine-passenger station wagon from the church and used "Miss Lucy," whom we introduced earlier, as bus driver. She was responsible for making the largest single pick-up—at a housing project some five miles away. Each teacher responsible for driving children had a list with names and addresses of the children and a daily check list. A duplicate list of all children being transported was kept in the Coordinator's office as a double check. Trying to keep lists current and keeping daily check of who was riding with whom on a given day became so complicated that we felt the need for some more effective means of transportation. Also, the responsibility for transporting their pupils seemed to be taking away from some teachers' effectiveness in their major roles.

A short-lived promise

With the promise of the use of an idle school bus which was owned by the church from which we rented facilities, we hired a vacationing city school bus driver. Our pleasure and relief at ending all transportation problems was short-lived, as this arrangement lasted for only a week. Alas, the church itself was funded for a recreation program of its own which required the use of the bus.

Saved by the yellow pages

The Classified Telephone Directory yielded a long list of various bus services available. Available were buses with drivers, with insurance furnished by the bussing agency; or buses without drivers with the driver and insurance being furnished by the project. What to do! Costs were amazingly high on a per day or per week basis. Such large expenditures for this purpose had not been anticipated in our budget and caused us some moments of real concern. Faced with no alternatives and the need for a safe and satisfactory transportation program which would compliment the effectiveness of other areas of our program, we were forced to contract with a bus company. The contract included weekly transportation, with the driver and insurance furnished by the company. It was also arranged that the bus and driver would be available all day between regular runs. In this way we doubled the buying power of our transportation dollar by having the bus transport groups on short field trips and on visits to the Health Department. The cost was enormous!

Arranging bus schedules

Bussing services enabled the parents to ride with their children on scheduled Parent Education days and on scheduled family outings, which added to their feeling of "community" and of being an integral participant in the Head Start program. In order to facilitate bussing procedures, lists were made up of each pick-up point with a weekly schedule to check children riding on a given day. A weekly schedule of "bus teacher" designated teachers and/or assistants to accompany the bus driver on specified dates and hours. The children wore name tags on the bus to expedite checking for all heads. The bus driver was skilled in routing, and, with the Co-ordinator, developed a schedule which we gave to parents and teachers. At last we effected a smooth transportation schedule which permitted teacher freedom, minimal program distractions, safety, and assurance to all that children would be picked up on time and returned on time.

We point out these difficulties as an indication of the problems which are potentially present in the operation of a Head Start program. Adequate advance planning might have prevented some of the problems in this area.

But, as we recall how the children were enrolled, and the unexpected necessary extension of our service boundaries, anticipation in this instance was hardly possible. Groups planning programs would find it practicable to include sufficient amounts of money in this budget item to cover transportation costs adequately. For lengthy programs some better financial arrangements than we were able to achieve may be worked out by planning, shopping, and comparing costs and taking bids. Long-term leases offer one possibility for reduced transportation costs.

The advantages of bussing

Bussing, in the instance of the children in our program, was a broadening and rewarding experience. Contrary to the oft-quoted supposition that removal of the young child from his immediate community via bus or other transportation media to go elsewhere to school is a traumatic experience, these children suffered no pangs of insecurity in being transported from their homes. To most it seemed an excursion—an adventure into the big wide never-never land outside of the restricted range of the projects and the confined neighborhoods in which they resided. It seems fitting to mention the case of Joe, a little boy who lived some distance away in a housing project. His mother related that he was left by the bus on one occasion when he was late in getting out to the pick-up point. From that day forward, he insisted on sitting outside at the pick-up point for fully forty minutes to an hour ahead of time to assure his daily adventure. It was an experience neither he nor any of his friends wanted to miss.

Section II

PROGRAM

5

the teacher

Tears of separation
Fears of the unknown
Insecurity of the unfamiliar
Joy of new experiences
Delights of new-found toys
Comfort in adult attention

Any one of these may characterize the Head Starter on his first day, shaping the focus of the teacher's actions and activities. There is never a clearly defined format to the Head Start day, whether it be the first day or graduation day. Ever present is the unexpected, which is normal to a situation involving a group of preschoolers marked with individual differences in physical development, emotional development, social development, and intellectual development. The teacher sets the stage for satisfactory growth and development in these areas through her personal qualities, ability to provide an environment for effective learning, and her ever-continuing awareness of children as individuals. In her awareness, she must deal with each one according to his own unique makeup.

An observational account by Mrs. Betty Simmons, a student from a nearby college, who visited our Project as an assignment for her Child Development class, projects a picture of the multi-faceted day facing the Head Start teacher.

OBSERVATIONAL ACCOUNT

"Today, I met the Director of Operation Head Start who gave me a schedule of the day and introduced me to Mrs. M., a teacher. I started the day by observing the children coming in. Until they are all present they are given the opportunity to play inside or out. This seems to be a good way for them to feel relaxed and independent in greeting each other before the day is started. Some of the boys were on the swings trying to see who could swing the highest. The girls were in little groups talking about what they did yesterday and making plans for today.

"When all but two of the children had arrived, the teacher's aide brought in some brightly colored clay. One group decided to pretend theirs was food. They sat at a little table and began to place it on the plates. No one made anything else with the clay. They tired of it after about 20 minutes and went out to play. Two little girls decided to play with the puppets behind a puppet stage, and when another started to use the telephone, they decided this would be more fun. They wanted all the adults to participate in this phone game. It was very real to them and they played this for about 25 minutes.

"Donny, whose mother is visiting for the first time today, decided to build a store with some wooden blocks. The teacher was helping him. He seemed to want a customer, so I asked him what I could buy in the store. He said 'cheese,' and handed me a block. I asked him the price, and paid $5.00 for a pound of cheese!

"His mother was a high school graduate and volunteered information about her son. She said he was an only child, that she worked all day, that he was cared for by the grandmother while she worked, and that he had never had any playmates his own age. She said he has been helped by this program in the following ways: he is less shy of children his own age and also of people in general; he is less energetic—by which she said she meant that he had a better outlet for what she realized was 'normal activity in a child'; and he sleeps and eats better.

"Some girls working with a puzzle asked the teacher to please help them. She did, but she did not put it together for them. A little boy next to me said he could do it all by himself. He did.

"Patty and Cora have now transferred the phone conversation to a toy that represents 'The Old Lady in the Shoe.' They said she was calling me. I talked to her and then told them she wanted to know how they were and wanted to talk to them also.

"*Clean-up Time*—Time to go for a *hearing test*. The teacher's aide sings, 'This is the way we march along,' as they all take partners, hand-in-hand, to go up the block to take the test.

"The lady who gave the test said she wanted to test them to see what good pilots they would be. She then gave the group instructions as to how the pilot puts on his ear phones and listens for a beep. She went on with full explanation about what they were to do. The others each waited in a chair and watched the one who was being tested. They seemed to enjoy this. Only one little girl walked back to the teacher's aide for reassurance.

The aide held her, diverted her attention, and when the girl's name was called, she went right up and took the test.

"When we returned to the classroom, the group I was with went to lunch. Another group had been painting egg cartons. They finished them and set them in the middle of the table. This was a good activity to observe. Here I could easily ascertain each child's previous experience with paints, his attitudes about doing something which taxed his skills and coordination, and his ability to observe what he was doing, to see if he was covering the whole carton, and whether or not he could finish something which he started. Two were unable to complete the project, and one almost didn't. For a group of ten, I think that is probably 'average.'

"The children placed the paint containers and brushes on a tray and went into the washroom to clean-up for lunch. They also had a quiet period before eating. The teacher put some of their favorite records on the phonograph and they sat on the floor in a circle to listen.

"List of experiences provided:

"Painting—easel and finger and other, paper mosaics, dress-up, house, block building, sawing, hammering, cutting, live animals, music, story telling, learning language, using group toilet, table manners, water play, sand box, jungle gym, cars, wagons, and tricycles.

"List of services provided:

"Physical examinations, hearing test, bus to and from school, nutrition and lunch, parent conferences.

"In addition to the women teachers and women assistants they had invited a number of men to be 'the father symbol.' These men were young and selected from State College on the basis of their previous experience with young children and the field in which they were majoring. Every effort was made to acquaint the children with things and experiences which they were not getting at home in an effort to bring them up to that level of experience which is desirable for the child starting school. For some of these children, the variety appeared to be overwhelming at first, but they soon attuned themselves to the situation and gained considerably. One of the teachers told me about a little girl who had been neglected by her mother to the point of being extremely undernourished. The grandmother convinced the mother to put the girl in the program—and also obtained custody of her. The grandmother said that, in addition to being undernourished, the little girl had seldom been loved or allowed to play with anyone. On the day I observed, the girl had been in the program four weeks. She was climbing the jungle gym, and playing with the other children as if she had never had such a handicap."

PLANNING THE DAY

To attribute a label of "typical" to a day in Head Start is presumptuous if not altogether absurd. This is not to imply that there is no planning involved or order to procedures and activities. Planning and orderliness are prerequisites to learning. If children are to be guaranteed a continuity of experiences and any sequential development of concepts, team planning and team evaluation, time for preparing activity materials, and setting up the environment are imperative parts of the teacher's day.

In our program, teaching teams were present at least one hour before the arrival of the children. During this first hour, relationships between teacher and assistants were strengthened as they evaluated the previous day's activities, became acquainted with general center-wide activities through the daily bulletin, and planned specifically for the day and each person's responsibilities. This was a time wherein the teacher was able to translate her professional knowledge and educational philosophy into meaningful functions as they applied to the day's activities. It was a time to answer questions, give practical assistance in "how to do it," to grow in mutual respect as each team member contributed, through his particular strength, in a *modus operandi* for the day.

When all share in the planning, all feel a mutual responsibility for implementation. The aide does not have the feeling of "being told" to do meaningless, servile chores, but sees through to the totality of the program and the necessity for each adult to carry his share of the load throughout the day. This means not only a follow-through of delegated duties, but a perceptiveness and alertness in anticipating and remedying on-the-spot needs.

Each day in Head Start demands a balance of activities which foster the intellectual, physical, social and emotional growth of the child. These are accomplished through a variety of techniques, and no less a variety of schedules. Certain routines for the effectiveness of center operations, as well as for children's security in doing some things at certain times is necessary. However, flexibility in programming the day from teacher to teacher, and from day to day, indicates an awareness of individual differences, group differences, and the nature of the young child.

A sample schedule for a day is offered here only in the interest of providing a picture of programs to our readers.

OUR HEAD START DAY

8:00— 8:20   Unit Team Meeting
                  1. Review the general activities of the center for the day

2. Re-evaluate the previous day
3. Make specific plans for the day's activities
4. Assign areas of responsibility
5. Discuss problems—solutions
6. Consider case histories of special children, needs, recommendations
7. Share knowledge of families, neighborhood conditions, and so forth, which may have bearing on the children's behavior
8. Give specific instructions in "how to" (as applicable)
   a. Mix play dough
   b. Prepare clay
   c. Prepare paints
   d. Serve nutrition
   e. Supervise outdoor play
   f. Prevent and handle accidents
   g. Meet parents
   h. Record observations and/or case histories
   i. Read a story
   j. Supervise and yet contribute to small group activities
   k. Handle discipline
   l. Increase awareness of children with special problems
   m. Work with other professionals

8:20— 8:50 Setting up the Environment
1. Activity Centers
   a. Easel painting—finger painting
   b. Play dough or clay
   c. Collage
   d. Doll house—dramatic experiences
   e. Books
   f. Blocks
   g. Music
   h. Science
2. Outdoor Areas
   a. Check for safe condition of wheel toys and apparatus
   b. Check if yards are free of hazards
   c. Put out wheel toys
   d. Refresh marked or painted areas

        e. Put out sand and water toys
        f. Have outdoor blocks and accessories accessible
     3. Nutrition Provisions
       a. Check with kitchen staff
       b. Have nutrition accessible upon arrival of children

8:30— 9:00 Arrival of children accompanied by parents
     1. Personal greetings and acknowledgements
     2. Informal parent conferences
     3. Informal play activities
     4. Informal nutrition
     5. Health inspection

9:00— 9:10 Arrival of children transported by bus
     1. Meet bus in parking area
     2. Greet and tag children with name tags
     3. Health inspection
     4. Induct new arrivals into informal activities

9:10—10:00 Planned small group activities—indoor
10:00—10:10 Bathroom and wash-up
10:10—11:00 Planned activities—outdoor
        Bathroom and wash-up
11:00—11:45 Lunch
11:45—12:00 Quiet activities on lawn, under trees, or in classroom; preparation for home
12:00   Departure

Satisfactory growth and good health demand adequate sleep and rest for the preschool child. Fatigue is to be avoided at all times. The short day for our Head Start program did not allow time for a planned sleep and rest period such as one finds in most full-day nursery schools. The teacher's skillful design for an alternating program of vigorous, active experiences, and quiet, sedentary experiences, was a precaution against over-exertion and fatigue.

An essential element of curriculum planning for preschoolers is the setting up of "activity centers," the repetition of a central theme, and the opportunity to "play out" newly learned concepts in a variety of ways. For instance, before the visit of the policeman, the teacher read or told a story. After the visit, she provided books, art materials, and situations for dramatic play so that the children could incorporate the policeman's role into their own make-ups.

The children's learning proceeds from their experiences with materials and their relationships with their teachers and companions. Because the children select their own activities, structured from materials provided, it is impossible to put down exactly what the teacher will do. However, the following chart is illustrative of some of the kinds of situations which may present themselves in any given day, emotional response to a "model" teacher, and what basic needs of the child are being satisfied through such responses.

Typical Incidents	Child's Needs	Teacher Response
Individual greetings	Self-esteem	Recognition, acceptance
New item of clothing	Recognition	Acknowledgement
Successful execution of a maze, puzzle, etc.	Successful experiences	Praise
Skinned knee in play	Sympathy	Love and affection
Spilled food, paint, etc.	Understanding	Tolerance, acceptance
Selects own activity	Satisfy curiosity	Permissiveness
Struggle to put on own sweater, coat, tie, shoe, etc.	Independence and self-reliance	Patience, appreciation for child's learning independence
Develops a rhythmic response independent of group	Create and experiment	Fosters creativity through recognition and promotion
Takes toy away from other children	Limits within permissive framework	Firmness, consistency
Cries when parent leaves; clings to teacher	Love and trust	Love, assurance, calmness
Does not participate in music activities	Acceptance as he is	Recognition of individual differences
Simultaneous interest in a given toy	Rights and privileges	Sense of justice
An "accident" before getting to bathroom	Acceptance	Tolerance, acceptance

And who shall dare to teach?

The teacher, it becomes evident, is the central figure in the team which serves the child in Head Start. She is in a position to do more good or harm in affecting children's development than any other single influence in the program. Aside from her responsibility to the children who are under her supervision, the teacher of Head Start must serve as the helmsman of her teaching unit. The effectiveness of the team—teacher, assistant teacher, aide, volunteer—is contingent upon the teacher's skill in inspiring, training and directing her unit. Because of the importance of her role and the weight of her influence, selection of the teacher for Head Start children becomes a grave and responsible concern.

Topping the list of any expectancies for the teacher who works with preschool children, is a *warm, giving nature.* The teacher becomes the children's model for learning to share, learning to handle aggressive feelings, learning to try, and even learning to learn. She must be free of inhibitions within herself. She must be a self-actualizing person.

How do we know when a person is free enough within herself to guide the learning experiences of young children? There are some questions we can ask.

1. Can this person work *with* other people?
2. Can this person own up to her own *mistakes?*
3. Can this person let others take the *lead?*
4. Does this person have the *patience* to let others find out the answers for themselves through problem solving techniques?
5. Does this person *dress* attractively and interestingly, yet appropriately for working with young children?
6. Is she ready to get dirty and *messy,* to bend down, to sit on the floor?
7. Can she translate educational principles to *understandable terms* for parents and non-professionals?
8. Does she *respect* other professional disciplines?
9. Is this person an *innovator* or does everything have to be *"just so"?*
10. If this person has been out of school for some time, does she keep *reading* and learning?
11. Is this person a *"giver or a withholder"?* (Blau).
12. Does this person have the patience to work with parents?

Adversely, there are certain characteristics of individuals which tend to inhibit their effectiveness. If any of the following attributes are present to a great extent, then this person probably has qualities which make her a "withholder."

1. Does the person want to be different for the sake of *"being different"?*
2. Does this person give many hugs and kisses *which are unsolicited* by the children?
3. Does this person have to let everyone know that *she is there* and in charge?
4. Does this person feel that if her children do not show growth, she has *failed personally?*
5. Has this person *stopped reading* professional literature?
6. Does this person feel she has "all the answers"?
7. Does this person believe that "telling" parents the "right way" should be enough?

At the center of this child's "home away from home" is the teacher. Every experience which she provides leaves its residue and influences the child's personality and character development. She creates the atmosphere for healthy learning through her personal qualities, her ability to provide a stimulating environment and her organizational skills in providing leadership for the teaching team. The ultimate effectiveness of Head Start is dependent upon the teacher.

6

bringing the community
to the classroom

In an age of television, telestar, outer space explorations, and imminent inter-planetary communication, we consider the world of today's child devoid of boundaries. But, for the thousands of children who live in poverty, the invisible boundaries imposed by their cultural heritage and limited opportunities loom as a specter to restrict and confine their world. The world of books, the world of song, the world of nature, the world of animals, the world of exciting sights and sounds, the world of beauty, the world of comfort and security, the world of fulfillment are strangers to them. Theirs is a world filled with the ever-present threat of hunger, failure, and defeat.

Inherent in the philosophical concept of Head Start was a commitment to add in every way to the breadth and depth of these children's lives. Through field trips, the spiraling purview of their world was dramatically augmented. The multi-sensory involvement of sights, sounds, smells, and tactile experiences through excursions into the community elasticized the boundaries of their world.

We planned to introduce the children to facilities in their own neighborhoods, to community services, such as fire and police, and to the cultural offerings of our city. This planned order prepared them in a gradual way for acceptance, with understanding, of the broader world that lay beyond their immediate community.

A great deal of planning was necessary before we could take the children from the school into the community. A Delta volunteer took charge of all advance preparations for field trips. The teachers sent home permit slips to be signed by parents. The nutrition staff was to plan snacks or sack lunches for trips. The Coordinator scheduled trips into the total calendar of activities and helped prepare the children through their teachers for their venture. She also acted as public relations specialist. A master planning sheet was made for each trip giving time of departure, class lists, extra adults who were assisting, destination, contact person and mode of transportation.

Visiting an elementary school

One of the first trips the children made was to the neighborhood elementary school. Arrangements were made with the principal of the local school to bring small groups of children at a time for tours of the school and grounds. The objective in the school tour was to acquaint the children with the world in which they would function in September. There was an implied purpose of "getting ready" for this bigger world of kindergarten.

Individual classes, accompanied by teachers and assistants, walked to the school. The children found the walk a delightful experience. The teachers sought to orient them to the school facilities in an unstructured way through directing attention to things, answering and encouraging the children's questions, and permitting a limited exploration of physical facilities. The playground coach acted as guide, since the school was closed for the summer except for the playground.

This trip provided the children with numerous language opportunities as they discussed their observations and later reenacted their experiences through dramatic play.

Community cluster trip

A cluster of community resources, including the telephone company, a bank, a supermarket, and a service station were scheduled for one trip. This itinerary was planned primarily as an observational tour with brief stopovers along the route. Through prearrangement, the children were able to view cars being serviced at the station. The grease rack showing the underside of the car, with the car gliding up and down, was particularly fascinating for the boys and girls.

These experiences were subsequently reflected in the play and conversations of the children.

Community services

We decided that the children would profit more from having the firemen and policemen visit them at the school than for the children to visit the stations. If the children should have subsequent contacts with firemen or policemen, it would probably be in their own neighborhoods. Hence, the value of the experience lay primarily in acquainting the children with the community workers as persons, and in learning to see their functions as helpful rather than punitive.

Although the policemen and firemen were accustomed to presenting their program to elementary school children, they were at first shy with our preschoolers. They "warmed up" to the experience as their presentations developed and the interest and enthusiasm of their audience emerged, thereby accomplishing the objective of portraying themselves as friendly helpers instead of "shy guys."

The firemen's visit to the center consumed most of one entire morning. All of the children gathered on the parking lot of the school. The fire truck, complete with hook and ladder, firefighting equipment, firemen dressed for active duty and the Dalmatian dog mascot, drew enraptured squeals from the assembled children. A demonstration of the firemen donning their suits and boots and a water display added to the realism of the occasion. The firemen explained everything to the children in a most understandable way as they encouraged them to look at the inside of the truck and to pet the Dalmatian dog mascot.

The policemen's visit was arranged through the Public Relations Department of the Police Department. In fostering the development of an attitude toward policemen as friendly authority figures, the Los Angeles Police Department produced a program entitled "Policeman Bill." Two police officers who were especially trained in working with children were assigned to this detail regularly. Armed with visual aids, they presented "The Badge," a story of the historical significance of badges. In addition, they employed an interesting cartoon technique inviting pupil responses and answers. Through this media, they developed the idea of traffic safety. The presentation was appropriately geared in both content and length to the interest and maturity level of the children. The boys and girls were greeted pleasantly by the officers as they each passed the patrol car and had an opportunity to observe the magic of the red light and siren and listen to the police radio.

Hopefully, this presentation did much to dispel the children's fears of police officers founded on previous experiences or on the attitudes of their home and community.

Trips into the extended community

To acquaint our children with the extended community we planned trips to a science center, the Los Angeles County Museum, the Museum of Science and Industry and Griffith Park Children's Zoo and Park.

All of these facilities were open to the community free of charge or at nominal fees. By acquainting the children and their families with these public places we hoped to help them reach out of their drab surroundings, partake of the cultural heritage of the community, and experience excitement and wonder in the joy of discovery.

The Science Center excitingly revealed the wonders of plant and animal life. The children were transported by bus and visited the City Schools'

Science Center in groups of approximately 75 for about 45 minutes. Teachers, assistants, volunteers and parents were enlisted to help with the supervision. Through this experience, the children became acquainted with the wonders of growing and living things. They were provided with an opportunity to develop a sensitivity to the beauties of nature. Here an opportunity presented itself to form the proper attitudes of respect for all living creatures.

On their return teachers furthered this interest through loans from the Science Center of small animals and chickens for their classrooms. One classroom had a bantam hen which laid an egg each day. Guinea pigs, turtles, rabbits, baby chicks—all found waiting homes in the classrooms and eager adoptive parents in the Head Start children.

Los Angeles County Museum was scheduled for a simultaneous visit with the Museum of Science and Industry, both housed in Exposition Park. Groups of 30 were taken on unguided tours of the County Museum as groups of 45 were led on guided tours of the Science and Industry Museum. Admission to these facilities was free and both nationally renown facilities were within a few blocks of our concentrated poverty area. Provisions for parents to accompany their children, arrangements for bus transportation, and advance field trip planning were similar for both excursions and were a prerequisite to their success.

Griffith Park Children's Zoo and Park provided one of the highlights of the entire summer's experiences. Much planning preceded the actual trip. Contacts were made for a free, guided tour of the zoo's facilities; bus services and refined time schedules were made; invitations to parents and other children of Head Start families and friends were extended; lunch arrangments were made; special parent consent forms were sent out to be signed and returned; the luncheon area was reserved; and arrangements were made for the exclusive use of all amusement park facilities. (The latter was paid for by Delta Sigma Theta Sorority.)

The nutritional staff made sack lunches for all of the children and went along to serve lunch. The services of six 75-passenger buses were required to transport all of the children and their families. Parents were picked up on the morning schedules with the children and returned in the same way at the end of the day. This schedule made it possible for practically every family to be represented. Many of them had never before had the opportunity for such an outing because of the cost of transportation and other restrictions.

The Children's Zoo was a new development of the regular Griffith Park Zoo, designed especially for young children. The setting was concentrated and could easily be covered by little legs without undue exhaustion. This made it especially desirable for little preschoolers with limited physical endurance. A unique feature of the zoo was the Animal Family Center where the children were able to observe animal mothers with their young. A special "nursery" section featured new babies and provided the unique thrill of seeing the habits of animal babies exploring, rooting and sucking.

The concrete, stark world of these city children faded to nothingness in the Happy Hollow. Here, the children were able to live for a brief moment the life of rural children as they fed and petted small lambs, goats, rabbits, and even a baby donkey.

After the zoo visit the group was bused to another section of the park for lunch. Children and their families, aides, teachers—all joined in a festive lunch and group games in the afternoon. The merry-go-round never ceased turning as these delighted youngsters took ride after ride.

Our worst fears at having such a large group of very young children in a loosely controlled setting were allayed as the afternoon wore on and our only casualty had been one skinned knee requiring the use of one Band Aid. Visible name tags, small subgroups with definite supervisorial responsibility, and a clear-cut time table made the organization orderly and smooth.

At the end of a fun-filled day, some 500 weary passengers journeyed the freeways to return to their world of reality. Bodies returned to the same stark world, but with minds full of memories to dream upon, and families to share them with. And who or what can contain the mind of a child who knows where to seek and find?

Library books and services

We sought to provide each classroom with a wealth of the favorite stories of early childhood. Because our budget did not include a provision for a purchase of a large supply of books, we sought the cooperation of the neighboorhood library. We found in our neighborhood librarian a true ally of Head Start. Before the program opened we acquainted him with our plan to establish a Head Start in the neighborhood. We asked if it were possible for the library to provide enough books for twenty classrooms. The neighborhood librarian channeled our request to the main branch of the library where our request was granted. During the first few days after Head Start opened the librarian came to visit. In this way he was able to get a feel for the children, the setting, and the teachers, thereby more adequately assessing what kinds of books would be suitable. He then made arrangements for the delivery of 300 books which he felt would be appropriate for our children. A program aide had the responsibility for listing the books in sets of 15, one set designated for each classroom.

Books rotated on a weekly basis to each classroom, thereby providing a wider variety of books for each room and each child. It was felt that this procedure of circulating the books would better fit our needs than attempting to check out new books from the library each week.

The Library Program

Each week the librarian came and paid a visit to the individual classrooms. During his visit he read a book which he had selected especially for the children, one which he felt would be of great interest value to them. Their response to him and their enjoyment of the book was accentuated by the familiar setting of their own clasroom. The librarian helped to bring his stories to life by embellishing them with flannelboard aids and other audio-visual materials.

After all the children were sufficiently acquainted with the librarian as a friend who brought them exciting stories, each class was scheduled for a trip to the neighborhood library, to visit him. The librarian made arrangements for the trip to the library in the early part of the morning before the regular opening hours. He felt that if the children could come to the library before the other people they would be more comfortable and their introduction to the library could be more leisurely.

The library was close enough for the children to walk there with their teacher and sufficient aides, volunteers and parents to make it safe. We tried to get one adult for every two children so that we could hold the children's hands while crossing busy city streets. Our children seemed to be greatly impressed with the new world of books which the library presented. They looked around quietly, almost spellbound. "Here," said the librarian, "is where you come to find out things. Here is where you come to have fun." Then he had a story-telling time for the children. First he selected a story that he had already read to the children in their classrooms. He told them that the book would be in the library any time that they wanted to check it out again. Then he selected a new story, one that they hadn't heard before and told them that there were many new books in the library. He urged them to come again with their older brothers and sisters or their family.

The children seemed to take him to heart, for the next week the librarian told us of older brothers and sisters being brought to the library by our Head Starters. In a small way we like to think that we have begun to make books part of the world of these children of poverty.

The importance of books to the Head Start program

Many of the homes of our Head Start children could not boast of even a magazine or a daily paper. Children living in homes of poverty with scarcely enough material things to supply the basic needs of housing, clothing and food, were not afforded the luxury of books nor of anyone to share them with. One of the new worlds which we hoped to open for our children was the world of books. We found that the world of books held a fascinating appeal for our children. Once they were introduced to them they found that their insatiable curiosity about "things" could be satisfied through books. Their basic need for security was realized in the setting of warmth, proximity and confidence which were engendered in the story-reading or story-telling situation. In this way books came to be a natural part of the life of a Head Start child just as books are a natural part of the home life of the middle-class child. Just as the parents of the middle-class child have the means and the time to surround their children with books, so our Head Start teachers surrounded our children with books and had time to read them. In this way the incidental motivation of a love for books was provided by the model of the teacher. By example we hoped to motivate our Head Start children toward a love of books and toward development of proper attitudes and the motivation to read.

We felt that our goals were partially reached when, by the end of the Head Start program our children would come into a room, pick up a book which interested them, and peruse it. When they would share an oft-told story with another child, when they would bring a new book for the teacher to read to them, we felt we had begun to make books a natural part of their world.

We feel that it is imperative that properly selected books be a prominent part of the Head Start school environment and that teachers be properly instructed in how to introduce and use these books.

How we taught our teachers to use books

The guide suggested by Todd and Hefferman in their book, *The Years Before School,* were helpful to us in our teacher's workshop. The chapter entitled "Stories to Meet the Need of Preschool Children" categorized books for the preschool child according to the needs of the children.

1. Books to further security in relationships
2. Books for self-confidence
3. Books to meet the need for achievement
4. Books for meeting the need to belong to a group
5. Books to meet the need for safety
6. Books for experience

We highly recommend the use of this reference to teach the proper utilization of books in the preschool setting.

Once the books were selected it was important that the teacher approached the bringing together of children and books in the proper way. Books were displayed attractively on the table, and were within easy reach. Children were attracted to the brightly colored pictures. As a child approached the book he was allowed to get acquainted with it in his own way so long as he did not tear it—looking, feeling, touching, even biting and smelling were a part of his introduction to the printed page. Next the teacher would call attention to the pictures that seemed to interest the child, supplying a word for a prominent object such as kitty, boy, chair, sky, tiger, girl, or house.

It was enough to look at the picture and say a few words in the beginning. Later the words became short sentences—"Girl on the chair"; "Yellow kitty cat"; "Dog says bow wow." Several weeks went by before the teacher attempted to read the text of more than the most simple book.

A good rule was, "The picture tells the story." Therefore, the teacher moved from the child's interest to the picture to vocabulary before she attempted reading the complete story. The story was usually for one or two children alone until the rest of the group listened, were interested, and chose to join, making a larger group. Story reading in a formalized first grade sense was not the way we introduced our children to books. We taught that a book is interesting, a book is to learn something new, a book is to be shared, a book is to be put down when I am through, a book is my friend.

7

the public health nurse

Our school nurse, Dorothy Jenkins, was a person of warm personality, gentle nature, humanitarian interests, and superior training. These qualities enabled her to conduct one of the most thorough medical programs in the county. From her experience as a public health nurse in a nearby elementary school, she brought skills in relating to young children, competent medical knowledge of the social and physical characteristics of disadvantaged children, and sensitivity to the problems and needs of the community.

Physical facilities for health care

A small office with adjoining bath was chosen as the nurse's station. Although the room was adequate for first aid, there was no space for doctor's examinations. A regular classroom was set up with screens and tables on days scheduled for the doctor's visitation.

Fortunately, the weather was warm enough for the children to play outside most of the time and to share another classroom when it became necessary to come indoors. It was not an ideal solution but one which was necessary under the circumstances.

The nurse checked the kitchen for sanitation, recommended sterilization procedures, and also checked the rest rooms for cleanliness, soap, and supplies. She made a thorough check of the premises to ascertain the safety of equipment, play yards, and room furnishings.

Record keeping

A daily log was kept of all children reporting to the nurse's office for medical care. The log book included provisions for the date, time, child's full name, presenting symptom, such as, "skinned knee" or "upset stomach," and treatment provided, such as "first aid" or "child sent home." These reports were made available to the teacher as well as the home, in order to keep each alerted to incidents involving the child.

Forms adapted from those used by the public schools were used for taking a health history for the doctor's examination and for recording laboratory results. The thought was that if the forms resembled those used in the local schools, better carry-over would be possible.

One of the major tasks of the health office was compiling the data collected for the U.S. Census Bureau, including family and health histories. A medical assistant who worked in the nurse's office was responsible for correlating all the information.

Laboratory tests

The public health nurse made arrangements with a private laboratory in the neighborhood to process the laboratory work *as it was taken.* Timing of lab work was held to be important for accuracy and efficiency of operation.

Blood samples were taken by the nurse for hemoglobin tests, and urine samples were taken for specific gravity, PH, albumin, sugar and micro-organisms.

If a child was unable to produce a urine sample "on request," the nurse accompanied the child home after school, explained the situation to the parent, and waited patiently until the child was able to produce a specimen. Next time we would recommend that parents accompany children to school or to the laboratory to assist in taking a urine specimen from small children. The vocabulary for asking a child to urinate takes on massive proportions, and makes one feel as if there are 100 tongues—wet, tinkle, go visit grandmother, oink-oink, whitle, go wee-wee, ah-wah, go-go, be a good girl, and so on.

Laboratory

Blood tests are important to assess hemoglobin content in detecting anemia. A low hemoglobin has a direct relationship to diet.

Whenever anemia is detected in Negro children, additional testing to determine if the sickling trait is present should be made. Sickle cell anemia is a hereditary disease with an incidence of about ten per cent among American Negroes. Untreated, it leads to mental deficiency and death. If detected and treated, it can be arrested and kept under control, much in the same way as diabetes is kept under control, that is, through diet and medication.

Urinalysis is a routine laboratory test given to assess kidney function and diseases. The sugar content also may be indicative of diabetes.

Tuberculin testing for preschool children is most effective if done by the Tine Method. A small cylindrical object equipped with four medicated tines is pressed into the skin of the forearm. Swelling and redness at the site of the tine pricks after 48 hours denotes exposure to TB organisms.

Both teachers and parents should be alerted to watch for positive signs even though the nurse will routinely check all children.

Any children who register positively should be referred immediately to the Health Department. We had one little boy with a positive reaction who was a recent immigrant from Haiti. The mother was not accustomed to any routine health measures, such as regular meals, serving milk, routine washing or the need for doctor's examinations. When presented with the findings that the TB test her son had was positive the mother shrugged indifferently, "En Haiti, tout le monde l'avez l'temp." ("In Haiti, everyone has TB sometime.")

It took continued contacts with the mother to convince her that something should be done. Finally the threat of permanent exclusion from school, with the knowledge that this would also apply to public school, motivated the mother to follow the referral advice of Head Start.

Such an experience is illustrative of the time necessary to devote to parent contacts. As one of our staff members put it, "What we need is an expanded parent education program—on a one-to-one basis!"

Physical examinations

Since physical examinations were performed throughout the session, a schedule was set up whereby all the children in a room were taken to the nurse's office for certain routine procedures, if these had not been completed at registration.

1. Taking of height and weight.
2. Screening for vision.
3. Taking blood and urine specimen for laboratory.
4. Recording family and health information and laboratory results on health history form.

All this preceded the physical examinations with doctor.

Assisting the doctor

On the scheduling of a child for a physical examination, notice slips were sent to the parents informing them of the time and day of the appointment and specifically asking them to be present.

A large classroom was partitioned off with screens to make one end private for examinations and the other end a place for parents to sit while awaiting their child's turn.

The class was brought into the room in a body. The parent asked to get her child undressed and move to the examining table in turn. The nurse kept the histories at hand, introduced the doctor to the parent and child, and assisted the doctor in whatever way he requested.

In all cases, letters were sent home notifying the parents of the doctor's findings and asking them to seek treatment in appropriate cases.

Inoculations

Arrangements were made with the County Health Department to administer inoculations for smallpox, D.P.T. (diphtheria, pertussis or whooping cough, and tetanus) and oral polio.

To make these arrangements, the nurse first sought cooperation from the Health Department. At first the local Health Department was reluctant to commit itself to providing vaccine for so many children. After explaining the nature of the Head Start program and the needs of the children, the public health nurse was able to arrange to take the children to the Health Department for the proper inoculations. Perhaps matters could be facilitated at the local level if federal, state, and county general offices could communicate with local districts corncerning the legitimacy of providing free vaccine for Head Start children.

Permission slips were sent home to be signed, and on the basis of the number of these parental permission slips returned, the nurse made arrangements with the Coordinator for transportation and supervision to the Health Department. Buses were chartered, parents were enlisted as volunteers, and a field trip to the Health Department resulted in most children receiving the desired inoculations.

A detailed outline of the responsibilities and duties of a public health nurse are given for a nurse responsible for setting up a new program. Health is one of the most important aspects of the total program, and we were fortunate in securing such excellent staff in this area. Any Coordinator will find it well worth the time and money necessary to staff this position with the best educated and most personable public health nurse available.

Some practical notes:

1. Collapsible lunch tables were used for doctor's *examining tables*. Blankets were folded for padding, old sheets for covering were donated, and sterile rolls of paper were purchased from the laboratory.
2. In the case of significant medical findings, the medical social worker *visited the home* to explain the diagnosis to the parent. Notes were sent home to *all* parents explaining the results of the doctor's examination.
3. We did not have as many doctors as we needed and many times the doctors were rushed. *Quality control* is desirable and was earnestly requested by the local pediatric society.
4. The nurse *always* checked the *master schedule* and gave out *appointments* the day before to both teachers and Coordinator, facilitating maximum cooperation.

5. All children receiving any health services were taken with their classroom group and teacher or aide who knew them. *All children* were *clearly designated* with name tags which were pinned on with safety pins. *Great care was taken that no mix-up would occur.*
6. Because of the fear and distress accompanying lab tests and inoculations, it is suggested that these procedures take place *away* from the Child Development site, either in a doctor's office or in a mobile laboratory which visits and leaves.
7. In some areas there was a lack of standardization in laboratory procedures which rendered the results invalid. Quality control is mandatory in laboratory work. Verify your laboratory. (At first we were criticized for using a lab out of the neighborhood with "high" rates. Later it was found we were one of a small minority who had valid laboratory results.)
8. Laboratory tests should be made in advance so that the doctor has the results *before* the physical examination.
9. To obtain optimum medical care, health education, and follow-up, the physical examinations should be held in the doctor's office or local established community clinic. If enrollments could be handled on an advance basis, the physical examinations might be made mandatory before registration could be completed. Then the nurse and staff could devote their time to needed follow-up.

The pediatrician's point of view

To get the pediatrician's point of view, we asked the doctor in charge of setting up programs from our county to write about Head Start Health programs. His views are included in the Appendix.

8

nutrition

Our organization was fortunate to secure the part-time services of a junior high school cafeteria manager to do the budgeting, purchasing and menu planning. Because we were allowed but 28¢ per child per day it was only through her professional experience in planning and purchasing that we were able to stay within the budget. Because she had been the cafeteria manager in a public school she was accustomed to planning menus that utilized food from government surplus, such as cheese, butter, powdered milk and dried beans. Through her efforts we were able to secure surplus food from the State Department of Surplus Commodities, and a milk subsidy arrangement with the State Department of Education.

While our cafeteria manager was able to do the planning, budgeting, and food ordering, she was unable to be on the site when food was prepared and served because of a previous job commitment. As a result, many problems ensued. The kitchen facility was equipped with kitchen appliances and large kitchen equipment for group serving. On the first day, however, we discovered that we didn't have enough of anything. Because we had scheduled both morning and afternoon sessions with overlapping food service we didn't have enough plates. We didn't have enough serving dishes. The children who were fed in the adjoining building were not only fed late but were fed cold food because of the trouble in transporting the food from the kitchen to the other building. Morale of the kitchen workers sagged because of the lack of equipment, the need to run from one building to another, and insufficient time to clean up before having to serve another group. Being non-professional in the food serving business ourselves, it was only through the painful experience of trial and error that we finally found that paper plates were too expensive and that it would be more economical to rent more dishes; that plastic forks were not only expensive in the long run but were not strong enough, and that additional silverware needed to be rented. It was found that it would be better to serve the whole group at the same time, so we rented a portable steam-table and more serving dishes. In this way we finally eliminated the long periods of waiting and the cold food. Having sufficient equipment also served to boost the morale of the kitchen workers. We found by hard experience that it is imperative to have a professional not only to plan food purchasing but also the *food serving*.

What and when to serve preschoolers

During the first week of the program the morning snack was scheduled for mid-morning, but the teachers noticed that many of our children came to school without breakfast. Also, the mid-morning snack came so close to the time of the serving of lunch that some children were not hungry at lunch. Therefore, we adjusted our written schedule to the needs of the children and made the snack available immediately upon the children's arrival. In rescheduling the nutrition period to provide the children with a snack when it was most needed we found that we also had to rearrange the schedule of the cafeteria staff. We made an arrangement whereby part of the staff was available at 8:00 and others arrived at 10:00 and 11:00. All the staff were present at the peak lunch hour time with a minimum crew for clean-up and afternoon nutrition snack. This procedure proved to be an effective solution for maximum utilization of staff within the prescribed budgetary allocations regarding hours. Fortunately our staff exhibited flexibility and the willingness to make the change in the interest of greater benefits to the children. Such a willing attitude on their part demonstrated to us the necessity for all staff members to be directly and primarily concerned with the children's welfare.

The snack menu was changed from the traditional graham cracker or cookie and milk to peanut butter sandiches with fruit wedges and milk. The peanut butter sandwiches were cut in fourths so that children could eat none if they were not hungry or several if they had not eaten breakfast. Such a schedule and menu change, as simple as it seems, was responsible for providing the additional nutrients necessary for our children, who lived in the "inner-city" environment ("inner-city" refers to the "city within a city," the downtown dwellings as opposed to the suburbs).

As we visited homes we soon discovered that the recommended daily intake of milk was impossible for families of several children to meet. In the majority of cases the milk that the children got in the Head Start program was the sole milk intake for the day. This lack of milk in the children's diet was reflected in their lethargic behavior, in their suscepti-bility to disease, and in their high incidence of tooth decay.

We found that many of our children came from families who had im-migrated into the inner-city from low income rural areas. In the rural areas they had access to foods commonly produced on the farm, such as greens, eggs and milk—foods which are rich in most of the nutrients. Now that the family had moved to the inner-city it was entirely dependent on *purchase* of foods. Because of the prohibitively high cost of many cuts of meat and of most fresh fruits and vegetables, our inner-city children were often missing the vital nutrients of protein and ascorbic acid found in abundant quantities in the eggs, milk and greens that were available on the farm.

Before we innovated the schedule of serving the children peanut butter, milk, and fruit when they first arrived, many of them were lethargic or restless in their play behavior. Our nurse pointed out to us that children from the low income brackets are typically deficient in protein, ascorbic acid and thiamine. After these essential nutrients were added to the diet there was more spontaneity, more interest in the play activities offered and more concentrated attention on the part of the restless children. Teachers also noted less irritable crying and clinging behavior. We feel that it is vital to be aware of the need for breakfast among Head Start children, as children who go without breakfast are apt to be unable to profit from the learning situation. We firmly believe that it is imperative that the nutritional area of Head Start programs be given primary emphasis. A snack is not enough. Children need both a nutritional snack and a complete meal. It is reasonably safe to state that the amount of milk that is drunk at Head Start is often the total amount that many children get. Therefore, we believe that anything short of a complete hot meal, nutritional snacks and a maximum milk supply is a denial of one of the promises of Head Start.

Serving lunch

We painfully discovered in the catastrophe of serving lunch on the first day that it is impossible for preschoolers to line up, wait, or eat in shifts. Therefore, we soon served lunch where the children were—in the classrooms near the kitchen, in the patio outside and in individual class-rooms of a nearby building. We found that it was easier to take the food to the children than to bring the children to the food.

Ideally, the food was served family style with each teacher serving small portions to her own children. Sometimes, in order to serve the food while it was hot, the kitchen staff had to serve the plates. In these cases, serving dishes with second helpings, and thirds and fourths when desired, were left on each table for the teacher to serve.

We soon noticed that on days when the children had finger foods they were better able to manage their food. Carrot and celery sticks or cabbage chunks were preferable to salad.

Mealtime was a social time

Many of our children had never before sat down to a meal with their entire family present, either because of some physical home limitation, such as no table, or not enough chairs, or the absence of one or the other parent at mealtime. Therefore, the teachers made a special effort to make mealtime a time for socialization and the setting a place of beauty. Teachers were responsible for creating harmonious routines at lunch time— washing hands, sitting at preset tables and waiting until all were seated before eating began. As the children became accustomed to mealtime they learned to help set the table, put name cards at the places and, in some instances, pour beverages. Teachers and children made placemats, picked flowers for bouquets, and set name cards at the children's places. Such a propitious environment seemed to have a calming effect on disquieting behavior such as yelling, grabbing and throwing food. In fact, such occurrences were not observed after a child's first few days of attendance. Flowers, placemats, name cards, and eating with regularity at a definite time and place seemed to be one of the most satisfying experiences for the children. A place designated specifically for a child and the use of his name on the placecard were significant features in the development of positive self-concepts and sense of identity. Their faces and bodies reflected relaxation, enjoyment and contentment at mealtime. The way in which foods were served had a direct bearing on the children's ability to independently care for themselves at the table.

Eating new foods

The customary diet of many of the children before their Head Start experience was mostly prepared foods such as bread, bologna, cheese and cereal. Therefore, to be greeted with such an array of strange looking dishes was at first disquieting to them. It was not unusual to see children eat only bread and milk their first day or two in attendance. Small portions were served first and then children were encouraged to taste "a little bit" of everything. If, after tasting a food, the child still refused it, no issue was made. Usually, after tasting a new food or a food prepared in a different way a child would continue eating it if no further comment were made.

Eating different amounts of food

Individual children varied tremendously in the amount of food eaten. Although small children usually eat less than larger children, we found this rule of thumb not applicable to our Head Start children. As often as not it was the smaller children who kept on eating after their average-sized friends were quite through. One little boy, the smallest in his room, consistently ate three or four plates full of lunch every day. He was small, thin, had a distended stomach, and apparently was very hungry. Our nurse told us that it is generally well known that children such as ours from poverty backgrounds are smaller in stature and weigh less. Perhaps our children are small because they receive insufficient amounts of food. Therefore, when food is available they need more of it to compensate for their previous inadequacies.

Feeding the afternoon group

We served lunch to the afternoon children on their arrival for the same reason that we served the nutritious snack to the morning session children on their arrival. The children were hungry.

The nutritious snack of fruit wedges and milk and sometimes peanut butter sandwiches was served before the children left for home.

One very hot afternoon, the kitchen staff sympathetically served punch and cookies for a nutritious snack. To the kitchen staff this was a special treat. It took more than a usual amount of tact to explain to them that the children's nutritional needs demanded milk and fruit rather than punch and cookies.

Facts from our nurse about nutrition

As we were trying to adjust to our children's needs by changing both the time and type of food of the snack, changing the menus somewhat, and getting more serving equipment, our nurse was an invaluable resource to us. At an early teacher's meeting she spoke on the effects of an inadequate diet on the nervous system. She pointed out that an inadequate diet will often lead to lack of energy, a lack of endurance, restlessness and misbehavior. She said that even a mild deficiency in thiamine, that is, vitamin B-1, may lead to emotional symptoms where children are inefficient, irritable, depressed, quarrelsome, uncooperative and fearful. After understanding the effects of a poor diet on our children we felt that we were better able to understand their behavior. Although it is impossible to isolate the effects of a better diet on our Head Start children we feel that it was one of the contributing factors to their increased well-being and socialized behavior.

OUR IN-SERVICE TRAINING ON NUTRITION

Later the nurse gave a talk to our entire staff on the nutrition problems of inner-city children.

Adequate nutrition is vital to the development and functioning of children and adults. Studies have shown that children with an inadequate nutritional intake suffer from retarded physical growth and development, including tooth and bone formation. Children in low income areas are found to be smaller in height and weight and to have more dental caries. In our group of 300 children, 200 were found to be in need of dental services. The effects of an inadequate diet on the nervous system lead to a lack of energy and endurance, restlessness, misbehavior and dullness.

In addition to causing certain emotional symptoms, emotional instability may in turn be a contributing factor to malnutrition. Emotional instability may be an etiological factor in undereating or overeating. In these cases it is necessary to understand the basis for certain eating habits as well as to prescribe an adequate dietary intake. Teachers should notice how children eat as well as how much they eat.

The effects of undernutrition on mental ability are not clear cut. However, mental accomplishment may be inferior because of less energy, inability to concentrate and low endurance. Bringing a malnourished child to a state of optimum nutrition should be a primary step in improving his expression of mental capacity in school work.

Ignorance, carelessness and extravagance may be as important in malnutrition as poverty. However, economic insecurity is a constant insidious factor because it prevents purchase of sufficient quantity of the right kind of food. It creates home conditions which render impossible a quiet, happy mealtime and it may undermine the emotional stability of adults responsible for setting the pattern for developing good eating habits.

Signs of inadequate vitamin C intake are manifested in the high incidence of gum disease and tooth caries and in the incidence of anemia. Although there was undoubtedly multicausation for the 66 per cent incidence of tooth decay in our children, inadequate diet was probably a contributing factor. Our children had an anemia rate of 15 per cent when 10.0 grams were used as a standard. It is important to note that a low hemoglobin does not necessarily mean low iron intake. A low hemoglobin points to a total nutritional inadequacy. Because vitamin C is necessary for the iron to be used, it is possible that, by increasing the ascorbic acid intake, the low hemoglobin may then automatically rise to a normal range. Notice should be taken that not *all* low hemoglobins should be treated in this way, but that when hemoglobin is low an evaluation of the child's total nutritional intake is mandatory.

Sufficient intake of complete protein is also associated with malnutrition of city dwelling poverty families because of the high cost of meat. Therefore, the family may need education in:

1. the vital importance of protein
2. the value of low cost cuts of meat
3. adequate substitutes for animal products such as nuts and beans.

In addition, the Head Start center should provide the nutrients probably missed by the children in the snack and regular mealtime.

Any problems that continue more than a week should be referred to the nurse for further study.

WHAT WE LEARNED ABOUT FEEDING HEAD START CHILDREN

We learned some important things about food services and nutrition of inner-city children that will be helpful to us in the future.

1. It is imperative to secure the services of a skilled dietician or nutritionist in purchasing and menu planning in order to operate within budgetary allotments. She must be a person who is able to utilize government surplus foods effectively, provide a nutritious menu, and plan foods that preschool children like.

2. It is desirable to have a director of food services present throughout the day to adjust the menu and food service to the particular changing needs of the children.

3. All staff members, from kitchen aides to teachers, need information concerning the general nutritional status of poverty children from the inner-city. While in this instance our public health nurse was able to coordinate the services so that the nutritional needs of the children were revealed, known, and met, another program may utilize the services of a professional dietician.

4. It is easy to teach children the values of a regular mealtime and the social amenities of group eating when calm, order, and beauty are as much a part of mealtime as the food.

5. If children are coming to school without breakfast they must be provided with milk and a nutritious snack on their arrival.

6. Preschool children require food prepared simply and served in a manner which enables them to feed themselves independently at mealtime. The nutritious snack should include the nutrients most commonly lacking in the diet of our children. These are proteins, ascorbic acid (vitamin C), thiamine (vitamin B-1) and sometimes iron. Adequate protein intake is dependent on a daily diet of some animal produce, such as eggs, milk, meat, fish or poultry, or legumes and nuts such as beans or peanut butter. Vitamin C is found in fresh fruits and is often the "missing link" in the maintenance of general nutritional status because of its function in the maintenance of tissues throughout the body and its relation to the metabolism of other nutrients. Thiamine is abundantly found in breads and cereals as well as vegetables. Eggs are a rich source of iron as well as protein and calcium. Therefore, each day's menu should include (1) raw fruits and vegetables for ascorbic acid, (2) enriched bread for thiamine, (3) meat products for complete protein and, (4) milk for calcium and protein.

7. Offering an adequate diet is not enough. It is important that *food be served* so that the children consume the important nutrients. Actual consumption of food is the vital factor. Teachers need to know that if vitamin C foods, such as fresh fruit, are served by themselves either at the nutrition break or at the beginning of the meal, they will probably be eaten. However, if they are served with a meal or at the end of a meal they may be left. It is equally important that high grade protein food be served to assure consumption. For instance, one half of a breast of chicken will supply a good portion of the daily protein requirement, but in a serving of chicken pie children may eat the crust and decline the chicken chunks or eat an insufficient number of them. Therefore, if the children are to consume the foods important to their nutritional status, it is vital to serve plain food in sufficient quantity, usually without sauce or spice unless the child is used to getting these at home.

All personnel responsible for the nutritional intake of children should be informed of these principles and urged to provide both the environment and the foods which are so necessary to the general well-being of children. We found an excellent reference to be Roberts' *Nutrition Work with Children*.

9

the social worker*

Since we had no precedent for the social work focus that Head Start demanded, our anticipated plan of operation in this area was based on the traditional concepts and approaches of established social work agencies. We perceived that the duties of the social workers would be primarily to acquire family data for reporting forms, to determine financial eligibility, to make home visits for the purpose of interpreting the program to parents, or to make referrals to community agencies in the implementation of family needs. We could hardly have imagined the variety of services which were to come within the realm of the social worker's functions.

Emerging roles

When registration did not "catch on" and build as rapidly as we desired, we became aware that many of the eligible families had not had sufficient contact with the "outside world" to be aware of the program. Apparently they had not read the newspapers, listened to the radio or television spot announcements, read the posters in the local stores, or attended church on the preceding week. The social workers were, therefore, cast into the role of recruiters, interpreters, or educators as the need for recruitment on a door-to-door basis became imperative. They held a brief orientation session with teachers, teacher aides and social work aides to prepare them for making home visits. Many of the staff had qualms about approaching strange doors and initiating conversation with strangers so far removed from their normal operational base. One of the things they needed to learn, for instance, was that a friendly and informal greeting, such as, "Hello, I'm Jane Smith," would be more acceptable and effective than, "How do you do, I'm Mrs. Roger Smith." Recruiters were instructed to make a simple statement of why they were calling, realizing that it had to be presented both succinctly and clearly if we were to have an audience

---

* Written in collaboration with Juanita Goodman.

at all. The gist of their remarks was: "The federal government has set up a special school for four- and five-year-olds who will go to school in September. The purpose is to help them get off to a good start. It is free and meets every day at Victory Church. Are there any children here who may go?"

Each door necessitated retelling the Head Start story. The first day out netted us many stony faces and "no thank you's." If, in some resistant homes there seemed to be children who appeared to be eligible, a note was made of the address. Another worker, on a subsquent call, would make a follow-up visit and plea. Repeated contacts seemed necessary to convince some people that:

> We were not selling anything.
> We were not from "The Welfare."
> We were not from the police.
> We really had something to offer.

After the initial suspicions were overcome, many relented and more and more children were successfully registered.

Obtaining the necessities

Material deterrents to attendance became a pattern as canvassing progressed. "I'd be happy to send him but he doesn't have any shoes. If I'd known ahead of time, I would have saved the money out. I was going to get him shoes in September when he starts to school, but just can't now." And so the stories went as we were turned away. Recognizing these as real and serious needs which would prohibit enrollment by a majority of pupils, our social workers sought out means of taking care of them. Thus, out of a felt need, another function had been defined for social workers in their unique positions in Head Start. They could not fall back on the comfortable structure of established public agency practice to dictate how to handle the situation. These were real, immediate needs for direct services, and we did not have the time to stand still and explore or apply to the usual gamut of referrals. Our unrealistic budget estimate had not foreseen any need for the provision of material things to guarantee school attendance (nor were such items allowable in the federal share of the budget). Through the generosity of Delta Sigma Theta (from its Project Budget), we set up a special fund earmarked for welfare purposes. From this budget we bought shoes, clothing, food, and other immediately needed items.

Exploding the myths

Our social workers scoured the immediate neighborhood and made arrangements with local merchants to supply the children and families with the necessary items of clothing. (Simultaneously, the workers were in contact with other agencies who were serving the families, to establish their eligibility or determine why these conditions existed in order to avoid duplication of services.) This arrangement with merchants worked satisfactorily and we did not experience the customary delaying process in wading through "the structure." Social workers or aides took the children to these stores, or sent them with an authorization, to be fitted with whatever items were necessary for school attendance. Our experience failed to support the common myth that all needy persons are pleading need in order to secure "something for nothing." Almost without exception, the families did not want "charity" and were reluctant to receive direct aid of this kind. Numerous families where children needed clothing to come to school were *not* recipients of relief nor did they desire to have clothing given to them. In these cases the offer of help had to be approached very delicately by placing emphasis upon their child's welfare. We admitted that the program had been hastily planned and it was reasonable that they had not heard of Operation Head Start, or been able to prepare for it. Only when prevailed upon not to deprive their children of the opportunity to attend a program designed especially for them did they consent to accept the help that was necessary to assure their attendance. This latter situation was the rule rather than the exception in our experience.

Many visitors in the program expressed amazement at the neat dress and physical appearance of our children. Obviously, the visitors were still wrapped in the concept of relating poverty to dirt. However, those of us who had visited the homes were aware of the personal sacrifices that had been made in order to dress the children "nice" and have them in attendance at school.

Moving into parent education

As the Head Start session progressed, parents came and went daily, having short, informal contacts with teachers and others. Few, however, remained and were actively involved in the program. An evaluation of this sparse parental participation led us to seek some kind of activity which would appeal to a greater number of families. Acting on a suggestion that an informal "open air" kind of parent meeting, with the emphasis on family service, might be appealing to a larger number of the families, our social workers found themselves cast in another role and wearing the hat of Parent Educator. Convinced that many parents who might have been uncomfortable in the structured setting of our weekly parent education meetings would respond, we planned such a meeting and held it on a very warm summer night in a public park near the school. Advertisements on the radio and in the newspapers advertised it as a "Family Night."

The park chosen for the meeting was especially selected because of its proximity, rather than for the comfort of its facilities. Our thought was that the utilization of this recreation unit in their own neighborhood, however sparse in nature, would result in the accrual of certain values and pride factors to the residents. There was a more subtle consideration in holding the meeting out-of-doors. Because a loud speaker was used to address the audience, we hoped that the message of the guest speaker would be heard by other parents in the area who had not attended the meeting but whose windows were open during the warm evening hours.

A very capable public school teacher, Ruth Mueller, spoke to the parents about the relationship which parental motivation and interest have to the academic success of the child when such motivation and interest are demonstrated to him. The highlight of the evening came, however, when we showed movies and color slides which our assistant director, Mary Lou Tolbert, had taken of the pupils, families and staff members at various times and places during the program. More effective than a thousand speeches, these media convincingly said to the parents and to the children, "See, you are somebody. You are important to us." The movies and slide presentation seemed to help them open up. A question and answer period in which parents were encouraged to ask any questions concerning their children, their own problems, or anything relating to the program was quite profitable and free of restraint.

During a social time which followed, fellowship and warmth permeated the air. Each parent was given a directory of area services which had been especially compiled by the social workers from a larger county-wide social service directory. They explained its use to the parents and how it might answer the questions often asked in times of family crises:

> Who to call?
> What is the number?
> Where to go?
> What to do?

Community resources in the following areas were included in the directory: Child Welfare and Attendance; Employment; Health; Housing Authority; Libraries; Neighborhood and Family Assistance; Parks and Recreation; Schools; Youth Serving Agencies.

Everyone present expressed gratification for this program and the warm, interpersonal relationship which had been established between the child's family, his teachers, and the other staff members involved in the process of his social development. More important, the idea of the social worker as family friend and helper gained footing in the minds of families whose previous concept of their role was negative.

From that time on, a more intensified program of home visiting and gathering of family data was carried out, with emphasis placed upon the special problems for which follow-up services could be initiated.

One example of the extent of the time and skill required to adequately follow up a case is presented here in detail.

CASE WORK SUMMARY OF GARY WILLIAMS

Contacts:

Day 1	Child came to our attention when he began to attend Head Start class. He was not enrolled, as the class was filled at that time.

Day 2	Social worker made home visit to baby sitter's home, where child is cared for during the day. Both parents work. Mother reports that Gary has multiple birth defects but is a bright boy, gets along well with other children and manages to take care of own needs in spite of handicap. Later same day, the mother came in to talk with nurse, teacher, and social worker. Father asked if Gary could be enrolled in Head Start because he felt the child would benefit from being with other children. He reports that Gary is being seen at the Orthopedic Hospital for birth defects, which include club feet (on which surgery has been performed), club hands, and absence of hip sockets. However, the boy is mentally alert and enjoys being among other children. He also reports that he and his wife do not treat Gary as though he were different and he is, therefore, encouraged to do things all children engage in. Father said child had good rapport with teacher and he thought Gary would benefit greatly from Head Start.

Day 3	Conferred with coordinator. Decision was made to allow child to be enrolled on a trial basis.

Day 4	Conference with supervisor. Suggestion made by Mrs. Epps that resources be explored through city schools as to education of handicapped children, with view toward helping parents make plans for schooling of this child.

Day 5	Child has been observed several times by social worker and seems to be making good adjustment. Although he is unable to keep up with all physical activities of the children, he is able to find many areas of interest, including tricycle riding, painting, blocks, and so on. He has a longer attention span than many children and engages in much purposeful activity. Manipulates materials, feeds himself, takes care of own toileting.

Day 6   Both parents were present at parent meeting and participated actively.

Day 7   Home visit by social worker. Mother no longer working because she is under doctor's care for ulcerous condition. Hopes to return to work. She was encouraged to attend parent education classes, seemed interested. Mother said Gary has appointment at Orthopedic Hospital Clinic. As she has no transportation we offered to help. She indicated Gary used to be seen once a month but has not been there for more than five months. Expenses are covered by husband's medical insurance and by Crippled Children's Foundation.

Day 8   Mother is not attending parent education classes. Social worker encouraged her to visit the site and follow Gary's progress by talking with the teacher.

Day 9   Volunteer transported Gary and mother to Orthopedic Hospital where he was seen in the clinic. Four return appointments were given:
            1. Hand specialist
            2. Club foot specialist
            3. Plaster specialist, to apply plaster for correction of spine
            4. Clinic and X-rays

Day 10   Volunteer transported child and mother to Orthopedic Hospital but could not stay. Social work aide returned to take them home.

Day 11   Home visit. Mother discussed problem of her unemployment. Although unable to work until released by doctor, she would like to find work in another field because she was not happy in former job. Referred her to the Department of Employment for job counseling. Counseled her on other family matters.

Day 12   Social work aide transported child and mother to Orthopedic Hospital for appointment with club foot specialist.

Day 13   Social worker took child to School Board of Education building for appointment with the doctor. Mother accompanied. After examination of child and giving vision, hearing and language tests, he recommended that child be enrolled in regular kindergarten class on trial basis, his department making selection of school and class that would best fit his special needs. Child would be bussed. He thought a long range plan might include regular classes, depending on child's mobility, with some emphasis on physical therapy during the elementary years. Should there be much hospitalization in the future for corrective surgery, home teaching would be provided.

Day 14   Conference with teacher. Regular conferences have been held with teacher to keep her apprised of all contacts with family, medical visits and other developments. Teacher is making arrangements to provide transportation to Orthopedic Hospital.

Day 15   Home visit by social worker. Parents did not keep appointment at Orthopedic Hospital. Parents were informed that child is badly in need of dental care, following examination by our dentist.

Day 16   Social work aide transported child, accompanied by mother, to dentist for follow-up work. Dentist unable to treat child because of structure and inaccessibility of areas needing treatment. Suggested special dentist.

Day 17   Conversation with mother. She said family may be moving shortly.

Day 18   Social worker transported child and mother to Orthopedic Hospital for clinic visit with the doctor. Extensive X-rays were taken on this visit. Social worker consulted with the doctor on this date and the following information was obtained.

Diagnosis of Gary's condition: Child has a disorder present at birth, affecting the muscles of many parts of the body and causing contraction of the limbs. This is essentially not a disease of the bones. There is also multiple scoliosis of the spine. There is an absence of hip sockets, and also asymetry of the head.

Treatment is very long range and is done by degrees. Scheduling of treatment depends on child's development and response to previous treatment. Correction involves: Feet—surgery has been performed once and further surgery is indicated in the future; hands—surgery is indicated but not before a year or two when further development will have taken place; spine— plaster will be applied in two weeks and over a period of time there should be considerable straightening out of the spine; no correction for hips.

Prognosis: It is difficult to say because of the rarity of the disease. Child will never be normal, although correction of various parts of the body will increase his mobility. Mental ability is normal.

Recommendation for schooling and evaluation of ability to function: School should be attempted. Child may be able to adjust up to about a second or third grade level but because of physical handicap the gap will widen between him and other children, and special school for handicapped will be necessary.

On this same visit, arrangements were made through Social Service Department for dental treatment at the University of Southern California clinic, to be paid for by Crippled Children's Foundation.

On evening of same date, social worker made home visit to see both parents. They expressed appreciation for all services of Head Start. Father said they had an opportunity to get better living quarters in another city and they were planning to move. Parents said they may need some help in getting Gary established in Head Start or school where they plan to move.

A total picture

The social workers' responsibility for bringing the family into the Head Start program and the Head Start program into the home was clearly identified as a primary function. Effective home-school coordination was mandatory for identifying problems and effectively working toward their resolution. A case illustrative of the full range of the social workers' challenges is included here:

A few things happened out of the ordinary this week. Of course, medical forms and immunizations, along with medical examinations, took up most of my time. I had two referrals from the teacher which I shared with the psychologist. One child was very withdrawn and cried very easily. I made a visit to this girl's home after observing her in classroom, and observed that her behavior was not the same. The mother offered a suggestion on how to work with the child to get the best results—leave her alone after you tell her something. It turned out to be just a matter of adjustment. I did have a conference with the teacher, and gave her a report of my home visit.

The second child was extremely withdrawn and thought to be somewhat retarded. This turned out to be a real concern of mine after making a home visit. The mother told me of some other concerns she has had about this boy. She expressed a desire for us to help and offered to do all she could. I consulted the psychologist and she is planning a home visit with me. In the meantime, the mother's father, in another state, became critically ill and she was needed there. I helped her to make arrangements with her BPA social worker to get an emergency food order so she could use her grocery money for the trip. Also, she had to get someone to come and watch her eight children. This was finally arranged.

A crisis came up with Mrs. F. and her family. Her check was late and I had to call her social worker to arrange for an emergency food order, for they had no food in the house. Also, Mr. F. had some forms to be filled out from the Department of Motor Vehicles regarding an accident his car was involved in, and he was not able to read or fill them out. I handled this for him and called several people to get information he was not able to get.

In a full day's work many other situations come up, things such as absent children, sick children, parent meetings, and parent conferences.

Subject: Monthly Report for July

1. Teacher—team conferences:
   Conferences were held weekly with all teams.
   Referrals accepted; followed through and reports made to teacher team.
2. Observations of children on site:
   Observed all classes. Observations were also made with speech therapist and psychologist.
3. Home visitations and consultations:
   Completed all referrals from teachers and nurse for home visitations, with follow-up visits in many cases. Most cases required consultation.
4. Medical follow-ups:
   All medical referrals are being seen as the cases require by the medical doctor and dentist.
5. Medical services:
   Obtained medical history from families in the field and at the site. Assisted the nurse in medical examinations. Transported children and families to the local health center. Made contacts re family medical follow-up.
6. Doctor, dentist and health center visits and contacts:
   Telephoned for information. Took children for inoculations. Worked with staff in distributing information re menengitis prevention measures.
7. Service to the child and family:
   Took family to Bureau of Public Assistance for aid. Offered assistance with food and clothing. Provided referral information re legal aid. Provided information re community resources.

8. Consultation with other staff:
   Regular weekly conferences were held with the child development specialist, speech therapist, nurse, social work aide and
   and other social workers. Weekly conference with immediate
   supervisor.
9. Referrals:
   Bureau of Public Assistance, Legal Aid Society, Community
   Center, Employment Agency and Pepperdine Speech Clinic.
10. Parent meetings:
    Took families to parent meetings.
11. Parent education:
    Participated in a series of parent discussions to set up classes
    in consumer education. Recruited parents for English classes
    at local high school.
12. Staff meetings:
    Attended Coordinator's staff meeting, area staff meeting, and
    social workers' staff meeting.
13. Contacts with other agencies:
    a. Committee on Poverty
    b. Community Services
    c. U.C.L.A. Marian Davis Clinic
14. Community participation:
    a. Coordinating Council luncheon
    b. Human relations meeting.

Summary

This brief resume cannot be a full report of the efforts, interest,
and enthusiasm which the social workers and their aides put into
the attempt to equalize the benefits which the children gained from
the Head Start experiences with some similar orientation at the
home and family level.

Most important is the fact that in achieving these gains in a relatively short period of time, the usual "red tape" processes for
determining eligibility before instituting the real aid program were
quickly discarded, and simple, direct, and effective ways to give
help where needed were implemented.

Community resources were utilized and their worth was brought
to the fore in a very positive manner and with very positive results.
In utilizing the small neighborhood businesses, the owners were told
that the process was a part of the national program to strengthen
small business operations, and their cooperation was assured.

In using an almost discarded public park, its overall value to the
community was recognized. Hopefully, such physical improvements

as are needed may well form the basis for some kind of job activity for parents in that area, and make the park a part of the community.

The willingness to devise new and direct ways to reach the "hard-to-reach" was probably the most significant contribution of the social work staff. Through flexibility, greater gains in *future projects* can be expected.

10

parent education

On the basis of an interest inventory circulated to parents and personal contacts made with parents by the personnel, a formalized parent education program consisting of one event each week was set up. There were five afternoon lecture discussion presentations and three all-community events during the course of the eight-week program.

Planning meeting

The first meeting was designed to acquaint the community with the goals of Head Start and to enlist the help of the residents in applying these broadly based goals of increased school readiness to their community and to their children. Accordingly, in addition to parents, representatives from various community organizations were invited to the planning session—the national congressman, the state assemblyman, the city councilman, Neighborhood Adult Participation Project (NAPP), the principal of the local school, and ministers of neighborhood churches. All invited guests came or sent official representatives.

Publicity for the meeting was in the form of releases to local papers and appeals through neighborhood churches. A disappointingly small group of parents assembled for the planning meeting. After an overview of the national "War on Poverty" by the congressman, and a speech on the local implications of the poverty program by the city councilman, the thinking of the residents was sought. Members of the Neighborhood Adult Participation Project (NAPP) spoke briefly about their neighborhood and what they believed their needs to be. They especially wanted neighborhood residents to be used for employment whenever possible. This request was carried out by arranging job interviews on the site.

Questions from the parents were centered on the operation of the actual program:

Q: How will Head Start compare to the program of the public schools in quality, especially regarding teachers?

A: *The children will get a comparable education as all our teachers are certified and the administrative staff is similarly qualified and experienced.*

Q: Will it cost any money for the school, or for lunch, or anything?

A: *No, all costs are borne by the federal government and the sponsoring organization.*

Q: What are the hours of operation?

A: *From 8:30 to 11:30 for the morning session; 11:30 to 2:30 for the afternoon session.*

Flexibility in the hours if children needed to come earlier or stay later was stated as a possibility.

The Coordinator summarized what we hoped to accomplish, mentioning, specifically, medical examinations and inoculations, increased language facility, and socialization. The need for volunteers among parents was stressed and a sign-up sheet circulated to the group resulted in few signatures. Refreshments were served during the social hour following the meeting.

Because of the small attendance at the first meeting, it was apparent that we needed to seek out how to increase parent involvement in subsequent meetings. We learned that there was a wide gap between the theoretical parent participation model and what was practically possible because of many very real problems:

1. Limited desire to participate
2. Lack of transportation
3. Working parents
4. Too many small children
5. Too many siblings
6. Poor health of one or more family members

To partially cope with these manifold problems, baby sitting and transportation were provided for future meetings. Within the framework of the existing problems which limited attendance, a full program of parent education was carried out on the following topics:

1. Child Development and Health
2. Nutrition and Purchasing
3. Creative Experiences for Children
4. Health Forum

Summary of presentations

Specialists in each field were asked to give short talks and encourage parent participation in the form of questions and, where feasible, give demonstrations. An outline or summary of each presentation has been prepared by each of the specialists for inclusion herein. While not a complete transcript, the summaries do serve as a record of what we were able to provide.

GETTING A HEAD START IN GROWTH

Topic: Child Growth and Development

Specialist: Clara M.D. Riley, Ph.D., Department of Home Economics and Family Life, Pepperdine College.

Format: First the parents were taken to the play yard and rooms to observe the children at play. Then they assembled to discuss the implications of the children's play for the child growth and development.

LECTURE

Children grow. As they grow, if they have toys and playmates and families who love them, they develop. As they get bigger in size, they also learn to think bigger thoughts, say bigger words, and figure things out for themselves. We all want our children to learn to take care of themselves in this world they live in. Learning to do things for themselves and to take care of themselves are two things we teach.

How children learn

Children learn by watching. You may have noticed the little boy standing by the swings—not swinging or talking—just standing there. But did you see his eyes? He was watching. *Watching* comes first, and when he's watched enough, then he'll swing. The same goes for singing and painting and talking and taking turns. First children need to watch—the other children and us—to see how it's done.

After they watch, they try it.

One of the things children need to learn before they go to school is to speak up for what they need. At first most of the children here watched me when I said, "Good morning, how are you today?" But now, one by one, they are trying out words. This morning Jamie caught on. He smiled and said hesitantly, "Good morning."

Alice has been watching the easel painting. This morning she held out her hands for the paint smock and painted for the first time. Painting is expressing herself and the beginning of writing. Putting on a smock is learning the rules. "If you want to paint, you must put on an apron first."

After they try it, they exercise it. Perhaps you noticed the group of boys and girls on tricycles as we came in. They are exercising their muscles—to grow stronger and more capable.

They are exercising their minds—learning to ride in the right direction, and learning to take turns.

They only learn to use their bodies effectively, to express themselves coherently, and to use their minds productively if they have opportunity to exercise abundantly.

As you go out, take another look at the play yard. Look for a child learning to get along, learning to share, learning to take care of himself. Look for a child learning to be happy in playing by himself. Notice the stages of learning—WATCHING, TRYING, EXERCISING; and all the kinds of learning—to think for himself, to solve the problems, to say what he needs, to play together, to use his muscles in his hands and arms and legs. Children grow. But, they develop, too, if we give them opportunity. We are happy you have brought your children to this "Child Development Center."

GETTING A HEAD START IN SPEECH

Topic: Speech Development

Specialist: By Glyndon Riley, Ph.D., Director, Speech and Hearing Clinic, Pepperdine College, Los Angeles.

Format: Dr. Riley addressed the parents concerning their importance in the speech development of their children. He encouraged questions from the audience, and remained during the refreshment period to talk with individual mothers.

Helping your child talk better

Parents are the important teachers. A child spends 90 per cent of his "school age" at home. So, naturally, the parent influences the child's speech more than anyone else.

Language includes listening, thinking, and talking. My talk concerns only listening and talking.

Listening

A child's listening habits can be improved by the parents. Anything that makes listening more profitable or more fun encourages the child to listen. You may follow these four specific suggestions:

1. Speak in a voice that is pleasant to listen to. Don't shout or whine.
2. Say many things that the child wants to hear. Keep "no" type speech and "orders" down to 25 per cent of the total talking. Seventy-five per cent of the time, talk to your child about things of mutual interest.
3. Use words that the child can understand. No one pays attention if he

is confused by the words being said. Has your minister ever preached "over your head?" Imagine how a child feels if most of the words said in his presence are meaningless to him.

4. Read to your child some every day. Read things that are of interest to him. Children like repetition. You may be bored at times with the story that is being read, but you need never be bored with the reading time. You can enjoy your child even while reading a story to him that you know by heart.

Talking

A child is encouraged to talk when someone will listen to him and is interested in what he has to say. Your child will talk *more* and better if you follow these four suggestions:

1. *Listen!* Listen to your child! Listen to what he is trying to tell you more than to how accurately he pronounces his words. Don't expect perfect speech of a four-year-old. Speech therapists expect good speech by age eight. When practical, do what your child tells you to do. Let him experience the feeling of controlling other people by words. Words are powerful—your child has a right to use them wisely.

2. *Do not interrupt when your child is talking.* You don't like him to "butt in" on you, so extend the same courtesy to him. After all, he is so much younger and less skilled socially.

3. *Help your boy or girl build a better vocabulary by explaining the meaning of new words.* Also, you can supply a word at the moment he needs it. For example, all animals may be called "doggie" by a two-year-old until other names are given, such as horse, kitty, or cow. Sometimes the child needs more experience to associate with a word. He needs to "touch and say" to learn how the object with the new name feels.

4. *Be a good speech model.* Pronounce words correctly and your child will learn to say them as you do. He will learn much of his grammar the same way. If you need to improve your own speech there are evening classes in voice and diction improvement for adults.

Conclusion

In general, your talking to your child encourages him to listen, and listening to him encourages him to talk.

GETTING A HEAD START IN HEALTH

Topic: Health Education

Specialist: Written in collaboration with Dorothy Jenkins, Public Health Nurse, Los Angeles City Schools.

Format: Mrs. Jenkins addressed the parents, giving them specific suggestions regarding health, and distributed hand-out sheets recommending the optimum amounts and kinds of food to be served. Since Mrs. Jenkins served Head Start as nurse, she used this meeting as an additional opportunity to become personally acquainted with the parents present. Added interest and clarity was given to the nurse's presentation, which follows, through the use of a *series of visual aids.*

LECTURE

A child's successful entrance into school and community life depends largely upon the understanding and support provided by the parents. Parents' feelings and beliefs so easily may become a child's own that he may find it difficult to develop new ones for himself in later years. Because of the receptivity of young minds, it is most important that parents and other adults provide the child with reliable standards. These standards find their way into the physical and mental, as well as social spheres of life.

Realizing that the child cannot benefit from any educational or social experience if his physical and mental condition are inadequate, health is, and should be, the increasing concern of parents and educators alike. The body which suffers from hunger caused by an inadequate diet can hardly house an alert, responsive mind. Weak legs that are restricted in their pace offer no match for the range of activities and physical skills demanded in a preschool situation. An unclean body or offensive teeth are incompatible with the goals of social acceptability and feelings of increased self-worth which are sought in Head Start. It behooves parents, then, to be alert to the nutritional and personal hygiene needs of their children if maximum gains are to be realized through this Head Start experience.

Cleanliness

Cleanliness, unfortunately, is not inherently a part of children's nature. It is a lesson which must be taught by parents. Cleaniness and impeccable neatness are not necessarily the same. Undue emphasis and rigidity in trying to extract neatness and perfection in young children may be damaging and restricting to complete expression and participation in expected activities at nursery school.

Habits of cleanliness, on the other hand, need to be acquired at an early age and maintained as the child grows. *Daily bathing* is good hygiene and is to be encouraged. Children naturally resist being bathed once babyhood is passed, but we may encourage them toward self-help by rendering praise in their "do-it-yourself" attempts. If parents provide children with the tools of cleanliness—their own wash cloth, towel, soap, toothbrush, toothpaste, comb and brush—body, face, hair, fingernail and tooth care may more easily be instilled in the young child.

Clothing

Clothing plays a big part in the degree of enjoyment and benefit which a child derives from Head Start. Loose and light clothing which do not hamper play and work at school are desirable. Water, sand, mud, clay, paints, and play dough are the tools for child's work. Therefore, shorts or trousers for boys and washable play dresses for girls are preferable. Sweaters, top coats, rubbers and hats are to be worn if the weather condition dictates but are to be removed indoors. Sweaters worn under blouses and shirts are ill advised as they may become uncomfortable and bulky as temperatures rise in the day. Good shoes are one of the best investments a parent can make. Sturdy, well-selected shoes guarantee healthy foot development. Well-fitting tennis shoes are recommended, but cowboy boots are unsafe, and, therefore, unacceptable.

Dental health

Good dental health is approached along three areas:

1. Proper nutrition and diet with adequate balances of food essential to sound tooth development.
2. Proper dental care through brushing and oral cleanliness.
3. Regular dental visits.

Head Start is concerned with proper dental health for your boys and girls. We are laying the groundwork for proper tooth development as we plan and prepare nutritious meals which are designed to promote proper tooth development. Milk, fruit juices, fresh fruit, vegetables, meats and starches, all in the proper quantities, add to sound tooth development. As this diet is implemented in the home we further the guarantee of healthy teeth for our boys and girls. A visit and examination by the dentist is a part of our Head Start services. After the dentist's visit you will receive a card which will tell you the condition of your child's teeth. It will certainly behoove you to accept his recommendations and follow up and do something about the problem areas which he relates to you. Proper dental care is a continuing process. A large part of the responsibility, parents, lies with you and the home for instilling the practice of daily tooth care.

Rest and sleep

Rest and sleep are important to a young child's growth and development. From your observations here at school you will note that our day is planned around periods of strenuous activity and rest. We recognize the needs of the bodies of young children for periods of rest and play. Parents can do a lot to guarantee the necessary rest for children by seeing that they get at least twelve hours of sleep nightly, with a daytime nap of one to one and one-half hours. The children who are assigned to our PM classes need to rest in the morning before coming to school. Their bodies will be more receptive to the activities in which they are to engage in the Head Start program. It is easy for us to spot the child who has had a morning of television or strenuous activity before coming to afternoon Head Start classes. He may be overly active, fretful, aggressive and prone to make trouble, or he may assume the opposite role of quiet, withdrawn and inert behavior. In either condition he is not in the best position to take advantage of the experiences which Head Start offers for his development.

Disease prevention

Disease prevention lies primarily with parents and the home. In fairness to your child and to others to whom he will be exposed, children should be kept home when they are ill or exhibit any symptom of illness. The closeness in which children live in a preschool program is comparable to or even greater than that in the home.

California State Law requires the *immunization* of all children prior to entry in school. We cannot urge too strongly that parents sign the parent consent forms and take advantage of this service as it is offered through Head Start. By receiving their polio, DPT and smallpox innoculations now we are guaranteeing better protection for our boys and girls as well as assuring them of being able to meet the necessary requirements for kindergarten. We have within our own community the resource of inoculations for all members of the family from babies to adults. At our own Southeast Health Center, clinics are held weekly for inoculation of all family members. It may be well for us to telephone and make arrangements to have our entire families inoculated if this has not been done. These simple preventive measures will insure better school attendance on the part of your child and, as a consequence, he will receive greater benefits from the continuity of experiences in Head Start through daily attendance.

Other health habits

Other health habits frequently overlooked by parents because they seem unimportant may be just as harmful as the more obvious cold or tooth decay. *Nail biting,* frequently a symptom of nervousness or fatigue, may be alleviated by insisting on adequate rest and relaxation. Faulty habits of *elimination* can contribute seriously to a child's attitudes and result in irritability or even illness. Encourage daily bowel habits. Young children do forget and may need to be encouraged to go to the bathroom frequently. It is better to avoid laxatives in young children and promote better elimination through increased vegetable and fruit intake. *Bedwetting,* often a habit in young children, may be the result of either poor habit training, nervousness, or a physical defect. A child may grow out of it, but a physician should be consulted to determine the cause. *Postural defects* in young chidren are more often the result of a slouchy posture than real orthopedic difficulties. We as parents can do much to alleviate the situation by frequent reminders to our children to stand and sit tall, and by encouraging play activities which contribute to sound physical development.

Lastly, we may contribute to the soundness of our children's health by encouraging them to play outdoors in the sunshine and providing them with activities for both indoor and outdoor play that are suitable, satisfying and appropriate to their level of development.

GETTING A HEAD START IN GOOD NUTRITION

Topic: Nutrition and Purchasing of Nutritious Foods at Low Cost

Specialist: Jewell Graham, M.A., Junior High School Homemaking Teacher, Los Angeles City Schools.

Format: Lecture and discussion followed by an actual demonstration during one afternoon at which the mothers planned and prepared an entire meal, using the techniques learned in class.

I— LECTURE

Food for children

Little children need foods that will help them grow—foods that build muscle, bones, blood and sound teeth. They need food which help them to stay well most of ' ime and to get over colds and other sicknesses. Children use trer mounts of energy—running, climbing, and pushing play ec

Good foo' food which gives plenty of building material, r rgy. A child will get the substances that do ome foods from each of the four food ly available at the food markets, th ple quantities of correct foods. gster needs for getting off to a really stem em too, but they are especially important to the the process of growing and developing the body he n che rest of a natural life.

Planning the m

Mothers have always wanted their children to eat a lot, and probably always will be worried when they don't. That's natural. When you think about the important foods listed on the sheet you probably feel that you have a big job to get it all in. Divided in the day's meals it becomes much easier to manage. By choosing different kinds of meats, vegetables, fruits, and cereals, you can provide variety, match your pocketbook and cater to your family tastes.

The following sample meal plan for a child shows how little adjustment, if any, needs to be made in the pattern you use for the whole family:

Breakfast
Fruit or juice
Cereal with milk
Toast or other bread
Butter or margarine
Milk

Lunch
Main dish—mainly meat (eggs, fish, poultry, dried peas, cheese, peanut butter)
Vegetable or salad
Bread—butter or margarine
Dessert or fruit
Milk

Dinner
Meat, poultry or fish
Vegetable
Relish or salad
Bread
Butter or margarine
Fruit or pudding
Milk

What happens when children eat inadequate diets

The effects of an impoverished environment in the early years upon physical growth, personal health, social relationships, and emotional development have been a matter of concern for many years. There is plenty of evidence to indicate that they seriously influence intellectual functioning as well.

Deprivation stunts growth and learning. The earlier it is removed or compensated for the less danger of permanent damage. Health authorities and nutrition studies agree that good nutrition is the sound foundation upon which the most effective, happy, and satisfying individual grows and develops.

It is our dream that the parent education program will enlarge and grow to include parent-child preschool classes—an adult education program that will help mothers develop attitudes and skills that will enable them to guide and motivate their children. It is further hoped that this program of adult and parent education will expand to provide homemakers with instruction in family budgeting, installment buying, consumer information on adequate clothing and food purchasing, improving existing housing accommodations, sanitary procedures and the use of various cleaning and refinishing materials. This is simply an initial step. Let us go forward together.

II— DEMONSTRATION

Preparation, serving and storage of food

In addition to the importance of planning and selecting the proper diet for growing boys and girls it is equally important to know efficient methods of storage before and after cooking. It has been discovered that over-cooking, poor storage methods and improper handling of food, cause losses of vitamins.

Demonstrations illustrating the correct methods of cooking vegetables, meats, and other dishes in order to conserve these perishable vitamins were made. In this pilot class the mothers were intensely interested in the best methods of preparation and eager to participate in a training program that would give opportunity for learning these methods.

After talking about the best way to cook and store foods, these parents planned menus from basic meal patterns and actually prepared and served these foods to their children from plentiful, economical foods in season. The mothers gave careful attention to make sure they included foods from each of the Basic Four Nutritional Groups.

Some of them were unaware of how they could save money by buying foods in season and seemed especially grateful for this information. All in all the demonstration seemed to have been an effective way to teach the principles outlined in the lecture.

THE FOUR BASIC FOOD GROUPS

1. *MILK GROUP*

Food included:

> Milk—whole, evaporated, skim, dry or buttermilk
> Cheese—cottage, cream, cheddar type
> Ice cream

Contribution to the diet:

> Milk is our leading source of calcium which is needed for bones and teeth. It also provides high-quality protein, riboflavin, vitamin A and many other nutrients.

Amounts recommended:

> Some milk every day for everyone. In the amounts shown below the measure is an 8-ounce cup.

Preteen children	3 to 4 cups
Teenagers	4 or more
Adults	2 or more
Pregnant mothers	4 or more
Nursing mothers	6 or more

2. *MEAT GROUP*

Food included:

Beef, veal, lamb, pork, variety meats such as liver, heart, kidney, poultry, eggs, fish and shellfish. Alternates—dry beans, dry peas, lentils, nuts, peanuts, peanut butter.

Contribution to diet:

Food in this group are valued for their protein which is needed for growth and repair of body tissue—muscle, organs, blood, skin and hair. These foods also provide iron, thiamine, riboflavin and niacin.

Amounts recommended:

Two or more servings every day. One serving equals two to three ounces of lean cooked meat, poultry or fish, two eggs, or one cup cooked dry beans, dry peas or lentils, or four tablespoons of peanut butter.

3. *VEGETABLE—FRUIT GROUP*

Foods included:

All vegetables and fruit. This guide emphasizes those that are valuable as sources of vitamin C and vitamin A.

Vitamin C—

Good sources—

Grapefruit or grapefruit juice, orange or orange juice, cantalope, guava, mango, papaya, raw strawberries, broccoli, green pepper, sweet red pepper.

Fair sources—

Honeydew melon, tangerine or tangerine juice, watermelon, asparagus tips, brussel sprouts, raw cabbage, collard greens, garden cress, kale, spinach, kohlrabi, mustard greens, potatoes, sweet potatoes, tomato juice, turnip greens.

Vitamin A—

Dark green and deep yellow vegetables—broccoli, carrots, winter squash, collards, cress, kale, spinach, sweet potatoes, turnip greens and dark green leaves.

Fruits—

Apricots, cantalope, mango, persimmon and pumpkin.

Contribution to diet:

Fruits and vegetables are valuable chiefly because of the vitamins and minerals they contain. In this plan, this group is counted on to supply nearly all the vitamin C needed and over half of the vitamin A. Vitamin C is needed for healthy gums and body tissues. Vitamin A is needed for growth, normal vision, and healthy condition of skin.

Amounts recommended:

Four or more servings every day, including one serving of a good source of vitamin C or two servings of a fair source and one serving at least every other day of a good source of vitamin A.

If the food chosen for vitamin C is also a good source of vitamin A, the additional servings of a vitamin A food may be omitted.

The remaining one to three or more servings may be of any vegetables or fruit, including those that are valuable for vitamin C and vitamin A.

4. BREAD—CEREAL GROUP

Foods included:

All breads and cereals that are whole grain, enriched or restored. (Check labels to be sure.) In addition to breads and cereals (cooked and ready-to-eat) grits, macaroni, spaghetti, noodles, rice, rolled oats and any foods made with cornmeal or whole gain and enriched flour.

Contributions to diet:

Foods in this group furnish worthwhile amounts of protein, iron, several of the B vitamins and food energy.

Amounts recommended:

Four or more servings daily. If cereals are not included in these four servings, add another serving of breads or baked goods, making a total of five servings.

Count as one serving: one slice of bread, one ounce of ready-to-eat cereal, ½ to ¾ cups cooked cereal, cornmeal, grits, macaroni, noodles, rice or spaghetti.

GETTING A HEAD START IN CREATIVITY

Topic: Creative Experiences for Children

Specialist: Rosalie Blau, M.A. Mrs. Blau was a National Consultant for Project Head Start, a visiting professor in UCLA Extension and Santa Monica College, and directs a nursery school in Santa Monica.

Format: Mrs. Blau set the stage for this meeting by having each adult pin a bow of ribbon in her hair. This simple act seemed to eliminate some of our adult inhibitions and put us nearer in thought to the level of the children as explorations were made into clay, fingerpaints, collages and paper sculpture. Mrs. Blau is a chronic "saver" of every scrap, every discarded item, everything, and consequently had enough materials in premade kits for every parent to have one to work with and later take home. Mrs. Blau's incidental comments as she circulated and encouraged participation were subtle reinforcements of the benefits to be derived by the children from these same creative experiences.

Clean-up time and evaluation of the activities with the parents tactfully and unobtrusively acquainted them with two further educational objectives in our preschool creative arts experiences.

The setting promoted conversation, gaiety, and socialization. The restraint overcome here served as the foundation for a continuing relationship among this group of parents. Using this experience and their mutuality of interest in their children's welfare as a point of departure, these contacts may well become forerunners of community interest groups and the assertion of active leadership.

CREATIVE EXPERIENCES FOR CHILDREN

If we could take our children to the beach for a day, the children would probably be very happy entertaining themselves with the sand, the sun, the waves and sea shells. What is the charm of the beach? What are the offerings there?

Nature as teacher

Before we all moved to the city and were enclosed in apartments, with tiny cubicles for yards, children had the creek and the rocks, the trees and the grass for their very own backyards. Perhaps some of you were lucky enough to grow up with Nature's offerings as your toys, actually your *teachers,* teaching you what the world was all about—the waters and pebbles, rocks and sand and twigs, the taste of water and of grass, the smell of wet earth and sod, the feel of cool moss and sun-baked stones, the sound of sticks hitting together—and sometimes it was the taste of the earth and the feel of the sticks!

Learning through our senses

At any rate, this is the way some of us learned—in the country—with mud and water and sticks and stones as our materials. And how did we learn? Through our senses. By smelling, tasting, touching, listening. And our children, all children, learn the same way today—through the senses. The reason we make such a fuss about children's learning today is that we have taken away their natural tools for learning, by and large. We have taken away the creek and the rocks and the beach and the mud. Now if our children are to grow and to learn we must provide other things in their places. *How?*

As we cook at home, we can let the children stir, smell, touch, and taste the dough. Let them learn that *"We put things together to make something else."* This is a wonderful lesson to learn while stirring, mixing, helping mother.

Sorting out is another wonderful lesson to learn. These two socks go together because they are the same *size* and the same *color*. The color of your shirt is blue, your sister's shirt is red. Put your shirt "here" and your sister's shirt "there." Children who know colors, sizes, and where to put things will be far ahead when it is time to go to school.

How parents may help

We could buy expensive toys and still miss out on what we can teach our children with what we have at home. *Parents are the providers and the givers of things;* tissue paper for pasting; greeting cards for cutting; greenery for beauty; seeds for collage; squeeze bottles for water play; cut-down soap containers for mud pies; spools for sorting and stacking; blocks of wood for building.

In their play, we must remember that *children must explore before doing.* If our children know how paste tastes, smells, and feels (all over hands—perhaps faces too) they will be more able to use it constructively to stick "this" to "that" and make "something else."

In Southern California where most of us have yards, nature has richly blessed us with sun and soil. Perhaps there is nothing quite so exciting as planting some carrot seeds, watching the plants grow, and finally, plucking the plump, yellow vegetables from the ground and biting into the product of our very own planting. We sing a song at Head Start school called, *The Carrot Seed*—"I water it, I pull the weeds—*carrots grow from carrot seeds"*.

Water, soil, weeding, waiting, growing, all these experiences will be theirs if they learn where food comes from in the *first* place. Will you make a garden with your children?

Although your preschoolers will need much help from you, they will learn many lessons from their own garden.

OTHER PARENT ACTIVITIES

Three all-community events besides the formal parent education sessions rounded out a full eight weeks. A field trip to the Children's Zoo for families and extended families, a community-wide carnival, and a social welfare forum in a neighborhood park all received popular support with the majority of the families participating. Detailed discussions of these community events are treated in the chapters on Bringing the Community to the Classroom and the Social Worker.

SUMMARY

Interested, vocal, active parents can become the catalysts that herald change, growth, leadership and sustaining prosperity in our communities.

Parent education, parent involvement or parent participation as related to Head Start parents are, in effect, one and the same. They each encompass a goal of effecting understanding and concomitant change in the parent and, in turn, in the home and in the community, for as a parent participates and becomes involved in the program his understanding and education increase likewise. The media through which interest is stimulated and the impetus for its perpetuation and growth is the child. With the primary focus on the child's interests and needs, parent education in Head Start holds enormous potential for an increased consciousness of the importance of the parental role.

Where does it begin?

Parent education in Head Start is far more than the isolated film, the capsule lecture, the coffee klatch, or even the interest classes commonly perceived as being the sum total of activities in this area. Where does it begin? Where does it end? In practice, parent education begins in the initial contacts with the home during the recruitment period. Breaking down the negative feelings toward schools and authority, feelings rooted in repeated unhappy experiences or simply based on fears and inability to relate, is the first lesson in this unique curricula of parent education. Teachers, social workers, social work aides—all those who recruit—are the initial instructors. The warmth, the tact, the confidence which they exhibit in initial contacts with the home may become the catalysts for emergence of new positive attitudes, interest, and a sincere desire to become involved in the Head Start program. Day-by-day contacts with parents as they bring children or pick them up are vital links in the educative chain.

Parents are people

Through our efforts to sensitize all personnel to meeting and working with parents, the slogan for our operations in this area became, "Parents Are People." Recognition of the parent as an individual with feelings and with concerns about his child and about himself went far in creating a warm cooperative relationship. It was at this point that we were able to take our departure into involving the broader spectrum of parent education.

Accepting limitations

It is important to respect the parents' degree of participation or involvement, *however limited* they may seem from our point of reference. For the parent who has ten young children, getting her Head Start child to school on time, clean, fed and dressed, may indeed be her contribution for any given day. The four hours once a week away from home, which involves finding a baby-sitter for the younger children and seeking transportation to get to Head Start, may constitute to this mother a great sacrifice and certainly limits the extent to which she may paricipate. Picture, if you will, the mother from one housing project who dispensed with home chores early enough to ride the bus with her child and engage in Center activities throughout the day in order to be present for the planned Parent Education Meeting at the end of the school day. She would not ask for a ride, however. She would take the bus rather than ask.

We learned early to accept, respect, and appreciate these efforts. They fell far short of the middle-class nursery school structure with the picture of the free housewife and mother who spends hours each week in planned observation and participation techniques; but for people to whom mere life and survival are the biggest challenges, involvement or participation, whatever the degree, is commendable. It behooves planners to be empathetic rather than condemning, but they must spark empathy with decisive action for stimulating and provoking interest and implementing practical procedures to encourage participation.

GUIDELINES FOR PARENT EDUCATION

In planning for parent education as a formal structured process we found certain guidelines which facilitated implementation of our program.

1. Establish a good relationship, build parental pride.
2. Invite and encourage observation and participation in the Center.
3. Guide the parent, through involvement in the program, toward increased understanding.
4. Find out where parents' interest is stimulated.
5. Schedule meetings at a time and a place convenient to parents.

6. Help parents discover hidden talent for greater participation.
7. Utilize skills and talents of parents, steering them towards self-leadership.
8. Solicit support and the exchange of "working ideas" of parents and teachers.
9. Make baby-sitting services and transportation available.
10. In bi-lingual communities have an interpreter and make communications available in both languages.

11

the speech and hearing specialist*

When Project Head Start was first announced, the executive secretary of the American Speech and Hearing Association sent a memo to each of its 11,000 members suggesting that we be ready to help the community wherever possible. So it was that whenever Delta Sigma Theta approached Pepperdine College Speech Clinic concerning the services that we could provide for their program we responded enthusiastically. Our first task was to screen all of the children who were present during the first two weeks in their speech and their hearing.

Developing a screening test and procedures

At that time an adequate test to screen the speech of low income preschool children had not been developed. At the clinic we had been working on such an instrument for several months. We decided that the time had come to try it out. This test, subsequently named the Riley Articulation and Language Test (RALT) proved to be entirely satisfactory. The most difficult problem proved to be not the development of a new test but bringing the test and the child productively together. We spent the first week at the school whenever we had a few free hours so that the children could get used to seeing us. At this time most of the children were without any verbal speech, to our knowledge; that is, they came and played silently but they did not talk to adults. When it came time to test the children we decided to bring them all together at the same time. We took the one or two "leaders" and gave them the test first. The shyest ones we put in the learning situation so that they might sit and observe, observe that nothing was going to hurt them, that nobody was going to yell at them, that they should talk back whenever they were talked to.

In this way the speech screening proceeded productively. At first we had

* Written in collaboration with Glyndon D. Riley, Ph.D.

an audiologist to give the hearing screening. However, at this stage, that is, the beginning of Head Start, the children seemed terrified not only of the strange person but of the earphones. Therefore, we found that it expedited things considerably for the same person who gave the speech screening to also give the hearing screening.

Screening for hearing losses

We found that children in the age groups served by Project Head Start were best screened by a process called "Pediatric Audiometry." It is a process by which each child is trained to respond to the sound of the audiometer by manipulating some kind of little toy. For instance, we asked one child to drop a marble into a box, another to fly an airplane from one side of the table to the other, another one to raise his hand when he heard a sound. Any procedure that is easily understood would have done as well. A suggested procedure that is easily understood is to ask several children to come together.

We set the audiometer at 80-DB and put the headset on the table before the children. We asked them to respond in unison as the test signal was turned on and off. Then the audiometer was set to 25-DB and we put the headset on one child who seemed to understand the procedure best. When we were sure that the child knew what to listen for we set the audiometer at the screening level. We screened at several frequencies including at least 500, 1,000, 2,000 and 4,000 CPS.

While we were doing this we let the others watch. Then those who were more shy could see how it was done. By watching they were able to learn and usually did it very well. We found that we had less than 2 per cent "no response" to the Hearing Test when we administered it in this way.

About 2 to 3 per cent of the children, we found, needed to have thorough audiometric evaluations before they entered school.

Usually on the screening we merely indicated whether the child passed or failed at each of the frequencies at which the test was administered. If the child passed all of these frequencies on both ears then it was indicated on the record that he passed the hearing test. If he failed any one of the frequencies in either ear then it was indicated that he needed further testing. If he simply did not seem to understand and did not respond to the testing situation we indicated that he needed to be retested in about a year or so when we hoped he would be able to adapt better. In this case we wrote a note, "Did not respond to testing situation."

Screening for articulation disorders

There are several useful methods of screening a child to see if he has an articulation or a speech disorder. One of the simplest is to merely engage him in conversation. A common test is the "Templin and Darley." This is a picture screening test of articulation available from the State University of Iowa. The test consists of fifty pictures. It takes about five to ten minutes to show the preschool children the fifty pictures and get their responses to each of them. Children's scores are then compared to norms available to see if they are behind the normal population in their speech development. If a child is substantially behind then he automatically fails the screening test.

We did not find this test satisfactory to use with the Head Start population and quickly switched to the *Riley Articulation and Language Test,* even though it was then in the beginning stages of development.

This test has two parts. The first is articulation and the second is language. The articulation part of this test consists of eight test words which were selected because they tested the sounds which, if they are defective, are likely to indicate the child will have a persistent speech disorder that will last into his adult life if he does not get therapy. The articulation test is very quick to give. The examiner says only eight words. After each word the child is asked to repeat the word after the examiner. It usually takes only thirty seconds to administer. The recommended procedure for screening the language function is to use the language subtest of the RALT. This subtest consists of a series of sentences which the examiner says and the child repeats. The sentences increase in length and complexity as they go along. A child who has difficulty with either understanding or with being able to put his words together to frame his own sentences will have difficulty in repeating these sentences back to the examiner. The RALT is now published and is available from Western Psychological Services, Beverly Hills, California.

After giving the RALT there were several results that could be scored— several alternatives. First, the child could have passed. Second, the child did not pass but his score was near normal. If this was true we recommended that he be seen by a speech therapist after he enrolled in public school. The third possible choice was that he failed the articulation test with a low score and he should be seen for thorough testing before he enters school or as soon as possible. Fourth, the child did not respond to the attempt to screen his articulation, that is, he refused to speak at all. In this case we recommended "retest" or "refer."

These same four possibilities are available for use on the language test, that is, there are four alternatives: (1) the child simply passes, (2) he doesn't pass it but he scores near normal and therefore he should have retesting after he enters school, (3) he fails with a low score and should have a thorough language evaluation immediately, (4) he refuses to respond at all. Anytime a child does not respond at all we recommend waiting until the next semester or next year to try to give the child the test again. In the meantime we usually refer him for psychological services or to the child development specialist.

CRITERIA FOR REFERRAL

After we had screened all the children we got together with the rest of the professional consultants in the program, including the nurse, psychological consultant, project director, and the head teacher to decide which children needed therapy and whether it would be best carried out in the clinic or hospital, special school, or the Head Start facilities.

Clinic referrals

We tried to set up some general guidelines for selecting children who should be referred to clinics. Head Start children are still quite young and it is hard to know for sure whether the difficulties will disappear with age or whether they are the type of defect that can be handled in public school therapy. Finally, we set up three guidelines for referral: first, a child should be referred to a clinic or to a hospital for medical examination if there is an *emergency* of some type which reqires immediate attention. For example, a child who has seizures, or complains of pain during the hearing test, or who has a cleft palate would fall into this category.

Special schools

Second, we refer if we doubt if the child will be able to go to regular public school. This is the child who may be deaf, extremely hard of hearing, cerebral palsied or mentally defective. We discuss the alternatives among ourselves and with the child's parents. We have to see what special schools are available. He might be eligible for certain special education services. He may be eligible for a school for the deaf and hard of hearing. He may be eligible for a cerebral palsy school or he may be eligible to attend certain specialized classrooms within a regular public school setting. One of the major considerations here is whether these referral facilities are available. An illustrative case follows.

CASE HISTORY OF REFERRAL TO SPECIAL SCHOOL

Reason for referral:

Ricardo failed to respond to the speech and hearing screening tests for no apparent reason (fear, perhaps). His teacher expressed concern that Ricardo did not speak in class.

Results of testing:

Ricardo failed to respond to most tests. He smiled and nodded when a task was present but made no attempt to perform. This occurred on the neurological signs test and a repeat-after-me speech test.

An oral-peripheral examination, in which Ricardo cooperated well, revealed a cleft line which appeared deep but closed extending through the alveolar ridge and hard palate. The lip appeared to have been repaired surgically and no adhesions were seen. The teeth appeared extensively decayed and seemed bunched and short at the lip. The lip appeared notched on the left side and too long in relation to the rest of the face. Ricardo was able to blow through a straw and drink through a straw.

Speech ability:

Although Ricardo failed the screening test, he was heard to say "fish" (one of the test items) very quietly and correctly after testing attempts were completed. His teacher reports that Ricardo never speaks in the classroom although he cries out and grunts while at play outdoors. He uses some gestures and nods his head for "yes" and "no," but gives no responses when indoors.

Observation of play:

Ricardo played with the other children while outdoors. They called him by name and included him in their game of "monster." As the title character, he chased them and growled, but did not speak. His coordination did not seem grossly abnormal as he ran and climbed on some boxes.

Teacher's report:

Ricardo's teacher reports that he does not attempt any activity that seems difficult. He is unable to work a simple puzzle which other children in the class can do. He does not follow group instructions and does not perform well in group activities directed by the teacher.

Interpretation and recommendations:

It was recommended that Ricardo see a dentist for his decayed teeth and to determine the likelihood of such conditions as extra teeth, misplaced teeth, and so on, conditions commonly associated with cleft palate. He found no present condition which would interfere with Ricardo's speech.

The examiners were unable to rule out hearing loss as Ricardo did not respond to screening attempts. His responses both to other speech tests and to his Head Start environment suggest the possibility of brain damage or retardation. The findings of the psychological team and a report on Ricardo's home activities would be valuable. A continuation of Head Start experience is recommended for the present and a special public school class might be considered in the future.

Referral to a university clinic

If a child's speech handicap is too serious to be treated during Project Head Start and if it is too serious to be treated very effectively in public school later on, it may be advantageous to get him to a university or a community clinic while he is still young enough for a very thorough diagnosis and for possible treatment. In general, then, we believe that the more serious disorders and those that are complicated by multiple problems or medical problems should be referred to the appropriate agencies in the area.

CASE HISTORY OF A REFERRAL TO COLLEGE CLINIC

Reason for Referral:

Willie has not spoken since entering the Head Start program.

Case History:

Willie was seen by the speech therapist for the first time in the classroom. At that time it was observed that he would not respond to directions (oral), that he did respond to the sound of a passing fire engine, and that he had great difficulty in fitting tinker toys together. When a toy was taken from him by another child, he cried out but used no words.

The following week Willie was observed in the playroom of the Pepperdine Speech Clinic. He failed to respond to the verbal directions of his father and used no language to communicate with his younger brother and sister. (No tester was in the room at this time.) When left in the room alone, Willie listened to a toy telephone until the tester entered some five minutes later.

According to the father, Willie has never spoken at home; however, he reports that the mother and grandmother claim to have heard the child say, "Good night" and, "Thank you."

Most testing has been inconclusive or inconsistent:

Mecham Language Development Scale: This parent interview form indicates a language ability of a two- and one-half-year-old. However, the father suffered a stroke when Willie was a baby and was unable to answer some items with certainty.

Peabody Language Development Scale: Willie was shown how to match, by pointing, a spoken word to one of four pictures on a page. Thereafter, when a test word was spoken, Willie responded, after a nudge of the elbow, by pointing to the same position on each page, regardless of what picture was there.

Neurological Signs Test: Willie failed to respond to any of the items except kicking (right foot) and throwing (right hand). This led to a game of pitch and catch in which Willie was able to catch with both hands cupped against his body.

Gesell Figure Copying: Rather than copying the circle, Willie made very weak scribbles on the paper. No other forms were tested.

Hearing evaluation: The audiogram indicated only a slight loss. It is possible that there is no loss but that a certain intensity was necessary to attract Willie's attention. He learned quickly by imitation how to raise his finger when he heard a sound. He appeared to be somewhat distractible and his responses were not always consistent. In a freefield test (no ear-phones, tester's voice broadcast at given intensity through loud speaker), Willie responded to his name but gave no response to, "Show me your nose," or, "Where's Daddy?" at the same intensity.

Interpretation:

Because of several factors—the very slight hearing loss, the ability to follow non-verbal directions, the apparent purposefulness of his actions—the testers feel that Willie's problems may stem from a confusion in the communication functions. He may be neurologically handicapped, and there may be some generalized retardation. There is certainly some degree of emotional overlay.

Recommendations:

Willie should be seen by a pediatrician for a thorough physical exami-nation and perhaps should have a neurological workup if the doctor so recommends. The available medical history is sketchy and should be completed with special emphasis on Willie's development. A report on the home situation has been requested from the social worker. Willie will undoubtedly profit from a continuation of his experience in Head Start, although it is uncertain whether he will be able to attend normal public school classes.

Willie's father also has a definite need for help with his speech. His stroke left him with dysarthria and some hearing loss. His speech disability creates a further problem in the environment of Willie and his siblings.

Providing therapy on the site

We provided therapy in the regular Head Start program to all those children who qualified for it. We sent graduate students in speech therapy to the Head Start site. There they took the children, either one at a time or in groups as large as four or six, according to the severity of the symptom, to a separate room where they talked with them or engaged in other types of play therapy.

The children were put together according to the type of difficulty which they had. The first level of therapy was for those children who had a relatively mild articulation and language problem, who scored just under the cut-off norms on the RALT and who showed no hearing loss and seemed to be getting along pretty well socially. These children were simply left in their Head Start classrooms and were treated indirectly through the teachers. We provided a special workshop for the teachers in language enrichment. This workshop was based on research which was carried out at Florida State University, Tallahassee, wherein we had systematically worked out a language enrichment program. An example of this type of child is included here.

CASE HISTORY OF A CHILD NEEDING LANGUAGE ENRICHMENT

Reason for referral:

Don scored 30 on the language section of the Riley Articulation and Language Test.

History:

The teacher reports that Don uses little language in the classroom, speaks in short phrases and is shy. Don's mother states that the child fell two stories and suffered a concussion and fracture of the left temporal bone when he was two years old. Treatment was rendered at an emergency hospital and no suspicious signs have been noted by the mother since that time. She did express concern about frequent nightmares from which Don wakes crying.

Results from testing:

The Peabody Picture Vocabulary Test, the Draw-A-Person Test, the Gesell Figure Copying Test and the Illinois Test of Psycholinguistic Abilities were administered. Don scored at his age level on the Gesell, just within normal limits on 8 of the 9 ITPA subtests, well above his age level on the DAP and well below his age level on the Peabody and the Auditory Decoding subtest of the ITPA.

Interpretation:

Test results indicated that Don has a marked vocabulary deficiency. Because other language functions appear to be intact, it is thought that this deficiency is a result of inadequate stimulation.

Recommendations:

Special attention should be paid, both in the home and in the kindergarten, to improving Don's vocabulary. He would profit from being spoken to and listened to as much as possible; and new words should be supplied to him at appropriate moments. In the classroom Don should not be allowed to fade into the background because he is a quiet child. Verbal responses should be encouraged and expected from him.

Prognosis:

If the above suggestions plus other standard language enrichment activities are used, Don should progress well toward a normal command of language. The testers would like to check his progress after a semester of kindergarten.

Language enrichment

Language enrichment is not something that the teacher does a few minutes each day; rather it is an approach to teaching which emphasizes language development at every opportunity. There are many specific ways in which the teacher can recognize and take advantage of language learning opportunities. What we sought to do was make the teachers sensitive to these language learning opportunities. After the workshop we put the major ideas into a memorandum so that the teachers could keep it on file and refer to it. The memorandum, in outline form, was:

LANGUAGE ENRICHMENT

1. Provide as much verbal output as possible.
    a. Do and Say (simultaneous activity and words at child's level).
    b. Verbalize what the child is doing.
    c. Use simple phrases. Three word groups for three-year-olds, four or five word groups for four-year-olds and up.
2. Keep verbal environment meaningful and helpful to the child.
    a. Relate to experiences *as the child sees them.*
    b. Be accurate phonetically. Use good diction.
    c. Use variety (not "hum-drum"). Must maintain child's interest and attention.
3. React to environmental sounds.
    a. Imitate airplane, auto, bird, door slamming, and so forth.
    b. Encourage children to join you.
4. Create a *need* for the child to talk.
    a. Listen and respond to his verbal attempts to control your behavior.
    b. Play games which require speech attempts.
    c. Expect speech attempts when the child wants something. NOTE— these speech attempts need not be accurate words.

5. Supply words when the child needs them.
   a. You are his "dictionary."
   b. Time the word so that it comes when he is interested or excited about the object, activity, color or concept for which the word stands; that is, at the "teachable moment."

Classroom activities

Activities which are standard to nursery school education were adapted to meet the language needs of the children.*

The activities described below may be helpful in setting up such a program but most of the games and activities have to be derived from those already in use by the classroom teachers.

Both structured and unstructured activities are described in order to give the speech specialist and also the classroom teacher some idea of the kinds of things that can be done to encourage language in the classroom.

Structured activities

1. *Discussion and story time.* Children listen to animated stories. They engage in finger play. They supply the words for the different animals, the words for the actions of the animals.

2. *Group singing.* The children can learn to sing several songs, many of them accompanied with finger, arm or other physical activity.

3. *Lotto games.* These language lotto or farm lotto games are standard equipment around most nursery schools. Each child draws a card with a picture on it. The teacher holds up a picture and asks the child to name the animal. They talk about it and the child with that particular picture comes up and claims it and places it on top of his matching picture.

4. *Listening to records.* Whenever possible, records and record playing equipment should be available in the classroom. Records should be provided which are stimulating for language use. Some suggested records are as follows:
   "The Carrot Seed" by Ruth Krauss, published by the Children's Record Guild
   "The Circus Comes to Town," Young People's Records
   "Train to the Farm," Children's Record Guild
   "Drummer Boy," Children's Record Guild
   "Musical Mother Goose," Children's Record Guild

5. *Field trips.* A field trip in which the children experience some interesting and exciting things that they are not used to, will give them something to talk about and will serve as a stimulus for their language.

* (Devised in collaboration with Susie Whitener, Florida State University.)

Field trips, of course, are planned in connection with the regular educational activities of the Head Start children.

6. *Jack-in-the-Box.* Several children can play this at a given time and the children are supposed to pop up at a given place in a song or rhythm or when a special word is said. This encourages them to listen and respond to verbal clues.

7. *Movies.* If available, the children should be able to watch movies that stimulate their language. Discussions of the movie or role playing where they re-act the movie with themselves as the characters is a very useful teaching device for language.

8. *Rhythm games.* Children love to use sticks, drums, their own voices, and various kinds of instruments to play and keep time with the music, perhaps in connection with their singing.

Unstructured activities

1. *Instruction.* Children need to learn to follow simple instructions. They need to learn the power of verbal commands, that they can be controlled by verbal commands and also that they can control others by verbal commands. Whenever they are to manipulate toys or able to participate in an activity—permitted to play with certain toys, encouraged to ride a certain direction on the playground with bicycles—any kind of instruction is healthy language instruction.

2. *Spontaneous utterances.* Spontaneous speech attempts should be listened to and encouraged by the teacher and the teacher should be willing to respond to the child. She should be willing to do what the child tells her to do if it is at all appropriate.

3. *Naming of environmental sounds.* Here the child can be encouraged to name airplanes, cars, motors, birds singing, the sound of the wind. He may want to imitate these sounds and to provide names for them.

4. *Sounds used in games.* Almost all of the outdoor and indoor games can use various sounds to enhance the enjoyment of them—the sounds of guns, airplanes, trucks—all of these things are in this category.

There are a great many opportunities for children to improve their language ability if the teachers can be encouraged to see the language potential of the activities they are doing and to incorporate language as a way of teaching—to recognize that they should encourage the child to talk and to manipulate the environment verbally whenever possible.

Children with moderate language or articulation dysfunctions

Although about half of the children in our Head Start failed the screening in speech or language, we felt that they did not require direct specialized therapy during the Head Start Project but would be able to learn from the teachers in the language enrichment program. However, those children who demonstrated a moderate language or articulation dysfunction were put into groups of three to five children for group therapy similar to that which is conducted in public school.

There are certain problems which seem to be more prevalent among children who grow up in socially disadvantaged areas than among children who are not so deprived. These problems include the following:

1. Inaccurate or immature sentence structure.

2. Limited vocabulary.

3. Incorrect use of grammar.

4. The misarticulation of certain of the diphthongs, especially the "i" as in kite and the "au" as in house.

5. The misarticulation of certain of the consonants and consonant blends, especially the "d" for "th" substitution—the word "this" is pronounced "dis" and "that" is pronounced "dat." Many of these sounds are not perfectly developed in normal children by the time they are four or five years old but there seems to be a more general inaccuracy in producing these difficult sounds among the socially disadvantaged children.

6. These children tend to leave off the endings of their words; for example, the "s" which ends a plural word. The "ing" also tends to be slighted or omitted.

7. Many of them need to work on their voice adequacy. They need to "speak up." Some of them are very shy and do not speak loudly enough.

Children with severe articulation and language dysfunctions

Those children who showed, by scoring in the lowest tenth percentile for their age, that they had severe articulation or language dysfunctions, were enrolled in what we called "Evaluative Therapy." To us, Evaluative Therapy means extended diagnosis. In Evaluative Therapy we saw the children individually, giving extensive testing.

Whether a child is deaf or has a language problem related to brain damage or is generally mentally retarded will make a great deal of difference as to what his rehabilitation program will include. As we went along we found that it was almost mandatory to give the Illinois Test of Psycholinguistic Ability to our children with severe language disorders. Many children who previously had been considered mentally retarded or deaf were found to be aphasic or have other problems associated with brain injury or dysfunction.

Training parents to improve language conditions in the home

One of the services which the speech and hearing specialist was able to render was to attend one of the Parent Education sessions and explain the importance of language to the parents. The main thing that he tried to get across to the parents was simply, "If you will talk to your child and read to your child, then he will learn to listen to you. If you will listen to your child and respond to your child, then he will learn to talk to you." (An outline of this speech is found in the chapter on Parent Education).

It is important that we do all that we can to improve the language environment of our Head Start children at home. Many of them come from environments that are dull and boring, that lack the kind of hope and sparkle that are customarily found in a home. Language is an expression of the hope and sparkle of life. The child who is tired or under-nourished or bored is not likely to speak up in a nice voice and with his best articulation and tell the stories about what he is doing and try to name things and do the other things that others do.

Besides talking to the parents about how to improve their children's speech we also found it valuable to send out a written note in which we made specific suggestions in simple, non-technical terminology that the parents could follow. We called the memorandum "How to Help Your Child Talk Better." It included the following specific suggestions:

1. Talk with your child as much as possible. Say things he enjoys hearing!
2. Read to your child stories that he enjoys, stories at his level.
3. Listen to your child and as much as possible do what he tells you to do so that he will learn the power of talking.
4. Don't respond to his gestures if you are sure he knows the word. Make talking necessary and important around your house.
5. Supply the word when he needs it. You are his dictionary.

Parent conferences

When a child was discovered who had a serious speech disorder it was necessary to call in the mother for a private conference. At that time the data from all of the various tests was explained to her and interpreted to her in terms of what the result would be for her child, that is, whether he should go to public school or whether he was likely to be a year behind his class or some other such interpretation in terms of the child himself. We found it wise to avoid panic words such as "brain damage" and "mentally retarded." We sought, rather, to help the mother and the father realize that, although the child's speech problem was serious, it could be helped with proper treatment. The children who were to be referred to the various clinics, such as the Cerebral Palsy Clinic, Speech and Hearing

Clinic or Mental Health Services, or to public school speech specialists, would need to have each of these services explained to the parent in order to overcome "fear of the unknown." We found the parents quite willing to accept guidance and share in the responsibility of contacting the agencies and providing the transportation of the children to them *when they understood their purpose.*

Filing reports and keeping records

A copy of the results of the Hearing, Language, and Articulation Screening should be placed in each child's folder and should become a part of his permanent educational record. Any child who is seen for Evaluative Therapy will have other test results. A report should be written which interprets these tests in a meaningful way which can be of use to the public schools and also to any other clinic or any other auxiliary service that may take an interest in the child and provide service for him, such as the hospitals, the cerebral palsy clinics or the psychological services. These reports should include:

1. Identification data.
2. Information as to the background of the child's problem.
3. A very accurate summary of the test results.
4. An indication of the speech therapist's evaluation of these test results.
5. Recommendations as to the kinds of therapy that the child ought to have.

If any therapy has been given, some indication of the effectiveness of the therapy and whether it should be continued is also in order.

Evaluation of speech services

Our evaluation of the language progress of the children during the eight-week Head Start term indicated that the program was quite beneficial to them. It is not realistic to expect that in a few short weeks or even in a school year a speech therapist could solve all the problems of the culturally disadvantaged children in her charge, but if the teachers are made aware of language enrichment techniques, if the parents are made sensitive to the situation and given the tools to help their own children, and if the therapist uses his imagination and professional ability to improvise the best types of therapy, then the children should better be able to meet the challenge of our highly verbal culture. They will be expected to take tests when they get to school that will be based on their ability to talk and to communicate. They will be expected to talk to their teachers and fellow students at school. All through life this ability to communicate will be vital to them, and it seems to us who are working in the program now that we can provide a genuine "head start" in language experience if we provide the right kind of professional services during the Head Start Project.

12

the child development specialist

Professional organizations in child development urged the membership before Head Start began to contact their local community to see what they could offer in the way of service to Head Start. At the time I was teaching Child Development at Pepperdine College and asked my students if any of them knew of an Operation Head Start in the area. A junior, Pamela, announced that she was volunteering to work in a Head Start sponsored by her sorority. I asked her if she could remain after class and give me more information concerning whom I might contact, as I also wished to volunteer. She stated that I should contact either the President of Delta Sigma Theta, Mrs. Harriett Williams, or the Coordinator, Mrs. Frances Epps. On checking through her notebook she found only the phone number of Mrs. Epps. On that bit of circumstance lay the beginning of the psychological service and the very existence of this book.

Initial testing

We had first planned to give some psychological tests to the children during their first and last week of Head Start attendance. Little did we realize then that testing would be only the beginning. As we began to observe the children by day and grade the tests by night we became very curious as to which child went with which test.

Who was this bright four-year-old boy who scored age seven on his developmental test? What were the play patterns of the children with vocabularies below the three-year-old level? What were the feelings of the child who drew a picture of a girl with ears twice the size of the rest of the drawing?

These and other questions prompted us to make an appointment with the Coordinator. We explained some of our findings and asked if we might be permitted to stay beyond the initial two-week period to study some of the children. Her answer was affirmative *if* the findings could be directly related to the teachers. We agreed.

Reporting to the teachers

By the time of the teachers' meeting of the second week we had already studied all the children's tests and were ready to make a group presentation of our findings. Since the children averaged 5.2 years in age, we arbitrarily selected 3.0 years as the cut-off point under which special help might be needed. In an attempt to get at every facet of school readiness we had selected several tests. Table 1 names the traits we chose to measure and the tests which attempt to measure them. (The reasons we selected these tests are described in detail in Section III.)

Instead of presenting test scores, which we believed might be misleading, we chose to make a list of children who had scored below three years on any subtest and make recommendations based on their low scores.

Table 1
TESTING FOR SCHOOL READINESS

DEVELOPMENT AREA	TESTS USED TO MEASURE
1. Physical Development	(1) Gesell Copy Forms (2) Draw-A-Person (3) Vineland Social Maturity Scale
2. Mental Development	(1) Peabody Picture Vocabulary Test (2) Draw-A-Person (3) Gesell Copy Forms (4) Vineland Social Maturity (5) Riley Articulation and Language Test
3. Social-Emotional Development	(1) Draw-A-Person (2) Vineland Social Maturity Scale
4. Language Development	(1) Peabody Picture Vocabulary Test (2) Riley Articulation and Language Test

For instance, if a child scored 2.9 on vocabulary, 3.4 on social skills, 4.0 on development, and was unable to respond to the Draw-A-Person test, we wrote, "Child has very limited vocabulary. Speak to him in two- or three-word sentences. He has a good learning potential but lacks the skill and the emotional maturity to progress independently. Probably needs patience and reassurance."

We dittoed off a class list entitled "Special Needs of Children." We assumed that all Head Start children would have many needs for a good nursery school experience. What we wished to do was to point out some individual characteristics which might be helpful to the teachers.

After the presentation some of the teachers asked if it would be possible for us to visit their classrooms and observe certain children further. This was the invitation we had been waiting for.

Developing into a professional team

Each day brought new challenges, some of which were beyond our individual capabilities and training. We sought out Dorothy Jenkins, the nurse, and worked together on the epileptic and the mentally retarded child. As we talked we realized we needed a report on the home to better understand the situation. In one case, the examining doctor had questioned the possibility of sexual molestation. About this time, Mrs. Betty Williams, a faculty member in the School of Public Health at Mt. Saint Mary's College, came to volunteer. Here was one skilled person who could certainly perform as well as she taught! Not one door was closed to her as she began making home calls on our most difficult cases. Her insights and recommendations were an invaluable resource, and her reports helped our limited information turn into a meaningful whole.

Child development specialist, nurse, social worker, speech therapist and teacher all soon came to form *the professional team* to service our most disturbed children.

Because the problems we encountered in Head Start were both more serious and more atypical than we had imagined, we are including several case histories showing the types of children encountered and the necessity of the team approach for therapeutic intervention.

CASE STUDIES

After presenting the list of children with special needs to the teachers, the child development consultant made a return visit to give added help where needed. Several of the children required further diagnosis before additional suggestions were possible. Case histories which are illustrative of children who need much specialized help are presented in this section.

A case of epilepsy

Case Study 1: Willie, male, age four years, seven months.

Behavior:

Willie was referred by his teacher because of his unsettled behavior. Observation of the child showed that he was unable to pay attention, listen, sit still, or play with other children. He would run or laugh, seemingly with no control.

Testing:

Neurological screening revealed that Willie manifested many signs of neurological impairment. It was impossible to achieve complete testing results because of his short attention span and inability to follow directions. On the basis of results achieved, a medical follow-up, including neurological diagnosis, was recommended.

Follow-up Observation of Behavior:

The following day at lunch, Willie gave a scream and fell unconscious to the floor. He lay there relatively motionless, with a gross muscular twitching and eyes rolling. An epileptic seizure!

A tongue depressor covered with cotton was inserted in his mouth to keep him from swallowing his tongue; the other children were taken outside, and his mother was summoned. He was unconscious about five minutes, then went to sleep. He slept about an hour. The mother and grandmother came to take him home. The mother seemed frightened and unable to understand the situation. The grandmother told the teacher she would not take Willie to a doctor, in spite of the nurse's insistence. Later that afternoon a Head Start teacher visited the home, and on her recommendation the mother consented to take the child to a doctor.

Three days later Willie was readmitted to school and put into a special class. (This special class for neurologically handicapped children is described elsewhere). Mother gave the teacher a bottle of medicine so that he could have his dosage every four hours.

On investigation, the Head Start nurse found that the medicine was for "allergy," that no E.E.G. had been given, and that no medication for epilepsy had been prescribed. Presumably, the mother did not relate the incident of epilepsy to the doctor.

Summary:

As the nurse and social worker worked with the family, Willie continued in Head Start. Some days he did not eat lunch; on other days he "ran wild." Sometimes he appeared sleepy.

Recommendations:

Willie must have medical diagnosis and treatment if he is to profit from the school situation. The mother may also need help. The school situation must be structured and have the elements he needs.

Willie needs a quiet atmosphere, free from distractions and disorderliness, noise, or too many objects for him to explore. He is "stimulus bound" to explore all his surroundings. When overstimulated, he may begin yelling and running about, unable to contain himself, until exhausted. The teacher needs to keep him in a quiet place with *only the materials he is working with* present. It is important to realize that his inner controls lack the power to inhibit his aggressive or exploratory behavior, and that firm, non-punitive discipline from the adult is necessary. For instance, he can be confined to a small area or help on a lap and then redirected into a less stimulating (to him) activity. Working with clay has the effect of slowing down children like Willie.

Willie is *not* a typical epileptic, and the recommendations for environmental manipulation should not be used indiscriminately with other epileptic children. However, Willie's behavior does typify the organically-driven, hyperactive child, and as such, generalizations may be made.

Comment:

Although Willie's mother walked him to school, came after him every day, and seemed to be friendly and open with teachers and staff, she had withheld his history of epilepsy from the school. She denied that anyone in the family had epilepsy, or that Willie needed medical treatment. Her speech was garbled and her comprehension seemed lacking. She was a "good" mother in the sense that she wanted him to go to Head Start, "behave," and get along with the other children. However, she lacked insight into causal relationships, and seemed to misunderstand often. One of her comments about Willie's behavior was that she was going to get him some glasses before he went to school. The glasses had no relation to his problem.

The Head Start program rendered a service to Willie and his family by helping the mother realize that the teacher and social workers would not ostracize her child because of his disability, and would recommend help for him. It will also be advantageous to the school to be aware of the child's epileptic history and need for follow-up. The social worker for the family under Aid to Dependent Children should better be able to minister to the needs of both mother and child.

A case of marked neurological disorganization

Case Study 2: Mark, boy, age four years, nine months.

Testing:

Extensive testing because of his low scores on the screening battery.

1. Gesell Geometric Designs: Could not draw a circle.
2. Draw-A-Person: Raw score of one; mostly scribbles.
3. Peabody Picture Vocabulary Test: Mental age of 2.6 years.
4. Vineland Social Maturity Scale: Social age of 2.5 years.

Behavior:

The teacher reported the child was inattentive and didn't seem to understand what was going on.

Home:

Public health nurse visited the home and reported that mother was concerned.

Testing and Interview:

Mark came with examiner to doll corner. His walk was awkward. He accepted the proffered hand and stood quietly. His eyes were crossed (strabismus) and he seemed to see with difficulty. When presented with crayon and paper, he scribbled and drew crude circles. His attention span was short, and he would stop activity and stare into space until spoken to. Neurological screening was attempted, but Mark seemed to have difficulty understanding, so not all items were completed. Neurological signs apparent were:

1. Brings *both* hands to nose when eyes are closed even when one hand is touched by examiner.
2. When arms are extended with eyes closed, hands come together immediately, right little finger turns down and left arm elevates.
3. Left eye turns in all the time.
4. He crawls on his toes, not knees.
5. Touches all fingers to thumb at once, not sequentially.

Diagnosis:

Neurological disorganization.

Referral:

Mark was being treated at General Hospital for an ear condition. A letter signed by the nurse was given the mother to take with her to the hospital to request neurological diagnosis. Because of waiting lists, nothing had been done to help Mark by the end of Project Head Start.

For the final four weeks of the Head Start program, he was placed in a small class with a teacher of special education. He learned to follow directions and to listen. The strabismus and general incoordination remained. A letter outlining diagnosis and referral was placed in his school folder to be sent to the school where he would attend kindergarten.

Comment:

The case of Mark was a frustrating one. The Head Start Center identified the problem; the mother was cooperative; but community resources were too overloaded to render prompt assistance. The problem was too serious in nature to be met by the Center, yet Head Start personnel were obligated ho help him to the extent possible. Head Start's main contribution here was giving the mother a tentative explanation of her son's behavior and making available a medical referral. (This is a case where adequate follow-up is imperative.)

A case of borderline mongoloidism

Case Study 3: Flo, girl, age five years, zero months.

Behavior:

Flo was referred by her teacher because of frequent crying episodes, running away, and her atypical physical condition. She was grossly overweight and had a tendency to walk on her toes. She did not know her colors. She liked to play all day with the puppet that talked when the string was pulled.

Testing:

Screening test results available yielded the following information:

1. Gesell Geometric Designs: age three.
   Drew circle well.
   Drew straight line for cross.
2. Draw-A-Person: score of one.
   She drew a circle completely around the outer edge of the paper.
3. Peabody Picture Vocabulary Test: mental age of two years, two months.
4. Vineland Social Maturity Scale: social age of three years, seven months.

Report of Home Visit:

Public health nurse reported that other family members bore a marked resemblance to Flo, and that although there was no mistreatment evident, neither was there any insight. The mother, age 33, had had nine pregnancies, nine children, and was expecting her tenth in October. The father, age 54, was a disabled construction worker. The family had been on Social Security and Aid to Dependent Children for eleven years and received $4,000 a year for the family of eleven.

An interview with the mother revealed she noticed no difference in the development of any of her nine children. She stated that Flo had had no medical examination in a "long time." She was vague about prior illnesses and she stated that her prenatal condition and delivery with Flo was uneventful, and that Flo delivered in bed at General Hospital. Immunizations included D.P.T. and Salk at Southeast Health District.

Family receives aid of Public Assistance and Social Security, for father has been disabled from construction work. Housing in project, sparsely furnished, cluttered, not clean. Communication in home between members observed as pleasant and calm. Mother offered very little information and appeared to lack awareness or insight in the slowness of Flo.

Refer to the Nursing Division, Southeast Health District, and to the General Hospital.

Interview with Flo:

Flo did not respond verbally to examiner. She grinned a wide, toothless grin. Many mongoloid tendencies (Down's Syndrome) were physically apparent: (1) constant drooling, (2) thick tongue, (3) obesity, (4) eyes did not converge, (5) tended to walk on toes, (6) grinned easily and, (7) easily upset.

Educational Procedures:

Help for Flo was dependent on daily to bi-weekly conferences with teacher and contacts with child. Teacher was advised of Flo's limitations, and suggestions were made to (1) keep the child near an adult at all times, (2) to *show* her as well as *tell* her, (3) to keep her environment ordered and consistent, and (4) to use rocking and singing to soothe her.

Progress in Flo's Education:

This was noticeable through written anecdoted records taken every week.

Observations: Week Two

Situation: Music time

1. Flo watched the teacher all the time. Smiled with mouth open a great deal. Listened to music being played on autoharp. Leaned forward on other child's chair. Easily distracted.

Week Three:

Situation: Parking lot for visit from fireman

2. When the fire engines came, Flo cried uncontrollably on hearing the siren. She seemed to "come apart at the seams." After the fire engines left, she continued to cry the entire morning. Same reaction with visit from policemen.

Week Four:

Situation: Group play directed by teacher

3. After four weeks of watching, Flo joined the Jack-in-the-Box game with great glee. She has stopped running away.

Week Seven:

Situation: Field trip to library.

4. Flo seemed to enjoy her trip to the library as long as she was near the teacher. Some spontaneous speech now. Librarian asked, "How many books do I have in my hand?" Flo answered aloud, "Two." She was correct!

Comment:

Without the supportive social experience provided by Operation Head Start, Flo might never have come to trust people nor begun to utilize her limited intellectual resources. Flo's teacher exercised consummate skill in giving success experiences to this frightened child. When she first came to Head Start, Flo had neither known nor played with other adults or children outside her own family. Subsequently she had successful social contacts with dozens of children and various adults. Perhaps even more exciting than her social skill was the unfolding of her intellect. Moving from no concept of numbers at all, at the end of eight weeks, Flo could take five pieces of felt from a box, and place them in a row, and count slowly, "one, two . . . . , three, ... , four, ... five!" She took obvious delight in this mysterious new-found skill as she grinned and fidgeted in her chair. She learned to copy a straight line and a small circle, though copying a cross still eluded her (as could be expected). She learned to name primary and secondary colors, to listen, to feed herself, to wait her turn, and perhaps most difficult of all, to relate experiences. For Flo, Project Head Start was the beginning of opportunity.

Placement and follow-up in public school should be facilitated by the diagnostic work-up as well as the intellectual stimulus of the Head Start program.

Referral:

Medical referral was made to Nursing Division of the Southeast Health Center and General Hospital. Complete notes on her behavior were sent to the school with recommendations to place her in a remedial class. No medical follow-up had been done by the end of the Head Start program.

A case of a motherless child

Case Study 4: Debra, girl, age five years, four months.

Behavior:

Debra was entered in the Head Start program during the third week by her foster mother who drove ten miles to enroll her in the program.

The teacher requested immediate help with Debra because she refused to join any group activities, especially music, art, or any planned group function. The teacher reported she liked to paint and play with water but appeared generally unhappy most of the time.

Observational Notes

The child development consultant visited the classroom and observed Debra at free play. No abnormalities were noted. An excerpt from the running record follows:

10:00   Water play situation. Debra mixes water and clay together on desk. Other children talk. She plays but doesn't talk. Neatly dressed and combed.

10:10   Girl: "Water is on the floor."
        Debra: "Wipe it up, please."
        Girl wipes up water. Debra continues playing in water and clay.

10:12   Girl: "This pan is hot."
        Debra: "Let's turn it down a little or it will burn up."
        Play continues as before.

From this observation, it seemed that Debra was new to the program and not ready for formal activities. A note was made to revisit in two weeks.

After two weeks the teacher reported that Debra still did not enter into group activities and asked the consultant to observe Debra again.

Anecdotal account

Situation: Time to wash up after clay (9:40).

Teacher carrying Debra. Arms locked around teacher's neck. Sober. No speech. Teacher carries her to washroom. Teacher leaves girls. To Debra, "You go. I have to go over to the boys' side." Debra looks at me soberly. I say, "You can go in here, Debra."

Debra used toilet. Flushed it. Washed hands with other girls. No speech. Teacher returned. Helped each one. Teacher: "Did you go to the bathroom?" Debra nods head yes. Continues washing. Lets water out of basin. Teacher washes clay off Debra's dress. No reaction. Goes to hall slowly. Stops. "Do you want to go in with the rest of the children?" Shakes head no. Waits three minutes. Walks to the door and listens a moment. I say, "Would you like for me to open the door for you?" No response. Then opens door and goes in. Stands by easel looking at teacher telling flannel board story. Goes to where she can see flannel board. Teacher, "Come on Debra, come over here and sit with us." Debra ignores her. Teacher continues story.

Debra fidgets. Works slowly forward to teacher. "I miss you, Debra; come and sit with me." Takes Debra into her lap. Debra puts arm around teacher, watches other children, and, occasionally, flannel board. Teacher gets up. Debra sits on floor. Teacher returns; Debra sits in her lap. Teacher asks children to point to various parts of the body. She watches, but does not participate. She looks at the book on teacher's lap. Replaces book. Gets up off lap. Gets pencil. Sits on lap again. Teacher plays "Pop-goes-the-Weasel." All children pop up except Debra, who sits on teacher's lap playing with piece of flannel. Is self-absorbed, but notices what is happening.

All children sit at table to eat lunch except Debra who stays sitting on the floor.

Recommendations to Head Start Teacher:

Let child join group at her own pace. Do *not* urge or coax her. Structure the activity—"Put on your apron and you can play with clay"—and then let child join when (if) she wishes. Ignore child's withdrawal behavior except when everyone must go to the bathroom, outside, etc. Then move her with as little aid as possible.

In following the suggestions made by the consultant, the teacher found that she was able to help Debra in achieving independence and social skills. Interviews continued between teacher and consultant. Though no direct work (except observation and testing) was done with the child, during a visit to the classroom Debra reached over suddenly and gave consultant a big hug and kiss. This affection was received tenderly but matter of factly and without comment. In general, Debra entered into more activities, became less demanding, and socialized better with the children.

Teacher's report: Child comes to school depressed. Will stand and look for a long time. When she gets upset, she won't talk. Otherwise, she will ask. She does better when she has a definite routine and knows what to expect. Enjoys art activities, clay, and so forth, and likes to participate.

Comment:

Debra was indeed most fortunate to have her first social experience away from an over-protective home with an understanding Head Start teacher who could devote love, time, and attention to her. The Head Start program should enable her to make a more productive adjustment to school since she has matured emotionally and socially, freeing her above-average intellect to learn. She would never have been able to get the individualized care in kindergarten that was possible in Head Start.

The case of an abused child

Case Study 5: Ramon, male, age four years, 11 months.

Behavior:

Ramon was referred to the child development consultant by his teacher because he did not enter into any of the activities. He was dirty and unkempt, and he did not respond to her in any way. The teacher's aide spent the entire lunch hour with Ramon, holding him, feeding him, and devoting herself entirely to him. During the third week of his attendance, Ramon responded to the aide, but still did not enter into any activities. He would sit and listen to a story, but did not speak. He had a brother one year older in the same room. Neither child had ever been to school. His favorite toy was a Woody-Woodpecker who talked when the string was pulled. He would pull the string and listen to the toy "talk" for long periods of time.

Observation by Child Development Consultant:

Ramon is a small, slight child with irregular features and brooding eyes that seem to notice everything that happens. His lower lip protrudes, and he appears dejected. He is dressed in faded blue jeans, a worn T-shirt, and old shoes. When first observed, he was sitting with the group listening attentively to the story. When the story was over, he stood up and remained standing in one spot while the children around him moved on to other activities. He stood, with feet wide apart, shoulders slumped and abdomen protruding, watching the other children but immobile himself. He refused the teacher's request to join in activities with a shake of his head and a scowl. He listened, but did not participate.

Physically, there were several other indications of neglect: His navel protruded about 1½ inches; he had many insect bites on his body; scars were evident on his arm, hand and face.

Interview with Ramon:

"I approached Ramon, stooped to his level, and spoke softly to him, asking him to come to the table with me and draw pictures. He shrank from my touch and looked at me darkly. I went over to the table and gave out colors and paper to two other children who expressed an interest. In about five minutes Ramon and his brother walked over and sat down at the table.

"The school day was over; the teacher's aide approached and told Ramon "Goodbye." He smiled slightly at her attention.

"I began to talk to him:
Consultant: "You like her, Ramon."
Ramon: Smiles shyly.
Consultant: "She is nice to you."
Ramon: Smiles more.
Consultant: "She doesn't hurt you."

Ramon: Smile disappears.

Consultant: "But someone hurts you."

Ramon: Frowns, shrinks back, puckers lower lip.

Consultant: "Who hurts you, Ramon?" "Could you draw a picture of him?"

Ramon: Nods head affirmatively. Continues frowning. Does not accept proffered crayon.

Consultant: "Could your brother Jose draw a picture of who hurts you?"

Ramon and Jose: Nod heads affirmatively. Jose accepts crayon and drawas a stick figure.

Consultant: "I wonder if that's a boy or a girl or a man or a wo- man . . ."

Jose: "It's a man."

Consultant: "I wonder what his name is. Tomas? . . . . . . Pedro? . . . . . Jorge? . . . . ."

Jose: "Jorge."

Consultant: "Jorge?"

Jose and Ramon: Nod "yes" solemnly.

Ramon looks very sad. Consultant reaches out and caresses Ramon's arm, then his cheek. Ramon seems comforted by the human touch, relaxes, and leans toward consultant.

Consultant: "No one will hurt you at school, Ramon."

It is the end of the day; the boys depart for home.

Recommendations:

Follow-up on home conditions and the child's physical abnormalities. Ramon is a very frightened little boy who needs a constant environment of acceptance and certainly no punishment. He is apparently bright, not schizophrenic, not retarded or neurologically handicapped. Teacher's aide should continue her tender, loving care. Ramon should be allowed to join the group at his own rate. He needs to know that at school he is cherished and protected from harm.

Comments:

The interview with Ramon seemed to effect a transformation in his behavior. He began eating lunch, and responded to the other children during the last hour of the day.

The consultant continued to make visits to talk with Ramon. He ultimately agreed to draw a person, copy geometric designs, and have a physical examination which he had previously rejected.

Doctor's routine examination revealed umbilical hernia, malnutrition, and excessive insect bites.

When the teacher drove to pick up Ramon and Jose for school Monday after the social worker had visited the home, no one answered the door. The apartment was vacant. No one knew where the family had moved.

Somewhere in this big city lives a little boy, still frightened and still hungry, but perhaps with a dream of a school with smiling faces, where he can play, and where no one will hurt him.

The case of the neurologically immature child

Case Study 6: Jimmy, age four years, 11 months.

Behavior:

Jimmy was referred early in the program by his teacher who said he seemed fearful of the other children and did not join activities.

Test results:

Jimmy was tested during the second week of school. The tests and their scores were:

1. Gesell Geometric Designs: Age three years.
   Perseverance on circles.
2. Draw-A-Person: Raw score of five.
   (Goodenough Harris) Much shading evident.
3. Peabody Picture Vocabulary Test: Mental age of 2.5 years.
4. Vineland Social Maturity Scale: Social age of 4.3 years.
5. Speech Screening: Articulation fair. Shy and did not respond well.
6. Neurological Screening: Although Jimmy had previously related well to the examiner, he seemed frightened by the physical activities he was asked to do. He began to cry and the test was terminated. However, he did show definite signs of neurological incoordination. His reactions were shyness, insecurity, and disorganization. Neurological signs included Achilles heel slap while hopping, hands spreading apart while eyes were closed, mixed dominance, poor balance, and difficulty in visual focus.

Home Visits:

Home visit by public health nurse revealed insight by the parent and the assurance of her help.

Social Worker's Report:

Project home clean, comfortably furnished. Mother interviewed—expressed herself freely and had good contributions concerning her observations of Jimmy. History of medical care good; no serious illness. Behavior at home described as staying very close to mother, wanting to do things for her; also very anxious to do what he can. Mother states each child is able to perform in the home. Atmosphere in the home warm. Jimmie sometimes prefers to be with mother rather than play with other children. Mother says he is easy going and others take advantage of him.

Mother seemed to understand his need for greater self-image; learning at his own pace.

Plan:

Mother will buy Frostig's book, *Visual Perception,* and along with husband (step-father) work with Jimmy. Will visit school with book and talk with teacher. Father to increase relationship with Jimmy.

Suggestions for Therapy:

Suggestions for helping Jimmy included:

1. No pressure to conform or excel should be given. He should be allowed to watch, and then enter in at his own rate. He should not be scolded or punished.
2. Routine language enrichment methods should be followed: (See chapter on the Speech Specialist)
3. An educational program to teach body image and neurological organization was suggested to the teacher.

   a. Teach him to name and point to parts of his body.
   b. Teach him to name and point to parts of a doll.
   c. Help him trace the figure of whole body.
   d. Teach him to put all parts of body together at flannel board. Show him the interrelationships of how the various parts fit together.
   e. Provide easel painting experience. Suggest he "paint a boy." Let him do it anyway he wishes. Praise him.
   f. Teach him colors of objects in the following sequence: Hold up cards with pictures on them.

      1. The ball is red. The sky is blue.
      2. Find the color that looks like this.
      3. Which one is red?
      4. What color is this?

Follow up:

Jimmy's teacher was able to incorporate special training in the classroom for him, and the mother helped him at home. Jimmy gradually gained self-confidence, became more relaxed, and was able to learn more easily. Although he remained reticent in joining group activities spontaneously, he was able to follow group routines and enter wholeheartedly into art and music activities.

Retesting at the end of the session revealed that Jimmy had progressed markedly:

1. Gesell Geometric Designs: from age three to age four.
2. Draw-A-Person: from a raw score of five to a raw score of eight.
3. Peabody Picture Vocabulary Test: from a mental age of 2.5 to a mental age of 4.3 (near normal).
4. Social age remained normal and speech improved.

Comment:

Jimmy is the typical shy child whose primary etiology lies not with the home or in the parent-child relationship, but within his own delicate and disorganized neurological make-up. Only careful diagnosis would have uncovered the underlying cause of his behavior and suggested an optimum program of therapy. Operation Head Start has in this case provided both parent and school with the key to understanding Jimmy's behavior as well as giving him necessary skills for coping with and profiting from public school.

CURRICULA DEVELOPMENT

During the course of the summer we offered two workshops for teachers to assist them in teaching language enrichment and body image within the regular classroom. The speech enrichment curriculum is described in the chapter, "Speech Specialist," and the workshop offered the teachers in "How to Teach Body Image" is outlined herein.

Teacher's workshop on self-concept

Many of the children failed to recognize simple verbs, such as *running* or *sitting,* and speech was seldom used for communication.

Many of the children did not know what they looked like and seemed unaware of their physical capabilities. They had to be taught to relate experiences verbally, to ride wheel toys with orderliness, to become aware of their bodies and their body functions. In order to teach the children to succeed in these areas, we must first understand how they learn or acquire "self-concept."

A child's perception of himself arises basically from two sources: (1) the feelings and impulses of his own body, (Bender, 1956) and (2) the reflected appraisals of "significant" persons in his life span, (Sullivan, 1948). Bender has stated that motor or muscle education is a preliminary step to all education in children. *A child only learns what he can do by doing it.* His physical capacities, however, have an emotional overtone in that all of his movements from sucking to running have their time and place, and are performed in a relationship with other people. "No more bottles." "Don't run in the street." "Don't pull the lamp." "Be quiet." "Don't hit your brother." "Leave me alone." These examples of adult expectations and restrictions upon the child's mobility carry with them important emotional ramifications.

Consider one example from a social worker's notebook:

Risa, age four, fell down, cut her lip, and ran crying to her mother seeking help. Her mother, talking to the social worker, reprimanded the child harshly, "What are you doing, running in here all dirty and filthy like that! You don't belong here!" Mother slapped girl across face and dragged her to kitchen where she washed her face, then cuffed her again, speaking harshly all the time. Finally the little girl, apparently terrified, tore from her mother's grasp and ran out the door. Mother remarked, "She'll be back when it gets dark."

What did the child learn about her body image and self-concept? Let us speculate:

1. That it is bad to be clumsy and fall.
2. That she hurts when she bleeds.
3. That to seek help brings more pain.
4. That she is dirty and not to be seen by company.
5. That mother is angry and punishes her for (a) being dirty, (b) being hurt and, (c) asking for help.
6. That the solution is to run away.

Inextricably, how she acts, her phsyical feelings, and her mother's feelings, are bound together. The result, if the example is representative of the kind of treatment this child consistently receives, is a self-concept which believes:

— "I am clumsy; therefore, I am bad. . . . . .
— "I am dirty; therefore, I shouldn't be with people like that . . . . . . (Generalized to professional people or authority figures.)
— "It's no use asking for help. It only makes things worse . . . . .
— "The only solution is to run away."

Note that the progression of feeling comes first out of behavior, and then out of the "significant" adult's reflected appraisals of that behavior. In this way a concept of oneself is acquired, and eventually, a child begins to act in terms of his self-concept. For example, "I'm no good. There's no use trying."

The preceding example is given to illustrate the vital importance of teaching the preschool child that he *is* capable, that he has good body impulses and feelings, and that there are "other significant adults" in the world that believe him to be worthy.

The methods outlined are specifically designed to teach body image. *The attitude and feeling of the teacher will determine the concept of self which is learned simultaneously.* She should be permissive, encouraging, and enthusiastic about her children's discovery of themselves and their capabilities.

Teacher's outline on self-concept and body image

A.   Learn to identify parts of the body with their function.

The teacher should teach the names of parts of the body with their function in daily conversation as the opportunity presents itself. A minimum vocabulary list with appropriate verbs may include:

Eye—see, look
Ear—hear, listen
Nose—smell, breathe
Mouth—eat, drink, talk
Tongue—taste
Throat—swallow
Finger—touch
Hand—hold, draw, open
Elbow—bend
Arm—raise
Leg—walk
Knee—bend
Hip—walk
Stomach—where food goes
Genitals—(if opportunity arises in bathroom, as in "clean your
          genitals"). Other bathroom words if the need arises
          may be B.M., feces, urinate or wet.
Hair—comb
Foot—kick
Waist—turn, belt
Chest—breathe

B.   Learning the location and interrelationships of body.
  1. Talk directly to children and help them point to body part as they use it.
  2. Put up flannel graph pictures of humans. Take down one piece at a time. Let children replace. Continue making it harder until children can put human body together.
  3. Sing songs
      Example: *Put Your Finger on Your Nose*

      a. Put your finger on your nose, on your nose
          Put your finger on your nose, on your nose
          Put your finger on your nose, and feel the
             cold it blows.
          Put your finger on your nose.
      b. Put your finger on your hair, on your hair, etc.

> Put your finger on your hair, and then just
>   leave it there.

    c. Put your finger on your cheek and leave it
       about a week.

    d. Put your finger on your ear and leave it
       about a year.

    e. Put your finger on your head, tell me, is
       it blue or red?

    f. Put your finger on your knee, and come and
       play with me, etc.

4. Do rhythm games
   Walk, stamp feet, run, dance, hop on one foot, skip. Children can pretend to be animals, or dance to music.

5. Finger plays are excellent preparation for writing activities. For example, this little game about fingers.

Verse 1	Where is thumbkin?
	Where is thumbkin?
	Here I am! Here I am!
	How are you today, sir?
	Very well, I thank you
	Run away, run away.
Verse 2	Where is pointer?
Verse 3	Where is middle?
Verse 4	Where is ringer?
Verse 5	Where is pinky?

6. Draw outline of child on butcher paper or newspaper as he lies on the floor. Then encourage him to color in eyes, nose, mouth, hair, ears, and clothes. Post these on sequential days.

Summary:

Our experiences in providing special diagnostic services for the children showed us that teachers need help in curriculum building in two areas—in building the body image and in language enrichment. One of the services that a professional consultant can provide is help in these areas. We were rather shocked to find such severely handicapped children in the program —severely disturbed emotionally or handicapped physically. We were able to render service to almost all of these children because we worked as a team. The volunteer physician, Dr. Elsie Georgi, who came one day a week from a local hospital, the volunteer speech pathologist who came from Pepperdine College, the volunteer child development specialist, also from Pepperdine College, the volunteer medical social worker, Betty Williams, and the superb school nurse, Dorothy Jenkins, worked in every way to help us function as a team.

We would recommend that each Head Start Agency retain a child development specialist to work in close coordination with other professionals, achieving accurate diagnosis, lending support services to the teachers in curriculum building and guidance techniques, in supporting the home, and in making intelligent referrals.

Although in this program most of these services were on a volunteer basis, in the future it would seem mandatory that these consultants be retained on a fee basis.

All of the records which were accumulated on the children during the summer were summarized and passed on to the public school. In this way we hoped that the head start that we had made in diagnosing and treating problems would go on to school with the children, making follow-up treatment more efficient and prompt.

In Section III of this book a model follow-up program is outlined which would serve to continue helping seriously disturbed children such as have been described in the case histories herein. Without adequate follow-up, the team treatment that these children receive in Head Start becomes an empty promise.

As we continued studying the children more closely, we became impressed with the fact that there were three major types of limitations in our children, (1) lack of language ability, (2) poor body image or self-concept, and (3) the neurologically handicapped.

A special class was established for the neurologically handicapped about half-way through the program. It became apparent that these organically driven children could not function in the ordinary classroom and also that a normal functioning classroom could not function with them in it! The teacher, Ettawanda Mason, had had extensive experience in special education and devoted the best of herself to the task. The children developed, thrived, and were happier than some of us had thought possible. Without the special class, these children would have needed to be excluded from the program.

Had follow-up been available, their teacher offered to take leave of her regular job and devote the entire year to the special education of Mark and Willie and their friends. Unfortunately we lost them to the anonymity of the public school.

13

the coordinator

The Coordinator acted as a filament connecting every aspect of the Head Start program. Her job began fully two months before Head Start opened and continued several months after the program closed with follow-up and neighborhood requests for assistance (as well as the writing of this book). The planning outlined in *Section I, Procedure,* was the responsibility of the Coordinator.

Once the program was underway, it was the Coordinator's task to inspire, organize, and sustain it. An essential task of any administrator is *communication.*

COMMUNICATION

Communication with staff

Communication with the staff was facilitated through

1. Informal contacts
2. Separate weekly meetings with teachers, aides, and staff
3. Daily news bulletins

There were ninety-seven employees in our Head Start program (some of whom were part-time or N.Y.C. employed), three hundred children, and three buildings. Effective internal communications were of the greatest import in maintaining staff morale and good relationships. Head Start seemed like a family operation with every worker therein having an interest in the totality of the program, and possessing a stake in making a "go" of the program. Daily bulletins from the Coordinator's office to all the staff kept every worker aware of the full program. These bulletins detailed all of the day's scheduled events, printed special messages or recognitions, and anticipated the morrow's activities.

Daily news bulletins tend to help a large staff achieve a sense of oneness, a unity of purpose, and to lend a sense of order to all the "disruptions" at the end of each day. The Coordinator dictated the *Daily Bulletin* which the secretary dittoed the last thing before she went home. The bulletin was dated, began with an inspiring quotation, and then listed the events and announcements of the day.

A sample staff bulletin of the beginning of the program is included as an example:

SAMPLE STAFF DAILY BULLETIN

Delta Sigma Theta's Head Start

GOOD MORNING!

> *Enthusiasm is the genius of sincerity, and truth accomplishes no victories without it.*
>
> Bulwer-Lytton

1. Your enthusiasm in recruiting children for our Project has been truly remarkable. Bouquets and thanks to all for your wholehearted support.
2. Callouses anyone? Take heart in the fact that our enrollment is swelling rapidly. To date, we have 60 children enrolled, with a promise of at least 100 within the next two days.
3. MASS MEETING of community leaders tonight in the Church, 7:30 PM. Please advertise to your friends and neighbors and make every effort to return yourselves. We want the church to be filled.
4. Mrs. D., cafeteria manager, over-bought on milk, anticipating more children during the first few days. If anyone is interested, you may purchase this surplus at retail cost.
5. We have encountered fine cooperation and a willingness to share on the part of all Victory Nursery School and extended day staff. However, in order to remain in the clear and adhere to our commitments to the State Department of Welfare and Health Department, let's try to keep our operations separate, so as not to jeopardize their position. All groups, please eat in your own area. All adult personnel, please eat in the patio area indicated.
6. Dr. Riley and Miss Beard will be visiting the premises again today. Thank you for your continued courtesy and cooperation with them.
7. Please note the *Sentinel* newspaper coverage of our Project Head Start. Some commendations are in order for this spread. Perhaps it will encourage future publicity of the fine work that is going on in our community.
8. We are covered by insurance in the transportation of children to the Project. However, let's all use extreme caution in driving and be sure that we have a clear understanding with parents on procedures for pick up and return. Bus services will be available next week.

MONDAY:

1. Bus service will begin (hopefully).
2. Research team will begin screening—Stations 1 and 2. Wait for call by monitor.
3. Nurse's office visits for Stations 5, 6, 7, 8. She will send for you.

Besides the *Daily Bulletin* to staff, there were memos of a more permanent nature regarding procedures such as registration, transportation, clerical work, custodian and building routines, emergencies, supplies, keeping records, general policies, safety, and completing government forms.

Monthly master calenders were distributed with all preplanned activities marked, so that things could be anticipated and personal adjustments made where irregular hours or schedules were necessary. These two communicative devices were most successful.

The Coordinator met weekly with teachers and teacher aides. Other workers, (kitchen, clerical, custodial aides) met departmentally, with the supervising head responsible for specific operations.

Communication with visitors

Visitors came every day! Parents, grandparents, uncles, grandmothers, siblings, ministers, Girl Scouts, Youth Opportunity Board, visitors from Washington, D.C., a group of businessmen, Los Angeles County Schools and Los Angeles City Schools representatives, newsmen, television cameras, State Board of Social Welfare, Sorority members, students from colleges.

People, people, and more people, all curious about Head Start, were daily visitors to our Center. Colleges sent students to interview and observe; other community groups wanted speakers to tell them more about the program; workers in allied fields sought information and ways in which they might help; businessmen sought to donate to the cause, others to sell their services; Girl Scout troops wanted to tour the school and assist; neighborhood groups wanted to see the program in operation; governmental representatives, program developers, the designers of the project, all sought to see Head Start in action. These all added up to many hours spent in public relations. This was a most pleasant aspect of the job. Everyone's genuine interest in the program kept the staff alert and motivated to a higher degree of effectiveness. But a word of caution was necessary—as we noted in the bulletin:

> VISITORS are always welcome at Head Start. However, let's make sure that all visitors clear through the office before visiting classrooms or interviewing or photographing. We have a visitor's permit which all visitors will display in the future. Notify the office immediately if you find persons wandering around without the proper identification.

To acquaint teachers with visitors, we put a note in the Daily Bulletin whenever possible, and sent an introduction slip with unexpected visitors who "dropped in."

Communications with parents

The most effective communication with parents is on a one-to-one basis. The teacher was found to be in the best position to maintain contact with parents. However, the Coordinator facilitated this contact by providing teachers with the necessary legal permit forms and information sheets.

It is important that the bulletins to parents be written in simple language —the median education level in our community was eighth grade—but without "talking down." Ideally, the bulletins to parents were delivered by teachers with opportunity for discussion.

MAINTAINING AN OFFICE

Office procedure

Contrary to most other programs in the country, our entire program was centralized in one site. With a program of twenty groups of fifteen children in each group, we had a full scale operation, necessitating much organization for effective operations.

We maintained two offices—one in the principal building, and one about a block away in the second classroom unit. The Coordinator was housed in the principal building, while a head teacher, assuming the role of assistant coordinator, occupied the other unit. Also housed in the main office were the coordinator for volunteer and N.Y.C. services, the secretary, who was a regular elementary school clerk, and a half-dozen part-time clerical aides from N.Y.C.

Because of the two sessions on which we were operating, the half-time clerical staff was on a staggered four-hour work schedule, thus enabling us to have adequate coverage and service throughout the eight-hour day that the Coordinator was on duty.

Checking daily attendance, providing an accurate lunch count, maintaining records of bus services and schedules, typing bulletins and calendars of events, enrolling new arrivals, and maintaining records of library books and services were part of the office routines. Perhaps some of the clerical work could be dispensed with in a center operating on a smaller scale, but adequate records were mandatory to assure the health, safety, and welfare of three hundred preschoolers in one center.

The secretary had responsibility for the proper maintenance of office records, enrolling children, telephone services, and supervision of the clerical aides. The coordinator of volunteers, who worked partly on a volunteer basis, provided direction for Neighborhood Youth Corps, and maintained the necessary records for reporting the time worked and payroll for these Neighborhood Youth Corps workers.

Government forms

The medical assistant and coordinator of volunteers worked eight hours a day throughout on filling out government forms.

Because the responsibility of interpretation, administration, and collection of the forms lay with the Coordinator, it was important to have an understanding of their function and importance. In order to refine and continue a Head Start Program, there must be research. The responsibility of the staff is providing information. Even though completing the questionnaires was time-consuming and thought-provoking, it was a vital part of Head Start.

Appendix III contains samples of several questionnaires. Coordinators are urged to familiarize themselves with them so as to assuage doubts and execute their completion in a professional manner. Included are:

1. Worker's Attitude Scale
2. Staff Member Information Sheet
3. Paid and Voluntary Worker's Evaluation of Operation Head Start
4. Parent Evaluation of Head Start
5. Psychological Screening Procedure
6. Behavior Inventory

It is suggested that duplicate copies of the Psychological Screening Procedure and Behavior Inventory be placed in the children's general file to be passed on to the school.

For most of the questionnaires, identification was accomplished by use of an IBM number. A special session had to be called to explain and issue IBM numbers to each staff member and child.

Other organizational procedures involved maintaining personnel records, supervising bookkeeping and signing authorizations for expenditures, and payroll. On one occasion when the payroll was ten days late (!) we managed to smooth things over through the following note in the *Daily Bulletin:*

> The wheels of government grind but sometimes not too well; they also break. Therefore—I have the unhappy assignment of telling you that we expect to have your checks in your hands on Monday. Mrs. ——— went personally to the Washington office but there was a delay because of computer troubles. Do you think Head Start gave them a headache? Seriously, we are very sorry if this delay causes inconveniences but it is a matter over which we have no control. The check from Washington is expected at any moment.

You can imagine the problems involved in maintaining morale with a delayed payroll.

We mention this particular difficulty to illustrate that all of the procedural matters so glibly mentioned here are not matter-of-fact events, but each entails problems of personality, bureaucracy, and time-space scheduling. It is the Coordinator's task to continue to give order and purpose to the program. But a motto on his wall might be, "If anything can go wrong, it will."

Scheduling

Maintaining a calendar without conflicts in activities was, perhaps, the biggest challenge faced by the Coordinator. Consider the total scope of Head Start programs in one brief span of time.

Health examinations
Dentist's visits
Field trips
Visits by community workers
Nurse's visits
Aides' meetings
Teachers' meetings
Social workers conferences
Bus schedules
Speech therapy sessions
Psychologist's visits
Government testing
Parent education
TV and news coverage

All demanded a slice of this capsule of time.

Considering the health needs of the child to be of greatest urgency, the Coordinator and nurse plotted on an eight-week calendar the schedule of doctor's visits, dentist's visits, trips to the County Health Department for inoculations, mass Tine tests, and other mass examination or testing procedures. The nurse was efficient and effective in keeping these activities current and in cross-checking calendars with the Coordinator's office.

Psychological screening, speech screening, hearing screening and vision screening were fitted into the next available slots on the master calendar. Once special needs were ascertained through these mass screening procedures, special weekly sessions with psychologist and speech therapists were established.

Meeting deadline dates for government testing instruments and forms was mandatory. Testing was designated for special weeks. The time grid gained in complexity as all of these activities were entered.

Field trips

A member of the sponsoring agency, volunteering in the capacity of Field Trips Coordinator, worked with the Coordinator in selecting dates for field trips: visits by the policemen, firemen, librarian, and community activities which involved the parents. Alternative dates had to be selected in the event that a chosen date was not available. These trips, the planning which went into them, and the expenses involved are given a detailed treatment in the chapter entitled "Bringing the Community to the Classroom."

All other activities were dovetailed into the schedule in the remaining time blocks. The order of this narration may give the misleading impression that all of the time slots and all of the scheduled activities fell neatly into the designated patterns. Anyone who has had any experience at all with Head Start would surely not be so misled. There was always the unexpected—a doctor volunteering some time which we sorely needed and welcomed at his convenience, but not in the scheduled slot, return trips to the Health Department for selected children, drop-ins by V.I.P.'s, and so on. But it can be honestly stated that we managed to cover all activities with a high degree of effectiveness and minimal conflict. One reason for the lack of major conflict was allowing the teacher to make the final decision concerning her children.

For instance, on the day the policemen visited, the following announcement was in the *Daily Bulletin:*

> Two policemen, as a part of our Community Helper Series, will be on campus today. This is a fine opportunity for our children to view law officers as friends and helpers. The officers will be in the patio area between the nursery and extended day buildings at 10:30 for all AM children. Classes from the day school will please come down at this time and plan to remain until lunch time. Please note that this is permissive; I realize that we have many things crowded into a short space of time in order to try to give our children a sampling of many things. If we can work around all other schedules I am sure that the children will benefit. Thank you for your cooperation.

In the case of field trips, preference was still given to children's needs. For instance:

> Science Center trip for afternoon classes. Departures are scheduled for 12:45. Teachers, please use your own judgment as to whether these trips are practicable. If testing and other matters are pressing, please feel free to cancel out. Let the office know so that bus schedules may be revised.

Meetings with other directors, coordinators, and program planners came in for their share of the Coordinator's time.

Parent education

With the social workers and an advisory body from the sponsoring agency and community and teachers, the Coordinator planned the parent education schedule. We sought to develop a program that would cater to the needs of the parents in the community, would be of sufficient interest and variety, and would parallel our concepts of development of the whole child.

A topic relating to some area of child development and family living was assigned to each week of the program. A balance in program format was sought through use of speakers, workshops, films, observations, panel discussions, and active participation on the part of the parents. The Coordinator established the program format, sought out and contacted resource people in each area, organized the meetings, sent home notices in advance of all meetings, and participated in each parent education session. This was a most valuable experience and served to strengthen our relationships in the community. Through this series, people got to know each other better, they enjoyed the experience of working and sharing together, and it afforded a view of the professional worker in a different perspective.

Post project activities

One can hardly put a closing date on Head Start. Long after the official closing date, a myriad of details still claimed the time of the Coordinator. In this instance, the sponsoring agency had undertaken Head Start as a public service project and much time was willingly donated by all workers on the project. But program planners need take this additional time into consideration in writing proposals so that adequate clerical services and compensation are possible.

A post-evaluation conference some weeks after the close of the project brought all of the workers back together again. Discussions and reports yielded many valuable suggestions for future programs.

Endless letters of recognition and thanks, final reports and summaries, disposal or storage of certain items, seeking places for storage, termination of utility services, return of equipment and rentals, final bookkeeping proceedures, and payment of bills which came in late are but a few of the items which demanded attention long after the final date of the program.

Section III
PROMISE

14

the influence of head start on school readiness

It was toward the end of the college year that one of us mentioned in class that we were interested in finding a Head Start project in which we might actively participate. After class, one of the students, Pamela, said that she had volunteered to participate in a Head Start that summer and would be happy to introduce us to her director. We set up an appointment to meet together and there we discussed the possibility of a research program. What would the children be learning? How could it be tested? Would a research team moving in on a preschool be disruptive?

There were many fears on both sides but we all agreed that the idea was a good one. We would try to work out the details as we went along. We had two weeks to set up an entire research program.

Just two weeks before Head Start was scheduled to begin, a group of us who taught Early Childhood Education on the college level were discussing the influences that such a nation-wide program would have on the lives of children. Although there was not much research in our academic journals to tell us either what children from low income backgrounds were like or what effects a good nursery school program would have, we were all confident that the outcome would be a positive one. As is true in most any college or university setting there was a skeptic among us who said, "But how do you know that a nursery school experience will be able to negate the experiences that the child has in his home environment?"

Previous research

At that time we were ignorant of the pilot project that the Ford Foundation had done with children from poverty areas showing, indeed, that a nursery school experience was beneficial to later school life. At that time about all we could do was sputter about researches done in orphanages and resort to the common sense of: "After all, it should work." We did remember three small studies done by two people named Bonney and Nicholson in 1958 on the social adjustment of children which matched and compared children with and without nursery school experience. Their findings were that if nursery school experience was going to be of any value to children's social adjustment then that social experience had to be of what they call a particularly high-quality level one—that is, they felt that the teachers had to be superior in being able to meet the individual needs of children. This certainly made sense to us. After all, if the children had been from a rather poor environment it seemed sensible to expect they would have to have adults for teachers who were particularly sensitive to their needs and able to give them individual attention to compensate for what they hadn't had before. Would Head Start be able to make adequate provision for meeting varying needs of individuals?

We began to do a little library research to see if other people had studied this whole matter. In 1942 a researcher by the name of Dawe had found that children in an orphanage had limited language experiences. He set up a 50-hour program, lasting over a period of time, which included reading to children and taking them on short trips and talking to them and explaining words. After this experience he found (naturally) an increase in their vocabulary and information about home living, more information about science, better scores on reading readiness tests and also better IQ scores. We wondered if there would be a parallel in the type of child we would be dealing with. Our library research began to run into the days and the nights. What would we measure? How would we measure it? We knew that children were in the Head Start program to get ready for school. We presumed that their language development would be retarded. We also presumed that their practice in thinking with abstract terms had been limited.

About this time a book came off the press entitled *School Readiness* by Frances Ilg and Louise Bates Ames which was of great value to us. These authors suggested that unless a child was developmentally ready for school he would profit little from the experience. A colleague of theirs, Arnold Gesell, had suggested that children matured developmentally as a whole but that this whole can be conceptualized in four different ways: (1) physical; (2) mental; (3) language and (4) social-emotional. If we could somehow get measurements from all these categories on the children at the beginning of the program and again at the end of the program we could measure the difference and see if the children had learned what would normally be expected or if it were more than would be expected.

FINDING TESTS TO MEASURE SCHOOL READINESS

Gesell Copy Forms

Then began the search for tests. To test physical development we borrowed from Gesell—the Gesell Copy Forms or Developmental Designs. Gesell first conceptualized this test in his book *Developmental Diagnosis* published in 1947. He found that a three-year-old can usually draw a circle, a four-year-old can draw a cross, a five-year-old can draw a square or a box, a six-year-old can draw a triangle and a seven-year-old, a diamond. These are average ages. They are dependent upon visual-motor maturation. If a child is retarded he probably will not be able to draw up to the age level. If he is average he will probably be able to draw the design for his age level, and if he is bright he may be able to draw a design far beyond his age level. The ability to draw these simple geometric figures does not seem to be based on experience but rather on maturity. Therefore, we felt that this test would be a relatively culture-free test, that is, it would not be necessarily dependent upon the children's experience with abstract thinking or language ability.

The Draw-A-Person Test

The other test that we selected from these researchers was the Draw-A-Person-Test. The Draw-A-Person Test is an old one. It was first developed by a lady named Florence Goodenough in 1926 as an instrument to measure intelligence. Since then this test has had wide use all over the world, not only to measure intelligence but to measure how a child feels about himself. It is a short test to give and takes but one or two minutes. It is usually enjoyed by the children and it can be given by someone without special training. The person giving the test just hands a piece of paper and a crayon to the child and says simply "Draw a picture of a person." To any questions the child may ask the examiner answers, "Do it any way you want" or, "Do the whole person."

We were quite excited about the results that we might get on the Draw-A-Person because of its use by some people to explore the child's inner world. Goodenough, for example, noted that although children might get the same intelligence scores on their drawings, the drawings could be quite different and that they seemed to tell a story about the children who drew them. She said, "The child exaggerates items which seem interesting or important; other parts are minimized or omitted—tentative experimentation suggests the possibility of devising a method of scoring drawings in such a way as to throw a light on functional mental disorders, but such a method has not been developed." (Goodenough, 1928). Twenty years later Dr. Goodenough wrote, ". . . the child and his drawings frequently give outward expressions to his inner life of thoughts and feelings, to his fears and his desires, to his hopes and his frustrations. . . ." We were particularly entranced with her words of his "fears and inner thoughts." What of the fears and inner thoughts of these children that we were to study? What would we find?

In 1949 another researcher, Karen McOver, wrote in the same vein as Florence Goodenough when she said, "The drawing of the human figure must be understood as an expression of moods and tensions and as a vehicle for the individual's projection of his problems and his mode of experience—organization as revealed in his body image."

We were to become very well acquainted with the term "body image" before the summer was over. Little did we know at that time how important body image was to be.

The Peabody Picture Vocabulary Test

We found one test to measure vocabulary. It was called the Peabody Picture Vocabulary Test (PPVT). This test was devised at Peabody Teacher's College as a non-verbal test of intelligence, that is, one in which the person being tested does not have to speak. The test includes a booklet of pictures. On each page are four pictures, simple line drawings of objects or people doing things. There are key words that belong to one of the pictures. The examiner shows the four pictures to a child and says, "Here is a kitty, a car, a dog and a chair. Show me which one is the chair." If there's no response, the examiner says, "Put your finger on the chair," or, "Here is the chair." After he is sure that the child understands the procedure he goes on to pictures where he will give no help.

We found that the Peabody Test had been used extensively and with rather good success in speech clinics where children's vocabulary was limited or where they were too shy to talk. Therefore, we felt that we had a good instrument to measure the child's passive vocabulary, i.e., the number of words he knew without actually having to pronounce them.

The Riley Articulation and Language Test

We were at a loss as to what test we could use to measure the child's articulation and language development until we found a test, then being developed, called the Riley Articulation and Language Test. Dr. Riley, husband of one of the authors, had been working on this test for some time and when we talked to him of our needs he agreed to get it ready. The test was developed and used, and is now published by the Western Psychological Association.

Vineland Social Maturity Scale

With speech, language, mental ability and physical maturation taken care of we still felt that we needed a test of social development. Although we did not find one that suited us completely, we finally compromised on the Vineland Social Maturity Scale. This test was devised at the Vineland Training School in New Jersey by Edgar Dawe as an instrument to measure the social age of mentally retarded children and adults. It provided a list of children's behavior according to the following categories:

1. Self-help
2. Self-direction
3. Occupation
4. Communication
5. Social relations

Examples of these are such things as—can put on his jacket without assistance—can go to the bathroom without being told—can finish a task— can talk to others in sentences of three or four words—plays cooperatively with his playmates. The total maturation score toward independence is considered to be a measure of progressive development and social competence. The author of the test states that besides giving a social age there are four other purposes to the test.

1. To aid in differentiating between mental retardation and social incompetence.
2. To assist in child guidance and training by providing an age level for performance expectations.
3. To evaluate the influence of environment, cultural status and other handicaps to development.
4. To be used as a research instrument to determine social maturity when adjustment is a consideration.

Therefore we hoped that, besides learning something about the social age of our children, we would be able to gather other information about them and guide the teachers in helping the children mature. For future references we noted that a summary of the test and its uses was published in 1953 by Dr. Dawe.

Getting ready

Once we had selected the tests we had to order them, and to get them on time we feverishly searched out catalogs, made long distance phone calls, and begrudgingly paid air freight charges to assure having the proper test materials ready for us by the opening of Head Start, now just one week away.

We wished to test all the children as soon as possible and it became apparent that we would need help. Our research team at that time was composed of Dr. Glyndon Riley, Speech Pathologist at Pepperdine College; Dr. Clara Riley and Dr. Helen Beard of Los Angeles State College. Dr. Beard assumed responsibility for the direction of the research and the statistical analysis. The Rileys assumed responsibility for enlisting the students in helping to administer and grade the tests. Fortunately there were several students in the master's program who could give both the speech screening, the Peabody and the Draw-A-Person tests.

Opening day

The research team was there on opening day. We had met together and decided it would be best to become acquainted with the children before we began the testing process. We had heard of what we considered to be an unfortunate research design elsewhere in the country, where teams of psychologists had gone into strange schools among strange children, yanked them from their classrooms and pounced on them with strange questions. We believed that there must be a better way to treat young children. Test results could hardly be valid under such circumstances. It was our desire, then, to work into the program slowly, to become known and trusted by the children and teachers as much as possible before we provided tests for them to take.

Our chagrin was as great as the rest of the Head Start staff that first week when enrollment was as slow as it was. We had hoped to test a hundred children, fifty boys and fifty girls, but at the end of the first week there were not even that many children enrolled. At that point the decision was made that testing would begin the following Monday with whatever children were available. So came the rude awakening from the ideal to reality.

Setting up the facilities

We arrived at the Head Start site rather nervously that second Monday morning and went to an empty classroom where we set up stations for testing. Our plan was to bring in one whole class at a time so that the children would not be separated from their new found friends nor their teachers. At the first table there was room for two children to write and two children to wait. This was the table to test them on the Copy Forms. Here we had plenty of paper, pencils and black crayons. As two little children sat down facing each other, two other little children sat at the end of the table in "ready" chairs watching them.

At the next table the set-up was exactly the same for the Draw-A-Person Test. At the third table there were two chairs at each end. Here we gave the Peabody Picture Vocabulary Test. Children were situated so that they could not see the pictures until it was their turn, but they could still see what was going on, so they knew that they need not fear. Over in the corner of the large room Speech and Articulation Tests were given. Although the tests were given individually there were several "ready" chairs where the children could watch and listen. It was felt that listening and watching would help the children respond better to the examiner.

After the speech screening came the audiology screening, both administered by the same person. In this way the children were able to get acquainted with the examiner, and the strange earphones seemed not to frighten them so much. As children finished the testing procedure they were taken outside to play by the regular teacher or the assistant.

Testing begins

One of us would go to a classroom and alert the teacher that we were ready. The teacher and the assistant would bring the children to our testing room. There we put the braver children, the bolder children to work at once. The shyer children were put in chairs to watch so that they might become accustomed to the situation. We asked the teachers to hold the tearful ones on their laps.

Since most of the teachers were sophisticated in testing techniques, once in a while we asked the teacher to give the test. Almost always, the child would then respond. The only child that we were unable to test was a little boy fresh from Haiti who spoke only French. Unfortunately, none of those on our research team were fluent in French.

We were successful in testing all of the children except for those in one classroom where the teacher informed us that she didn't believe her children would want to come but that we could ask them. We were not at all surprised to find that, whenever we asked if they wished to come, they did not. We remained to play, and a little later, after the snack had been served, we asked if we could test the children in the classroom. There we set up our materials on a table and in the informal situation the children were able to overcome their fear of the strange examiner and the reticence of their teacher to support them in this work.

In this fashion the testing proceeded morning and afternoon, Monday, Tuesday, and Wednesday until all the children in attendance were tested. Each night we took home the test results and graded them, for we were most curious to see the results as we went along.

One of the ways in which we were able to enlist the teachers' cooperation in the testing was to tell them that we would get the results to them as soon as possible so that they might use these results in devising better teaching methods. We wanted to have the results to them by the end of the week if at all possible. Late at night the graduate students had coffee drinking parties where they stayed up until the wee hours of the morning grading Peabody's and Draw-A-Person's and Gesell's!

The graduate students soon caught our enthusiasm for the project and made real sacrifices in order to help us complete the testing. Dwayne Carlson, for instance, worked the graveyard shift, showered, had breakfast and came to the project to work until two in the afternoon before going home to sleep. Herman White, father of three children, working the swing shift and going to school in the morning, took time off from studying and being with his family in order to test long hours. Donna Hazel Larson and Thelma Brown, graduate assistant and student assistant to the Speech Department, worked long hours in the evening grading the tests that had been given during the day, often staying up until midnight or after. Doris Sundean, who was studying double time to make up some incompletes that she had received during the previous semester due to illness, sacrificed two afternoons. Don Bone, recently returned missionary and father of two children, was the most successful in working with our shy children. It was he who was able to go to the classrooms with the reticent teacher and test the children who had retreated from the rest of us. Without the spirit of self-sacrifice on the part of these students the testing could not have been completed in the short time in which we had.

The teachers help us with the Vineland

We soon realized that we would have neither the time nor the skill to administer the Vineland Social Maturity Scale. The interviewer who makes out the scale has to talk to a member of the family who knows the child very well. Since the teachers were usually in daily contact with one member of the family it seemed more logical to us that they would be the ones to interview.

What we found out about our children

At the teachers' meeting the following Friday we were able to present the results. It was 3:30 on a hot sultry afternoon as we all gathered into a classroom which was also used part-time for storage. We took secret delight in the comments which we overheard from the teachers, who said, "My, it's hard to believe that you are giving us the results so quickly," or, "In the city schools we're lucky if we ever find out what the research is all about." The enthusiastic cooperation of the teachers confirmed our belief in sharing any and all research information with the entire staff as quickly as possible.

It seemed wise to us at that time to present the research results in terms of the children's needs rather than as test scores. Since our children had a minimum chronological age of 4.7 (four years, seven months) we felt that any child in Head Start with characteristics below the age of three would need special attention. We tested 89 children in all. Of these children 60 of them had one or more severe limitations. Many of them had multiple limitations. Table 2 lists the limitations of our Head Start children.

Table 2
LIMITATIONS OF HEAD START CHILDREN

Limitation	Number
1. Vocabulary extremely limited	36
2. Social deprivation	28
3. Social maladjustment	29
4. Mental retardation (constitutional)	3
5. Perceptual and neurological handicap	8
Total number of Limitations*	104

Explaining the test results to the teachers

Our account to the teachers went something like this: "You will notice that 36 children have an extremely limited vocabulary. This means that the vocabulary is below the language age of a child three years of age. We noticed as we went through the tests that the children know many nouns such as chair, table, kitty, fork, or ice cream cone, but that as a whole their use of verbs, such as sitting, peeking, or baking, is somewhat limited. Therefore, we can roughly say that a little less than half of the children have very limited vocabularies. You will need to talk to them in short sentences, often illustrating the verb that you want them to understand. Another way to teach them verbs is to talk about what the children are doing, especially if they are outside, such as, 'Johnny is riding the tricycle' or, 'Mary is climbing the jungle gym.'"

"We have made a distinction between social maladjustment and social deprivation. By social deprivation we merely mean that the child does not know, has not been taught interpersonal relationships. This is the child who drew on his Draw-A-Person Test a head, a couple of arms and maybe a leg or two. In the classroom you may see him standing around watching, not knowing exactly what to do. He may not even know that the chair is to sit on. These children should respond rapidly to teaching.

1. We hang our sweaters here.
2. A chair is to sit on.
3. The books are there.
4. When you want Johnny's toy, ask him. Say, 'May I have it?'"

---

* Based on 60 children

This is the type of teaching that the child with social deprivation will probably respond to best.

"On the other hand, those children whom we have classified as socially maladjusted seemed unable to organize their drawing environment at all. They scribbled or made drawings which were wild or distorted. They seemed tense in their entire make-up. The one child whom we knew had been mistreated was able to draw only jagged lines on the paper, with one circle for the head and huge ears. These children with social maladjustment will take special tender, loving care, firm limits and telling many times over. They are not apt to trust us. They must learn by experience that we are their friends. Perhaps we will need to study these children further to find out how we may best help them.

"Although we found 36 children who had a vocabulary of age three or less, we have found only three children that we believe are constitutionally mentally retarded. These are; Faye in Room 1, Nadine in Room 8 and Christopher in Room 14. We will want to observe them further, however, to see if our first impression is correct. We would like your opinion on this. If you have not taught mentally retarded children in the public schools, perhaps we can have a meeting or transfer these children so that they can be in classrooms where the teachers have had experience with mentally retarded children.

"We have found eight children that may have a perceptual or neurological handicap. These children seem to have few controls and we would like to know if your perception of these children was the same as ours."

At this point we had a lively group discussion. The teachers wanted to know which of their children had what limitations, what could be done regarding speech enrichment, and how could they better teach self-concept. The most pressing problem seemed to be how to handle the neurologically handicapped children within the regular classroom. At that time we had no answers but the problem and challenge were clearly there.

Giving the Vineland

At the conclusion of the discussion we handed out the Vineland Social Maturity Scale with the directions to the teachers on how to gather the information. We asked them to try to remember exactly how the child was during the first week of school, to interview the parent, and to return them to us as soon as possible. Since the teachers administered and graded the Vineland Test of Social Maturity, they were immediately aware of the strengths and weaknesses of their children and of the importance of learning independent self-help communication and other skills toward building independence. Many of them commented that this had been a most valuable experience and that they were very happy to have been included in the research. Many of the teachers were surprised to find that their students were used to going around the neighborhood alone, that they were often left with only slightly older brothers and sisters, that about a fourth of them put themselves to bed at night without any help, and that many of them went to the store, purchased materials, and brought home the groceries and the change. When compared to the low scores that the children as a group had made in language age and motor and perceptual skills, we were all quite surprised to find that the children had made as much progress as they had toward social maturity. Of course, there were many individual differences. Some children could not hold a pencil or crayon or cut with scissors, but on the whole we were gratified to find, during the weeks before the final testing that we were to learn much more about our children.

Results of speech screening

By the middle of the following week the results from the speech tests were available. Three children had not passed the hearing screening. Six children had articulation disorders, 22 had language disfunctions and 12 had both language and articulation disfunctions. Forty children in all needed speech therapy. This was 45 per cent of the total number tested.

Initiating remedial programs

The therapy program that evolved as a result of the initial research testing was primarily clinical in nature. In the time between the first testing during the second week of school and the last testing in the last week of school many of the original research teams turned their talents to therapy.

Small group placement, individual attention and special language enrichment programs were advised to meet the needs of these children. Due to budgetary limitations it was impossible to place the children in small groups as we advised or to provide individual attention. Later in the program a small group was established for neurologically handicapped children under the direction of a special education teacher.

Specialized curricula were developed about midway through the program in two areas, (1) speech enrichment, and (2) body image or self-concept. The teachers were encouraged to integrate these enrichment programs into their regular day. There was general acceptance by the teachers for these programs.

Testing at the end of the summer program

During the first three days of the last week of school the original research team reassembled, the testing room was set up, and the children were brought in for testing in exactly the same fashion as at the beginning of the program. Sixty-two were retested at the end of the program. Some

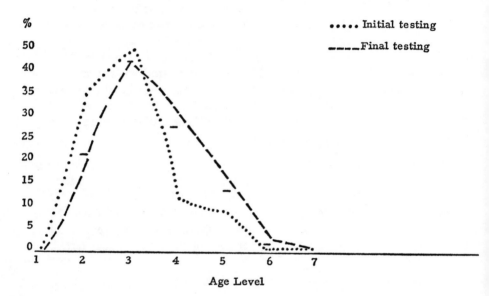

Peabody Picture Vocabulary Test

Age level	Initial		Final	
	N	%	N	%
2 - 2.9	21	33	13	21
3 - 3.9	30	48	26	41
4 - 4.9	7	11	16	26
5 - 5.9	5	8	7	11
6 - 6.9	0	0	1	1
Totals	63	100	63	100

children had dropped out, others were absent. Some few had left to go on vacation by the end of the summer. Although the testing conditions were as similar as possible, we do think it is important to record that very hot, humid weather descended upon the city during the final week of testing. This was the week that broke all heat records. This was the week of the Watts riots. Although the rioting did not enter our area until later in the week, there was still an atmosphere of unrest among the children. Because of the intense heat and the social unrest we were unable, until two weeks later, to grade these tests, record the results, and make the comparisons of how the children had grown toward school readiness.

SUMMARY OF RESULTS

Although we were delighted with the gains that we saw in individual children of one year, 18 months, two years, even 25 months, we were at first puzzled by the minus scores. We realized that there were several reasons to be considered. First of all, the children could have been ill, or in a bad mood because of something else that had happened that day, or resentful of being taken away from the room to the testing situation. Second, the examiner possibly did not take enough time or was unable to gain rapport with the child. Third, the child could easily have been distracted by heat or noise, especially by heat. Four, errors in recording were reduced to the minimum by double checking all tests, but this was still a possibility.

Peabody Picture Vocabulary Test

Although the group on an average had gained eight months on their language age, most of them still scored below their age level. We decided to make a breakdown of the scores and see what the gain was. The chart entitled "Peabody Picture Vocabulary Test" gives a graphic representation of the children of the first and the last testing. The percentage of children scoring between 2 years and 2.9 years of age decreased from 33 to 21 per cent. The percentage of children scoring between 3 and 3.9 years of age decreased from 48 to 41 per cent. The percentage of children scoring between 4 and 4.9 years of age increased from 11 to 26 per cent and the percentage of children scoring between 5 and 5.9 years of age increased from 8 to 11 per cent. One child scored between 6 and 6.9 at the final testing. Although as a group our children had made tremendous gains, only 12 per cent of them achieved a language age of 5 years or higher on the Peabody Vocabulary Test. Out of the 62 children we tested, 49 of them scored higher, two scored the same and 11 scored lower. The range of difference was from minus ten months to plus 25 months. The average gain was eight months. Eight months of vocabulary achieved in only seven weeks!

Draw -A- Person

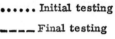

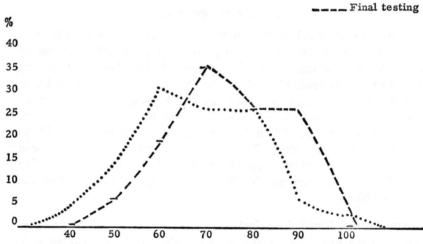

Standard Scores

Standard Score	Before		After	
	N	%	N	%
41---50	2	3	0	0
51---60	7	12	3	5
61---70	17	28	10	17
71---80	14	23	20	33
81---90	14	23	14	23
91---100	4	7	13	22
101---110	2	3	0	0

The Draw-A-Person Test

Standard scores were computed for all children on the Draw-A-Person Test, according to Goodenough-Harris Standards. However, our clinical judgment of the analysis of the scores is that these results are not primarily indicative of the mental maturity but are a reflection of the children's self-image. Out of the 60 children who were retested on the Draw-A-Person Test, 36 scored higher, six scored the same, 18 scored lower. The range of difference was from minus three years to plus five years. Since there were such tremendous individual variations in this particular test we were somewhat surprised to find that the gain made by the group was statistically significant at the .001 level.

Our interpretation of the scores

We feel that the results on this test reflected more than any other the tensions which were in the lives of many of these little children during the last week of heat and civil disorder. The results of the Draw-A-Person Test were given in standard scores instead of mental ages. In standard scoring, from 90 to 110 is considered normal, from 70 to 90 below normal, and scores below 70 are considered to be indicative of retardation. Clearly this was not so in our case. Children who gain eight months in vocabulary in six weeks are certainly not retarded in intellect! Since the sum total of our research illustrates beyond any doubt that these children are capable of learning at an accelerated rate, we feel that the Draw-A-Person is not a valid test of mental age for Head Start children. However, it may be a valid test of the ability to function or of emotional maturity. The chart entitled "Draw-A-Person" gives a breakdown of the changes of scores of the group. The percentage of children scoring between 41 and 50 dropped from 3 to 0. The percentage of children scoring between 51 and 60 dropped from 12 to 5. The percentage of children scoring between 61 and 70 dropped from 28 to 17. The percentage of children scoring between 71 and 80 rose from 23 to 33. The percentage of children scoring between 81 and 90 was 23 per cent in both cases. The percentage of children scoring between 91 and 100 rose from 7 to 22 per cent and the percentage of children scoring between 101 and 110 fell from 3 to 0. These scores are graphically illustrated on the chart entitled Draw-A-Person. If this same Draw-A-Person Test were being used in the public schools as a test of intelligence or mental age only 22 per cent of the children would have scored within the normal range of 91 to 110.

Certainly the children who score low on this test need individual attention. They need to know themselves better. They need many sensual physical contacts with both the world of things and the world of persons so that they and their teachers may become realistically aware of their true potentialities.

Gesell Developmental Designs

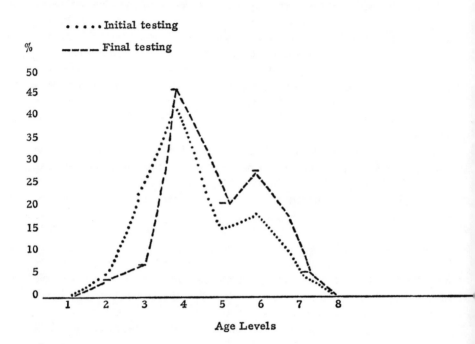

Age Level	Initial		Final	
	N	%	N	%
2.0 - 2.9	2	3	1	2
3.0 - 3.9	14	22	4	6
4.0 - 4.9	26	41	27	44
5.0 - 5.9	8	13	11	18
6.0 - 6.9	10	17	17	27
7.0 - 7.9	2	3	2	3
Totals	62	99%	62	100 %

The Gesell Developmental Designs

The Gesell Developmental Designs or Copy Forms were used to measure developmental maturity, visual-motor organization and coordination. Since this test is supposed to be dependent upon neurological maturity rather than environmental experience it was to be expected that it would be a relatively stable test and show little change.

Of the 60 children who completed the Gesell Developmental Designs Test, 24 scored higher, 27 scored the same and nine scored lower. Among the children who scored higher there was an average gain of 1.5 years.

The chart entitled Gesell Developmental Designs graphically illustrates the difference in the children between the beginning and the end of the program. The percentage of children who scored less than 3 years dropped from 3 to 2 per cent. The percentage of children scoring between 3 and 4 years dropped from 22 to 6 per cent. The percentage of children scoring between 4 and 5 years of age increased from 41 to 44 per cent. The percentage of children scoring between 5 and 5.9 years of age increased from 13 to 18 per cent. The children scoring between 6 and 7 years of age increased from 17 to 27 per cent and the percentage of children scoring between 7 and 8 years of age stayed the same at 3 per cent.

From the results of the Gesell Developmental Designs we concluded that our children were developmentally immature as a group, that they needed more practice in visual-motor activities and that they needed more creative play experiences with the world of things. The children, as a group, were about one year behind average children in their ability to conceptualize and reproduce symbols—a primary skill for learning writing and reading.

As a clinical footnote we would like to point out that we found the Developmental Designs to be a sensitive instrument for selecting perceptual and neurological handicapped children. Special education is needed for these children.

Vineland Social Maturity Scale

The greatest gains were evident in social maturity. Out of the 64 children we tested, 47 of them scored higher, 5 scored the same and 12 scored lower. The average gain was 1.9 years and the average loss was .5 years. As soon as we saw the results we began to ask ourselves how children were able to advance so far in such a short time. Part of the answer lies, we believe, in the fact that the children were granted freedom and encouraged to grow up, as was evidenced by their being sent to the store alone, by being able to put themselves to bed, and so on. The Head Start experience provided them with the tools for self-help that they needed. In other words, at Head Start they learned the skills to go with the attitudes that they already had. They learned to be independent, to be self-reliant,

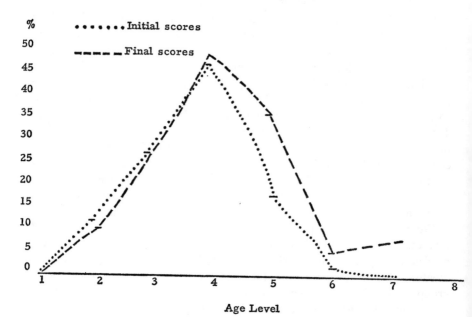

Vineland Social Maturity Scale

Age Level	Initial		Final	
	N	%	N	%
2 - 2yr 11 mo	6	11	0	0
3 - 3 11	15	26	5	9
4 - 4 11	26	45	27	47
5 - 5 11	9	16	19	33
6 - 6 11	1	2	2	4
7 - 7 11	0	0	4	7

to ask for what they needed, to button their own shirts, to cut their own meat.

However startling the results may be, however, it must be remembered that almost half of the children were a year behind their age level, with 47 per cent of them scoring between 4 years and 4 years 11 months. The extent of the social retardation is not as great, and probably all but about 10 per cent of the group are continuing to learn social amenities in the school situation. However, we recommend that a social enrichment program should be maintained for the lower 10 per cent, as they score under 3.9 years of age and probably would be lost in the shuffle of regular school. The children who scored under 3.9 years of age were also those same children who scored in the very lowest percentiles on the other tests.

The Riley Articulation and Language Test

The Riley Articulation and Language Test measured two functions of speech: (1) articulation, which is how clearly the children enunciate; and (2) language, the ability to remember meaningful sentences of various lengths.

At the beginning of the program 7 per cent of the children had articulation disorders which were so severe as to interfere with communication. At the end of the program this number had decreased to 3 per cent. The percentage of language disfunctions decreased from 25 to 17 per cent. The percentage of children with both articulation and language disorders decreased from 13 to 5 per cent. The total percentage of children needing speech therapy at the beginning of the program was 45 per cent whereas at the end of the program it had decreased to 25 per cent, a 20 per cent differential.

The value of the Head Start program for speech dysfunctions is abundantly clear. Within seven weeks of speech enrichment in the classroom and speech therapy for the most seriously disabled, 20 per cent of the children were able to bring their speech up to normal standards. In our public schools children are not usually screened for speech disorders until the second grade. By this time many speech patterns of the disadvantaged become fixed habit patterns and are much more difficult to treat.

Summary

That our Head Start children made phenomenal gains in every area tested is certainly self-evident. However, the seriousness of the emotional disturbances and intellectual retardation which has been environmentally produced must be recognized. Since the number of constitutionally retarded children appears to be about three per cent or normal for the United States population as a whole, we can only conclude that the seriousness and the limitations of our children in vocabulary, ability to draw, self-image and speech is due to their cultural environment. That these children are capable of learning their progress over the summer makes abundantly clear, but they still need specialized help before they can function competitively in an academic situation.

REFERENCES

Barrett, H.E., and Koch, H.L. "The Effect of Nursery School Training Upon the Mental Test Performance of a Group of Orphanage Children." *Pedagogical Seminary and Journal of Genetic Psychology,* (1930), 37, 102–121.

Bonney, M.E. and Nicholson, E.L. "Comparative Social Adjustments of Elementary School Pupils With and Without Preschool Training, *Child Development,* (1958), 29, 129–133.

Crissey, O.L. "The Mental Development of Children of the Same IQ in Differing Institutional Environments," *Child Development,* (1937), 8, 217–220.

Dawe, H.C. "A Study of the Effect of an Educational Program upon the Language Development and Related Mental Functions in Young Children," *Journal of Experimental Education,* (1942), 11, 200–209.

Doll, E.A. *The Measurement of Social Competence: a Manual for the Vineland Social Maturity Scale.* Minneapolis: American Guidance Service, 1953.

Dunn, L.M. *Expanded Manual for the Peabody Picture Vocabulary Test.* Minneapolis: American Guidance Service, 1965.

Gesell, A. and Amatruda, C.S. *Developmental Diagnosis.* New York: P. B. Hoeber, 1947.

Goodenough, C.L. "A Preliminary Report on the Effect of Nursery School Training upon the Intelligence Test Scores of Young Children," *Yearbook, National Society for the Study of Education,* (1938), 27, 361–369.

Harris, D.B. *Children's Drawings as Measures of Intellectual Maturity: A Revision and Extension of the Goodenough Draw-A-Man Test.* New York: Harcourt, Brace & World, 1963.

Havighurst, R.J. and Janke, Leota Long. "Relations Between Ability and Social Status in a Midwestern Community. I: Ten-year-old Children," *Journal of Educational Psychology,* (1944), 35, 357–368.

Ilg, Francis L. and Ames, Louise B. *School Readiness: Behavior Tests Used at the Gesell Institute.* New York: Harper & Row, 1964.

Kirk, S.A. *Early Education of the Mentally Retarded; an Experimental Study.* Urbana: Univ. Illinois Press, 1958.

Landreth, Catherine. *The Psychology of Early Childhood.* New York: Alfred A. Knopf, 1958.

Riessman, F. *The Culturally Deprived Child.* New York: Harper, 1962.

Riley, G.D. "Construction and Standardization of a Quick Screening Test." Paper read at American Speech and Hearing Association, Chicago, October, 1965.

Siegel, S. *Nonparametric Statistics for the Behavioral Sciences.* New York: McGraw-Hill, 1956.

Silver, A.A. "Diagnostic Value of Three Drawing Tests for Children." *Journal of Pediatrics*, (1950), 37, 129–143.

Skeels, H.M. and Fillmore, E.A. "The Mental Development of Children from Underprivileged Homes." *Journal of Genetic Psychology*, (1937), 50, 427–439.

Skeels, H.M., Updegraff, R., Wellman, B.L., and Williams, H.M. "A Study of Environmental Stimulation: an Orphanage Preschool Project." *University of Iowa Studies in Child Welfare*, (1938), 15, No. 4.

Swift, Joan W. "Effects of Early Group Experience: the Nursery School and Day Nursery." In M. L. Hoffman and Lois W. Hoffman eds., *Review of Child development research*. New York: Russell Sage Found., 1964.

Templin, Mildred, C., and Darley, F.L. *The Templin-Darley Tests of Articulation*. Iowa City: State Univ. Iowa, 1960.

Wellman, B.L. "IQ Changes of Preschool and Non-preschool Groups During the Preschool Years: A Summary of the Literature." *Journal of Psychology*, (1945), 20, 347–468.

Woolfolk, A.S. "Social Adjustment Through Kindergarten Training." *Child Education*, (1929), 5, 264–268.

15

the development of a quick screening test to select children with special needs

After the full enrollment of 300 children had been achieved, the teachers came to us requesting help in testing the newly enrolled children. They said they wanted to be able to plan curricula for them and know which children to refer, just as they had with the children who were first enrolled and in the research program. Since we had neither time nor personnel to engage in another extensive testing program for such a large number, we tried to think of a method that would help the teachers know what they wanted to know within the time limits which we had to offer.

The problem posed was this. Many of the children exhibited behavioral tendencies at the beginning of school which, if they persisted, would signal the teacher to ask for help. Examples of such behavior were withdrawal, refusal to speak, crying, overactive behavior and so on. However, these same behavioral tendencies sometimes disappear after a week or so in nursery school. The teachers wanted to know quickly and efficiently which children had pathological symptoms that would involve consulting with the psychologist or referral and which children would probably outgrow their behavior with the normal nursery school experience.

After a clinical appraisal of what we had learned so far through testing and observation of behavior it seemed possible that we might be able to devise a screening test by using the Gesell Developmental Signs and the Draw-A-Person Test alone. In an effort to find some basis of comparison for the test, we compared the drawings of the children who had been judged by the teacher, nurse or psychologist to have problems to the drawings of the children who showed no signs of problems in the areas of:

1. Neurological handicap
2. Mental retardation
3. Social maladjustment
4. Very low verbal comprehension
5. Unintelligible speech

On the basis of this comparison the following criteria were abstracted to be indicative of the need for referral:

A. On the Gesell Geometric Designs
    1. Perserverations: Traced the original design; drew several circles on top of each other.
    2. Failure to complete circle: Did not join the circle together.
    3. Failure to copy cross: Lacked two intersecting lines at approximate right angles.

B. Draw-A-Person
    1. Refused to draw anything
    2. Scribbled only
    3. Drew circle or head only
    4. Drawing did not resemble human body
    5. Drawing of human body was recognizable but disjointed
    6. Drawing had five or less clearly designated body parts (Goodenough-Harris standard of scoring)
    7. Heavy shading

Procedure

We set aside one entire day for testing the children in groups in their classrooms. Teachers were instructed in how to give the tests. As the psychologist went from room to room she and the teachers worked with the children as a group and individually in order to test every child. Directions for the testing were very important in that they had to be identical. The procedure was as follows: A 7″ x 9½″ sheet of white mimeograph paper was dittoed on one side with Gesell's Geometric Designs in a vertical row beginning with a circle and continuing in order with a cross, square, triangle and diamond.

The piece of paper and a black crayon was presented to each child with the words, "See this circle?" (Examiner puts finger on circle.) "I want you to make another circle just like it right here." (Examiner traces circle with finger as he talks and then traces a circle with his finger in the blank space as he says "right here.") Note: Both verbal and physical cues were given in the directions. If the child did not comply, the examiner repeated the cues up to three times. If the child made any kind of mark on the paper, verbal approval was given. However, if a completed circle was not made, directions were repeated for not more than a total of three times.

The directions for each succeeding geometric design were exactly the same as for the circle, except for substituting the words "cross," "square," "triangle," and "design" (not diamond), in that order. If the child appeared confused by any term, the examiner substituted, "these lines."

After two consecutive misses, i.e., cross and square, or square and diamond, the test was terminated.

Directions for Giving the Draw-A-Person

After the child completed the designs or the test was terminated by the examiner, the examiner turned the paper over and, according to the sex of the child said, "Draw a picture of a boy," or "Draw a picture of a girl." Encouragement was given by smiling or saying, "Try," "Make it any way you want to," or "Make all of him (or her)."

(Note: Children seemed not to understand the concept "person," usually used in DAP directions, so early in the testing procedures "boy" and "girl" were substituted. In a sample of 10 boys and 10 girls who were asked to draw the opposite sex, the child either refused or drew substantially the same thing. Subsequently, boys were asked to draw only boys, and girls only girls.)

Tentative findings

After the tests were administered and evaluated according to the aforementioned standards those children whose drawings showed any of the previously mentioned attributes were seen by the child development specialist for further diagnosis. Tentative findings based on this clinical evidence are as follows: (1) Children whose drawings do not resemble the human body need much teaching in body image. (2) Children who complete the circle and cross successfully but who have one or more scoring symptoms on the DAP probably have psychological or social adjustment problems. (3) Children who fail to draw a circle correctly are likely to have neurological or physiological involvement.

Summary

We found that it was possible to identify children with serious problems by giving two tests, the Gesell Developmental Designs and the Draw-A-Person Test. We have identified certain criteria for grading these tests which are indicative of problems which need to be studied by a child development consultant or a psychologist. For the future we urge that our teachers study the directions for giving these tests and administer them exactly as directed to each child on his enrollment. Two to five minutes spent in a drawing test may lead to early identification and treatment of children with serious problems.

In progress is a statistical analysis which we hope will lead to the development of a psychological screening test which can be universally given in Project Head Start to identify children who need psychological follow-up and treatment.

REFERENCES

Abt, Lawrence E., and Leopold Bellak. *Projective Psychology.* New York: Alfred A. Knopf, 1950.

Allport, G.W. *Personality.* New York: Henry Holt & Co., 1937.

Anastasi, A., and Foley, J. "A Survey of the Literature on Artistic Behavior in the Abnormal," *Psychological Monographs,* (1940), 52, 6–32.

Anderson, Harold H., and Gladys Anderson, *An Introduction to Projective Techniques.* New York: Prentice-Hall, Inc., 1951.

Bender, Lauretta, *Psychopathology of Children with Organic Brain Disorders,* Springfield, Mass.: Chas. C. Thomas, 1956.

Born, W. "Art and Mental Disease," *Ciba Symposia,* (1946), 7, 204–218.

Doll, E. *Vineland Social Maturity Scale, Manual of Directions,* Minneapolis; American Guidance Service, 1947.

Dunn, L., *Peabody Picture Vocabulary Test Manual,* American Guidance Service, Minneapolis, Minn., 1956.

Goodenough, F.L., *Measurement of Intelligence by Drawings.* Yonkers, New York: World Book Company, 1926.

————. "Studies in the Psychology of Children's Drawings," *Psychological Bulletin,* (1928), 25, 272–283.

————. "What Children's Drawings Tell Us," *Parent's Magazine,* (June, 1944). (June, 1944).

Harris, D. *Children's Drawings as Measures of Intellectual Maturity.* New York: Harcourt Brace, 1963.

Hinrichs, E.E. "The Goodenough Drawing in Relation to Delinquency and Problem Behavior." *Archives of Psychology,* (1935), No. 175.

Ilg, Frances, and Ames, Louise. *School Readiness: Behavior Tests Used at the Gesell Institute.* New York: Harper and Row, 1964.

Machover, Karen. *Personality Projection in the Drawing of the Human Figure.* Springfield, Illinois: Charles G. Thomas, 1949.

Pottenger, Martha. "An Analysis of the Human Figure Drawings of Orthopedically Handicapped Children". Unpublished Master's Thesis, Pepperdine College, Los Angeles, 1953.

Riley, G.D. "Construction and Standardization of a Quick Screening Test." Paper read at the American Speech and Hearing Assoc., Chicago; October, 1965.

Simons, Nancy. "An Analysis of the Human Figure Drawings of Orthopaedic and Non-Orthopaedic Children," *Psi Chi Newsletter,* October, 1951, pp. 11–13.

16

teacher performance
and children's growth

Evaluating her performance

From the time of the first testing of the children, when one teacher declined to bring her children to the testing room because they were "too afraid," we became interested in discovering what effect, if any, the teacher had on her children's progress.

The same incident might promote a completely different response on the part of different individual teachers. Take the response to spilled milk at lunch time, for instance. Since we often ate lunch with different groups of children and since spilled milk was a common incident, we were given ample opportunity to observe many such occurrences.

Miss "Hattie" McClure, the senior teacher on our team, was easily the most patient soul among us. She would recognize the spilled milk as an incident to be expected of youngsters and make some remark such as, "We all spill our milk sometimes. Let's see what we can do to clean it up. Johnny, can you find a sponge? We'll clean it up together."

When the milk was all mopped up she would smile warmly, thank each child for helping (for several usually volunteered) and make a comment such as, "What good helpers we have today."

A teacher assistant (whom we shall mercifully allow to remain anonymous) exclaimed at the same incident involving another classroom, "Oh, Johnny! You spilled your milk again! How many times have I told you to be careful!" She then nervously got up and mopped up the milk by herself, all the while engaging in a verbal tirade:

"You'll never learn to be a good boy and grow up to go to school if you don't learn to take care of yourself. I bet if your Mama were here she'd spank you! You are a bad, bad boy. . . .!"

There is little doubt in our minds as to which adult was most effective in turning a common mishap into a positive learning situation. But we had neither the time nor the inclination to observe each teacher and assistant systematically. We needed an objective means to appraise their teaching methods.

Objective evaluation

After doing some library research about how to measure teacher performance, we came upon a test entitled the *Minnesota Teacher Attitude Inventory*. It was composed of a list of questions concerning teachers' attitudes toward children, teaching, and discipline, to be answered on a five point scale. For instance, "Children are usually cooperative"—(Never, Seldom, Undecided, Usuallly, Always). The teacher with positive attitudes would be expected to answer, "Usually." We liked the test because it was objective, easy to take and easy to score, and had norms for kindergarten teachers.

After exhausting local bookstores in attempting to secure two dozen copies of the test booklet, we placed a long distance call to the publisher, the Psychological Corporation in New York, asking them to please ship the test immediately by air parcel post. (Since all of the money for expenditures of this type was out of our own pockets, we were in conflict between the extra expenditure and getting the tests as soon as possible. As was usually the case, time won and our budget lost.) The tests were delivered in three days and administered by the end of the second week.

So that we could remain objective concerning the results, we asked Donna Hazel Larsen, one of the research team, to score the tests and keep the results to herself until after the summer program was over.

At the end of the summer we asked the Coordinator to select her six strongest and six weakest teachers and teacher assistants. We also asked her to rate the teachers and teacher assistants as excellent, satisfactory, weak or unsatisfactory. (Since part of her regular job in the schools was to rate teachers for evaluation, she had both the skill and the experience to render valid value judgments.)

Results of testing and rating

We then compared the scores the teachers made at the beginning of the program to the evaluation of the Coordinator at the end of the program. In five out of six cases, the test scores and the evaluation were identical; that is, the highest scores were made by the best teachers five times out of six and the lowest scores were made by the weakest teachers in five cases out of six. In no case did a teacher with a strong evaluation score below average and in no case did a teacher with a low evaluation score above average.

The test was similarly effective in selecting the strongest and weakest teacher assistants.

The six teacher assistants evaluated as weakest by the Coordinator were the same ones who scored lowest on the MTAI. Of the six teacher assistants evaluated to be most effective, five scored among the top six and one scored below average.

In the case of the assistant who scored low on the test but rated high in classroom performance, further inquiry revealed that she was frightened to take the test. Therefore we concluded that her low score was attributable to her attitude toward test taking and perhaps lack of understanding of what some questions meant.

We had asked the Coordinator to rate the outstanding, satisfactory, weak or unsatisfactory teachers to see if there was a definite correlation between performance and a definite score. We found no teachers who scored below the 33rd percentile (using Kindergarten-Primary norms) who were satisfactory and no assistant teachers who scored below the 20th percentile who rated satisfactory.

As a result of this little study on our teaching personnel we concluded that the Minnesota Teacher Attitude Inventory (MTAI) was a promising test for predicting teacher performance and might profitably be used as *one* of the considerations in hiring. We do not believe that a teacher should be rejected solely on the basis of one test score, however. For instance, one of our six strongest teachers discovered at the very end of the testing period that she had taken the test backwards—that is, she had misread the instructions and checked the answers in the wrong column. She changed her answers just in time.

We also found that assistants needed to be told to utilize all five scoring categories, as they often tended to use only the extremes, thereby making their score much lower than if they used all alternatives.

Comparing teacher effectiveness to children's growth

We were hard put to know how to make a just comparison of teacher effectiveness to children's growth, although we felt we had adequate measures of each. In the first place, in the team of teacher and teacher assistant, one might have been rated excellent while the other was evaluated weak. (We found it interesting that there were no unsatisfactory assistants coupled with outstanding teachers.) Finally we decided to use the teacher as the major deciding factor to use in the comparison, as she was the leader of the team who was responsible for the total classroom performance.

We evaluated each child in each classroom according to his total gain or loss on each of the tests. Then we added up the total gain for the class and divided by the number of children to get an average gain score for each class, according to test. Then we grouped the teachers into their evaluation classifications: (1) Excellent, (2) Satisfactory, (3) Weak, and (4) Unsatisfactory.

Next to the classification of the teacher we put the *average gain* of the children in her classroom. By charting the results in this way it was apparent that the best teachers brought forth the most growth in their children. Table 3, entitled *Teacher Effectiveness and Children's Growth*, shows these results in more complete detail.

Besides taking account of the average gains in each classroom we were very curious to see who the teacher was of the children who had made the most gains in each subtest. In every case, the child came from the room of a teacher evaluated to be excellent or satisfactory. There were no great individual gains in the classrooms of weak or unsatisfactory teachers. Table 4, *Top Achievers According to Evaluation of Teacher,* portrays the dramatic achievements of children with good teachers.

Table 3
TEACHER EFFECTIVENESS AND CHILDREN'S GROWTH

Teacher Rating	Average classroom gain by test			
	Peabody	Gesell	DAP	Vineland
Excellent	+ 18 mo.	+ 2 yrs.	+ 21	+ 2.0 yrs.
Satisfactory	+ 10 mo.	+ 1.4 yrs.	+ 5 pts.	+ 1.5 yrs.
Weak	+ 3 mo.	+ 2 yrs.	+ 2 pts.	+ .4 yrs.
Unsatisfactory	+ 1 mo.	None	None	+ .4 yrs.

Table 4
TOP ACHIEVERS ACCORDING TO THE EVALUATION OF TEACHER

Name of Test	Top Achiever	Teacher Evaluation
Peabody Picture Vocabulary Test	+25 mo.	Excellent
Gesell Development Designs	+4 yrs.	Excellent
Draw-A-Person	+72 pts.	Satisfactory
Vineland Social Maturity Scale	+3.3 yrs.	Satisfactory
Riley Articulation and Language Test (Articulation)	+43%	Satisfactory
Riley Articulation and Language Test (Language)	+75%	Excellent

This evaluation is not to be construed to mean that the best results are always achieved by superior teachers. If a child is already functioning to potential, then only the average amount of growth could be expected. What we wish to convey is that only teachers who rate "satisfactory" or above are able to adapt their teaching ability to the needs of their individual pupils, and that teachers rated weak or unsatisfactory are unable to fulfill their responsibility.

Standards for teachers

Based on our experience of the importance of outstanding teachers to the success of Head Start, we urge that highest standards for teachers be maintained.

Based on the importance of the teacher to the personality, social, and intellectual development of children, the International Council on Early Childhood Education (ICEA) has formulated educational standards for nursery school teachers.

These standards include:

1. A Bachelor's degree from an accredited institution.
2. A major in Early Childhood Education, Child Development, or the equivalent.
3. Guided Observation and Participation in working with the preschool child.

The teacher of young children needs extensive professional preparation to acquaint her with principles of child development, the sociology of the group, and how children learn. Because nursery education includes acculturation as well as intellectual education, the teacher must have a full grasp of the principles of psychology and guidance.

In a University Child Development laboratory, the teacher usually holds an advanced degree and her assistants are students working toward their degrees. In a Parent Cooperative Nursery School, the teacher usually meets ICEA standards, and her assistants are participating parents who spend some time in in-service training. What shall be our standards for Head Start?

Based on our research results and experiences in Head Start, our tentative thinking is that the following standards should be established on a nation-wide basis.

1. *The Administrator* should hold an advanced degree in Child Development or similar subject matter area (i.e., Education, Social Welfare, Family Life).
2. *The Teacher* (who may be responsible for one center) should meet ICEA qualifications.
3. *The Assistant Teacher* (who may assume responsibility for a small group with the guidance of a teacher) should have a junior college

education with at least twelve units of Child Development and Early Childhood Education, plus yearly institutes.

4. *The Aide* may be lacking formal education. It is most desirable, however, that she possess the attributes of a "giving" person, and should attend an in-service training program.

That the degree of responsibility should vary according to professional training may be clarified by the analogy of hospital staffing. The teacher may be compared to the registered nurse who has primary responsibility for the care of the patients and organizes the rest of the staff accordingly. The assistant teacher may be somewhat analogous to the good practical nurse who has a certain amount of training and undertakes much of the "daily care" aspect. The nurse's aide, like the teacher's aide, is an important part of the team, functioning in routine tasks which, though simple to perform, are vital to the on-going program. (Who, during a stay in a hospital, has not been grateful to a very understanding aide in time of deep distress?)

A professional program of training

If these high standards create a greater demand for personnel than is available, we urge that a crash training program be initiated throughout the country through the Home Economics Extension Division of the Land Grant Colleges and other interested universities.

In the meantime, provisional certificates could be granted for one year only, and renewed on the condition of continuous formal academic schooling until the person satisfies the credential requirements for his position.

We firmly believe that the depth and breadth of the teacher's professional training will predetermine the excellence and ultimate success of Operation Head Start.

Child development—a distinguished history

Medicine, home economics, and psychology have a distinguished history of leadership in bringing nursery school education from the custodial care concept of the nineteenth century to a science of Child Development in the twentieth century.

Around the turn of the twentieth century, *Dr. Maria Montesorri,* an Italian physician, founded schools for four- and five-year-old slum children, giving her teachers intensive training. Her methods spread to the United States, and institutions everywhere began to think of the nursery as a place of learning rather than as a custodial institution.

Dr. Arnold Gesell, a pediatrician, founded the Institute of Child Development at Yale University in the twenties and began a systematic study of the behavior of children at home and in the nursery school. His classic,

Infant and Child in the Culture of Today, is still a model of how middle-class children act and learn in the first five years of life.

The University of Iowa, at Ames, began its Child Development Laboratory in 1928 under the Department of Home Economics Extension Service. Following the excellent leadership of Iowa, graduate schools in Home Economics throughout the United States have trained teachers and engaged in research concerning the nursery school child. These teachers have usually been employed in other university laboratory nursery schools or by upper-class schools wishing to give their children the best educational opportunities possible.

If Head Start is to fulfill its promise of enriching the lives of our children we must secure personnel able to apply the principles of child development. To do less would be a mockery of all the scientific accomplishments of the century.

Leadership for the twentieth century

A brief account of the history and educational institutions of nursery education is included to (1) help directors of programs know which universities may give leadership in Head Start and, (2) provide access to the results of the many years of research and experience that have gone into learning how to best prepare teachers for working with young children.

Nationally known universities whose Schools of Home Economics include Child Development programs are Cornell, Florida State, University of Iowa, and Oregon State. Columbia, Stanford, Yale, and Minnesota have excellent programs in Child Development within their Psychology Departments.

Specializing in Child Development and Family Relations are two privately endowed institutions, the Merrill-Palmer Institute in Detroit, and Pacific Oaks School in Pasadena, California. Both of these schools have been recognized nationally for their leadership and excellence since the thirties.

Every state will have its own training facility. In California, the State Colleges at Los Angeles, San Fernando Valley, San Diego, San Jose, Sacramento and Long Beach are providing leadership. The private colleges of Chapman and Pepperdine offer excellent programs at the Bachelor of Arts level. Many Junior Colleges have excellent two-year programs. The Department of Home Economics at Fullerton Junior College is the oldest and most widely acclaimed.

17

parents' evaluation of
the effects of Head Start
on their children
and families

What parents told us about Head Start

On Thursday of the next to the last week of Head Start we received a letter from the National Head Start Office directing us to send a standardized questionnaire home to all families with children enrolled in Head Start. Enclosed with the directive were nine copies of the questionnaire—nine copies for 300 children? A call to the downtown office told us that there were not enough forms to go around and that we would have to do the best we could. No one seemed to care that we were frantically trying to rent buses for the final field trip, schedule doctor's appointments, arrange for the final testing for the research project, secure a job for a young father, and find 20 missing library books! It was "beside the point" that our ditto machine had just groaned its last sigh, refusing to give multiple birth to any more communiques without the services of a repairman who said that he "might" be able to make it by the following Monday. The weather was unbearably hot and sticky, the typist was out ill, and we knew we had, somehow, to send out those forms! (Unfinished business meant unpaid checks!) Although underneath the trouble and turmoil we could see the worth of the survey of parents' attitudes, at the time it seemed that the request was intolerable.

"Unreasonable requests sometimes call for unorthodox solutions," we rationalized as we "borrowed" the mimeograph services of another "institution" over the weekend. We were ready to send home the questionnaire (see Appendix Three) and a cover letter eliciting the parents' cooperation by the following Monday.

By the end of the week, of the 262 questionnaires that were sent home, 78 had been returned. Because of the late date, the lack of time for follow-up, and the hot weather, we felt that the 30 per cent return was adequate.

One teacher was surprised to find any return at all. In fact, she was so sure that the parents would not return any form that she did not even bother to send the letters home! On the last day she turned in her blank forms with a note attached, "It was too late to send these out. Not enough would have answered anyway."

Fortunately her attitude was in the minority, so that we were able to receive some valuable comments from the parents.

The questionnaire

The questionnaire contained groups of questions under five headings:
1. Activities of value to parents.
2. Activities of value to children.
3. Changes in children's behavior.
4. Changes in family activities.
5. Change of attitudes concerning family and community.
(A copy of the questionnaire is included in the Appendix)

Activities of value to parents

There were seven activities listed for the parents to check (see Table 5):

1. Talking with child's teacher.
2. Meeting with other parents.
3. Speaking with social workers.
4. Special events, including:
   a. Child Care
   b. Homemaking Skills
   c. Employment Opportunities
   d. Housing Conditions
   e. Personal Problems.
5. Group trips in community.
6. Films shown in connection with Head Start.
7. Other.

The parents could check one of the five columns after each question, thus describing how they felt about the services. These descriptions were

(1) Very Helpful, (2) Helpful, (3) Occasionally Helpful, (4) Waste of Time, and (5) Not in Program. The table entitled *Activities of Value to Parents* lists the total number of parents responding to each question and the tabulation of their answers.

Table 5
ACTIVITIES OF VALUE TO PARENTS

Activity	Total	Very Helpful	Helpful	Occasion- ally Helpful	Waste of Time	Not in Program
1. Talking with child's teacher.	62	42	20	—	—	—
2. Meeting with other parents.	65	10	25	30	—	—
3. Speaking with social workers.	65	20	20	25	—	—
4. Special events:						
a. Child care	15	0	0	15	0	0
b. Homemaking skills	32	10	0	20	0	2
c. Employment opportunities	21	10	0	10	0	1
d. Housing conditions	18	7	5	5	0	1
e. Personal problems	22	5	6	10	0	1
5. Group trips in community	40	20	20	—	—	—
6. Films shows in connection with Head Start	50	20	30	—	—	—
7. Other	45	45	—	—	—	—
Total responses	—	189	126	115	0	5

Discussion of parents' responses

"Talking with child's teacher" was checked as very helpful by two-thirds of the parents and "helpful" by the other one-third. Although other activities listed provided more direct help to parents, no activity matched teacher-parent contact in degree of helpfulness. Without a doubt, "talking with child's teacher" proved to be the most valuable service to the parents themselves.

Speaking with social workers and *meeting with other parents* were widely accepted as valuable experiences, while group *trips* in the community and *films* shown in connection with Head Start were deemed helpful by about half the parents. Special events were checked as valuable by some: *child care,* 15, *homemaking skills,* 32; *employment opportunities,* 21; *housing conditions,* 18; and *personal problems,* 22.

A look at how many activities were evaluated gives some indication of the acceptance of what we offered. A total tally of 169 was checked for activities which were "Very Helpful", 126 for "Helpful" and 130 for "Occasionally helpful." No one checked "Waste of Time" for any activity. There were five tally marks for "Not in Program," but all except one of these were checked by one person and were in the special events section.

Forty-five parents checked "other" as being "Very Helpful." From this response it would appear that well over half of the parents were very pleased with some aspect of the program that had special meaning to them. A sample of these comments have been picked up at random to illustrate the variety of experiences for which the parents expressed particular gratitude.

"Being around live animals."

After a trip to Griffith Park Children's Zoo, many teachers secured animals for their rooms, through the cooperation of the Los Angles City Schools' Science Center. Turtles, guinea pigs, hamsters, rabbits, and chickens which laid eggs in their cages became a part of the children's experience for the first time.

"Having new toys to play with."

A parent who had been able to provide only hand-me-downs or used toys took a sense of pride in the new toys made available at the school.

"The various inoculations given the child."

The children were bussed by classroom groups to the neighborhood County Public Health Office for polio and D.P.T. inoculations. Since children needed to have this protection before enrolling in school, this service was appreciated by many parents who lacked transportation or had other little ones to care for at home.

"Andy has really enjoyed Head Start. I'm so glad I did register him in this class. He's always talking about Miss Lucy."

Here is a parent who found delight in her child's affection for his teacher. Many parents mentioned at one time or another how pleased they were with the teachers. In retrospect, we believe that insisting on high standards in the selection of teaching personnel was one of the factors contributing most to the success of the program.

"The children enjoyed the carnival immensely."

The entire neighbrohood was invited to attend a carnival. We rented the amusement equipment of a local carnival and brought it to the grounds of the play yard for an entire Saturday. Staff, parents, and community contributed their efforts toward serving refreshments, making decorations and providing the necessary supervision. The neighborhood does not have a facility of this kind. Many people expressed both gratitude and the wish that the neighborhood could have such wholesome recreational outlets for its children on a full-time basis.

"The meeting in the park."

Parents were invited to attend a question and answer forum focused on family welfare in a local park. There was excellent attendance and general surprise that the event had been so successful, as the park was one usually frequented by many unruly toughs and other undesirable persons.

"My child won't be afraid of contact away from home."

For many children, Head Start was the first experience away from home. Heretofore, brothers and sisters had been their only playmates, and there had been little or no contact with other adults. Although some parents had wished for play opportunities with other children, until Head Start there had been no vehicle to carry out these latent wishes. In general, we found parents cared deeply about their children's welfare, but lacked the personal or material resources for the execution of their concern.

"I think the Head Start Program is a wonderful program." "It gave my youngster an advanced head start for his kindergarten program in the fall. My son has enjoyed this experience tremendously and has been greatly benefited by it. I feel that I was benefited, too, by meeting other parents and exchanging ideas and having many informative speakers on various subjects. Many thanks to the sponsors." (Signed) "John's mother."

ACTIVITIES OF VALUE TO CHILDREN

All activities listed on the questionnaire were checked as helpful to children. However, some were chosen more often than others. From looking over the actual questionnaires it appears that parents may have checked the items they felt strongly about and declined to check those for which they had no particular interest. If such be the case, the activities can be listed in order of importance according to the number of times they were checked as follows:

1. Medical examination.
2. Increased experience with variety of games and toys.
3. Opportunities to participate in group activities with other children.
4. Increased experience with blocks, stories, and music.
5. Dental examination.
6. Opportunity to attend school at an early age.
7. Individual attention given to children by teachers.
8. Trips into the community.

Table 6, entitled *Activities of Value to Children,* contains a complete tabulation.

Table 6
ACTIVITIES OF VALUE TO CHILDREN

Activity	Total Number	Very Helpful	Occasionally Helpful	Helpful
1. Medical examination	71	65	1	5
2. Increased experience with variety of games and toys	65	35	30	—
3. Opportunities to participate in group activities with other children	53	50	1	2
4. Increased experience with blocks, stories, music	52	50	2	—
5. Dental examination	49	8	1	40
6. Opportunity to attend school at an early age	32	10	15	7
7. Individual attention given to children by teachers	30	7	3	20
8. Trips into the community	8	6	2	—
Totals		121	55	74

Medical examination

Advance notices of health appointments were sent home and many parents made a special effort to be present on the day their child was examined. In the event that a parent was not present, a note always accompanied the child home informing parents of services received.

Dorothy Jenkins, our nurse, revealed that the physical examinations had uncovered conditions requiring further medical attention in 70 per cent of our children. Of 163 defects discovered, 60 per cent were known to parents but less than 1 per cent of these defects were under treatment. Of the conditions unknown to parents, she considered 90 per cent of them to be urgent and in need of immediate attention.

Since 60 per cent of the defects were already known to parents, and had gone uncorrected, it seems reasonable to assume that they were unable to afford medical care and hoped that Head Start would provide remedial as well as diagnostic services.

Dental examination

In contrast to the importance attached to the medical examinations, which were checked as very helpful by 65, were dental examinations, checked as very helpful by only eight and occasionally helpful by 40. The results of the dental examinations revealed 100 children in need of further dental attention. Of these, 28 cases were known to the parents and 72 cases were unknown. Therefore, the need for dental work was as great numerically as for medical attention. Apparently, the parents responding did not consider dental health as important as medical health. Most of the children had never been to a dentist's office.

Preschool play experiences

Increased experience with a variety of games and toys received the second most checks as the activity of most value, with opportunities to participate in group activities with other children and increased experience with blocks, stories, and music ranking close behind. Such choices indicate to us that most parents were sympathetic to the goals and purposes of the preschool program—that of providing creative experiences for children in a human relationships laboratory.

An opportunity to attend school at an early age and individual attention given to children were deemed helpful by about one-third of the parents, although individual attention was generally viewed as being only occasionally helpful. We were surprised at this latter finding, as we considered individual attention to be most helpful.

Trips into the community

Only eight parents checked trips into the community as helpful. In light of the many laudatory oral sentiments expressed by parents about the field trips, we believe that the parents were thinking of the one field trip called "community helpers" where children visited places in the immediate area rather than the field trip experience as a whole. (See chapter on *Bringing the Community to the Classroom.*)

Change in children's behavior

"Getting along with children" and *"Finishing what he starts"* were chosen as the most significant changes parents noted in their children's behavior. These items would reflect a value judgment of "desirable" assigned to both interpersonal relationships and task performance, both objectives of the preschool program.

"Speaking ability" was noticed to be "Better" in 36 cases, with no change noticed in five cases. The speech evaluation showed that at the beginning of the Head Start program 45 per cent of the children needed speech therapy and at the end the percentage had been reduced to 25 per cent. Apparently the improvement in some children's speaking ability was sufficient to be noted by their parents.

Self-confidence

It was significant that, among a group of people stripped of faith in their own self-worth by virtue of repeated failure, there was the high incidence of awareness of growth in self-confidence. Growth in self-confidence in their own children was checked by about one-third of the parents.

Everyday manners

That everyday manners were better was noted by 10 parents, but 20 parents checked "no improvement" here. A similar ratio of fewer "Better" to more "No Change" categorizations were observed in *"Can do things on his own."* Such an inverse proportion in contrast to the other items may indicate that more change in "acceptable" behaviors, such as manners and completing tasks, was expected than realized.

Changes in family activities

Relatively few people reported any change in family activities (see Table 7). Fifteen people repaired or added things to their present living quarters, ten people were helped by a social agency, five planned to continue their education, and three reported that a child not enrolled in Head Start received medical attention. Since these activities may be termed secondary activities in that their performance would be an outgrowth, rather than a direct result, of Head Start, it may be that eight weeks was too short a span of time to expect changes in family plans or activities. For instance, one mother checked the "No" column on finding a job but wrote along the side that she was going to work in two months. No parents checked that they were moving to better living quarters but, to this author's knowledge, several families had done so by the beginning of school in September.

Table 7
CHANGES IN FAMILY ACTIVITIES

Check any of the following which apply as a result of your contact with Head Start:	Yes	No
1. My husband or I have been helped by some social agency.	10	20
2. My husband or I received medical and/or dental attention	0	10
3. A child not enrolled in Head Start received medical and/or dental attention	3	25
4. Moved to better living quarters	0	20
5. Repaired or added things (furniture, new curtains) to my present living quarters.	15	20
6. A family member got a job or switched to a better job.	0	25
7. My husband or I plan to continue our own education.	5	0
8. My husband or I have sought legal aid or financial assistance.	0	30
Totals	31	150

The wording of several of the questions in this section may have precluded some people answering them. The first two and last two questions began, "My husband and I . . ." Over half the families were headed by the mother and there was no father present in the home. Therefore, the wording of the question may have been an affront to some. In fact, one mother wrote across the side of this section of the questionnaire, "Don't have no husband. Take care of my kids by myself and with the help of the Lord." Such a poignant comment would tend to indicate that because she had no husband, none of the questions were applicable to her situation.

It is interesting to note that 30 people answered the questions, "Have you or your husband sought legal aid or financial assistance?" negatively and none positively. That 30 people took the trouble to mark the question rather than to ignore answering it may be suggestive of a felt need for legal aid or financial advice, but they did not know how or had not been able to secure these services. The same idea seems to be expressed by the preponderance of negative responses to "A family member got a job or switched to a better job" and "A child not enrolled in Head Start received medical and/or dental attention," and "Moved to better living quarters." We would suggest that there is an awareness of a need for these services as manifested by the large number of persons taking the time to respond to the questions.

CHANGE OF ATTITUDES CONCERNING FAMILY AND COMMUNITY

Table 8, entitled *Change of Attitudes Concerning Family and Community,* tabulates the responses to all of the questions.

The most significant change of attitudes concerned increased community awareness. Forty-five people reported that they were *"much more aware of new things my family and I can do in the community,"* and 25 reported that they felt a reciprocal relationship with the community, *"the community cares about me and my problems."* Since one of the prime goals of the poverty program as a whole is to enhance a sense of belongingness to and identification with the community, these responses were particularly gratifying.

Forty-five people also stated that they had *"learned new things about raising children."* In contrast, 25 out of 35 stated that the program had helped "not at all" in giving new ideas about *"how to take care of my family."* The reason for the contrast seems clear: They were helped in understanding their children as persons, but they were not given substantial help in providing material resources for the family such as food, clothing and medical care. Two parents wrote, "We need to have medical help for our other children," and "We need help to find better jobs."

Fifteen out of 18 felt *"a little more hopeful"* about their children's

Table 8
CHANGE OF ATTITUDES CONCERNING FAMILY AND COMMUNITY

Item	Total Number	Much more	More	Little more	Not at all
1. Am aware of new things my family and I can do in the community.	45	45	0	0	0
2. Feel that the community cares about me and my problems	25	25	0	0	0
3. Have learned new things about raising children	45	20	0	25	0
4. Have been given new ideas about how to take care of my family	30	5	0	0	25
5. Feel hopeful about my children's future.	18	3	15	0	0
6. Feel better able to handle family arguments when they arise.	9	2	0	7	0
6. Made new friends	10	8	2	0	0
Totals		108	17	32	25

futures. We believe that much more help is needed to enable these families to achieve economic independence so that they may break through the walls of discouragement and into the promise of hope for a better life for their children. Without hope there is little impetus to try. And without trying there is no chance of success. An avenue of escape from poverty through self-effort must be made possible and communicated to these families.

Summary

One mother attached a letter to her evaluation form which we believe summarizes how a good many parents feel about Head Start.

> *"The program of Operation Head Start was very helpful and enjoyable to my child.* He has improved in many aspects and I have been able to help him with problems that were revealed through the program. All of the field trips were educational and useful in developing self-confidence.
>
> "I do feel that there should be a better parent-teacher relationship. Mothers who send their children by bus or car have less chance to communicate with the teacher. Therefore, I feel more parent meetings, meetings with counselor and parents, and group

meetings should take place. Here problems in home, community, and group environment can be discussed and improved. In doing this a parent can continue the progress of the child because he or she is equipped with the necessary knowledge needed.

"I also feel that an individual evaluation of each child in regard to improvements and general information should be given the parents at the end of the program so that the child's parent can see the progress needed for his or her particular child.

"The Operation Head Start is a valuable program to each child and parent in the community. I was very pleased with my child's progress. The community is grateful to all the workers, and hopes with all sincerity that the program will continue for many years to come."

The evaluation of Operation Head Start by these parents carries several underlying feelings. Parents are generally enthusiastic about Operation Head Start for their children, are accepting of the goals of early childhood, and wish to see the program continue. There is a hopelessness born of being tied to dilapidated housing, of being limited to unskilled jobs, and to an inability to provide adequately for their families. But, given the means to help themselves, we believe that the people would actively seek better jobs in order to secure better housing and provide medical care for their children.

18

health services: a summary of services, findings, and implications*

The summer health program was designed to assess the physical, mental, and social status of children. Medical examinations included hearing and speech surveys, vision screening, dental examinations, tests for tuberculosis, anemia and kidney disease, immunizations against polio, diphtheria, pertussis, tetanus, and smallpox. Most of these services were rendered in the Center by Center medical personnel and volunteer doctors. The immunization series was administered through the local Health Department.

Of the total number of children receiving physical examinations in Delta's Head Start Program, 70 per cent had conditions requiring further medical attention. Tables 9 and 10, which follow, list the types of defects, distribution, whether known or unknown to the parent, and if the child was under adequate medical supervision.

The effects discovered represented most of the body systems. Among these systems there are varying degrees of urgency for follow-up. Mere identification of health problems is not enough. This is clearly shown in that of the 163 defects, 60 per cent were already known to the parents. Yet, of this number, less than 1 per cent were under adequate medical supervision. Of the conditions unknown to parents, 90 per cent were urgent.

---

* Written in collaboration with Dorothy Jenkins, P.H.N.

Table 9
IDENTIFICATION OF DEFECTS: KNOWN OR UNKNOWN TO PARENT

Type of defect	Unknown to parent	Known to parent	Under care
6 CARDIO-VASCULAR			
Blood pressure high	1		
Murmurs	3	2	Yes
1 CHEST			
Tuberculin Test Tine (Positive)	1		
100 DENTAL	28	72	
3 DERMATOLOGY			
Icthyosis (Fish-scale type skin manifestation)		1	
Keloid—Back		1	
Keloid—Face	1		
5 EAR, NOSE, THROAT			
Wax in ear canal	1		
Rhinitis (chronic runny nose)		1	Yes
Enlarged tonsils	3		
1 ENDOCRINE			
Hypothyroidism	1		
3 EYE			
Amblyopia (Blindness in one eye)	2		
Strabimus (Cross-eyes)		1	
7 GENITO-URINARY			
Circumcision		4	
Meatal stenosis (Stricture of urinary passage)	1	2	
12 MEDICAL			
Anemia	11	1	Yes
1 MENTAL			
Depressed	1		
3 NUTRITION			
Malnutrition		1	Yes
Obesity	2		
4 ORTHOPEDIC			
Chest—Asymmetry	1		
Head—Asymmetry		1	Yes
Leg Length		1	
Pronation	1		
1 SEIZURE			
Epilepsy	1		

IDENTIFICATION OF DEFECTS: KNOWN OR UNKNOWN TO PARENT
(Continued)

Type of defect	Unknown to parent	Known to parent	Under care
16 SURGICAL			
Hernias			
Inguinal	6		
Umbilical		9	
Ventral (abdominal)	1		
Total = 163			
Unknown 66 = 40%			
Known 97 = 60%			

Need for follow-up

There is a clear indication of the need for a follow-up that goes beyond mere discovery and even beyond merely advising the parents of a health defect. Any realistic follow-up must, of necessity, provide the implementative means for correctional services. These would include scheduling the necessary medical appointments, making fee arrangements, providing transportation, and educating the parents concerning the desirability of corrective and preventative health measures.

Preschool health programs embrace prevention as well as correction. Therefore, the earlier health problems are identified, the better the prognosis. Since this Head Start Project was located in the Los Angeles City School District, and since the majority of pupils have come and will come from this district, it is appropriate that certain aspects of this District's health program be considered in this evaluation:

Routine physical examinations are done in the first, fourth, seventh, and tenth grades.

Elementary: Height, weight, vision screening, review of systems.
Junior High: Add tuberculin testing.
Senior High: Add tuberculin testing and blood pressure.

Table 10 lists the type of defect, age Head Start detected, and the age public schools would detect through existing examination scheduling. The period of delay in detecting defects ranges from no delay to never discovering defects until the pupil should become ill and be referred for evaluation (as might be the sequence in a case of anemia).

Table 10
HEAD START DETECTION VS NORMAL PUBLIC SCHOOL DETECTION

Type of defect	Age Head Start detected	Age public school detected	No. years delayed in detecting
Cardio-vascular (Murmur)	4-7	6	1
Blood Pressure		16	11
Chest (Tuberculin test)		13	8
Dental		5-6	0-1
Dermatology		4-7	0
ENT—wax in ear canal		6	1
Rhinitis (runny nose)		4-7	0
Enlarged tonsils		6	1
Endocrine		6	1
Eye—Amblyopia		6	1
Strabimus		4-7	0
Genito-Urinary			
Circumcision		6	1
Mental Stenosis		6	1
Medical—Anemia		Not done	
Mental—Depressed		4-7	0-1
Nutrition—Malnutrition		6	1
Obesity		4-7	0-1
Orthopedic			
Chest—asymmetry		6	1
Head—asymmetry		4-7	0
Leg length		4-7	0
Pronation		4-7	0
Seizures—Epilepsy		?	
Surgical—Hernias			
Inguinal		6	1
Umbilical		6	1
Ventral		6	1

None of the anemias detected by Head Start were tested for sickling trait. This is a birth defect which occurs in about 10 per cent of American Negroes. Since there is a high correlation between this disease and mental retardation, it is humane that these children so diagnosed be given top priority in follow-up health programs. Also high on the list of priorities would be follow-up of the pupil with suspected high blood pressure. Since cardio-vascular diseases are a leading cause of death, adequate and immediate follow-through in this area is strongly urged.

Special and immediate follow-up is provided for pupils with positive tuberculin tests. If the pupil with a positive tuberculosis reading had not been detected through out Tine testing in Head Start, he would not have been discovered in a routine survey until junior high school age. As a result of the Project and its comprehensive medical program, many hidden horrors that could plague a child's whole life have been made known.

The follow-up phase of Head Start programs, then, suggests:

1. Need for follow-up based upon identification of defects.
2. Need for early detection of defects.
3. Need for coordination of findings with other agencies, including schools.

Health records were maintained for each pupil enrolled in Head Start. It was agreed that these records, along with recommendations, be sent to the children's prospective school. Since people are so mobile within this poverty area, the problem of the records catching up with the children becomes real. A test check of the school nurses at three elementary schools has not confirmed enrollment of some pupils who should have been there on the basis of summer addresses.

What happens to all of this valuable information? Where will these records be housed? If the pupil moves to another school, how would the new or second school know about this child's contact with Head Start? These questions and many more pertain to the "lost" Head Start pupil.

There are questions that need to be considered concerning the pupil who *is* enrolled and has been recommended for follow-up. Does follow-up start at the school door? Who contacts the school nurse to see what is being done for this child? Are progress reports recommended? How would funding for corrective work be handled? How close does Head Start personnel work with school personnel? Who introduces private sponsors to the school systems?

No answers are immediately forthcoming to many of these questions and the problems which they pose. They must, of necessity, be our concern, and serious efforts must be made toward a workable solution if the positive and continuing effects upon the child envisioned in the concepts of Head Start are to be a reality.

Children with serious psychological symptoms

In about the fifth week of Operation Head Start we received communication from Head Start offices in Washington, D.C., asking our teachers to fill out a check list on each child. This IBM form, named "Psychological Screening Procedure" is included in the appendix. There were two parts to the procedure. On one side of the page was a symptom check list with items like "wets bed," "hits other children," "has nervous ticks," "refuses to eat," and so forth. On the other side of the page was a behavioral description check list describing certain clinical syndromes which are considered to be indicative of possible serious emotional disturbance. After the teacher had filled out the psychological screening procedure check list we copied the answers on 211 of the children so that we might compare these results with our research when the project had ended. (The reason we came up with the total number of 211 was that this is all that we had time to copy off before the forms had to be sent on to Washington for analysis there.)

In the table entitled, "Children Needing Psychological Help" we have detailed the description of emotionally disturbed children, number of children with each symptom, and the percentage based on the total sample. Of the total number of 211 children 48 per cent of them had one or more serious behavior syndromes chosen from the following categories:

1. Disruptive
2. Provocative
3. Isolate
4. Fearful
5. Silent
6. Does not learn
7. Separation anxiety
8. Unhappy, depressed
9. Hyperactive

We feel that it is important to emphasize that the behavior syndromes described on the psychological screening procedure are of a serious nature. The children with these characteristics will *not* tend to "outgrow" their problems. Indeed, without specialized help and prompt attention these children are apt to become progressively worse. These are in need of professional help and must have it within a short time in order to profit from the school situation and eventually become contributing members of society. It is our firm belief that no investment in the therapeutic treatment of these children is too expensive. Without intensive, prompt attention these are the children who will become the future schizophrenics, criminals, prostitutes, dope addicts and others alienated to and dependent upon society.

POSTSCRIPT: A MODEL FOLLOW-UP FOR HEAD START CHILDREN

A model follow-up proposal based on the research results

Because the children in Head Start did show the capacity to learn at an accelerated rate during the summer program, and since the group still has much "catching up" to do in order to benefit from the school situation, a follow-up program has been outlined which, if incorporated in *all* its aspects, should serve to help the children grow toward emotional health,

CHILDREN NEEDING PSYCHOLOGICAL HELP

AS BASED ON TEACHER JUDGMENT AND RECORDED

ON THE PSYCHOLOGICAL SCREENING PROCEDURE

Description	N	%
1. Disruptive child	31	15
2. Provocative child	17	8
3. Isolate	25	12
4. Fearful	18	9
5. Silent	22	11
6. Does not learn	25	12
7. Separation Anxiety	7	3
8. Unhappy, depressed	20	10
9. Hyperactive	25	12
Total	190	

N in table = number of children with specific symptom.

% is based on total N of 210 children tested.

intellectual maturity, and fulfillment of their potential as contributing members of a free society.

The heart of the follow-up program is to bring children of like needs together in small groups of six or less for a two-hour session once a week.

Character and extent of professional services

We believe that follow-up services should be provided in the following areas (in addition to the more obvious areas of health).

1. Social adjustment
2. Social enrichment
3. Language development
4. Speech improvement
5. Special education for the retarded, neurologically handicapped, and so on.
6. Gifted

Services to these children is envisioned to cover a five-fold program including (1) diagnosis, (2) treatment through enriched play experience in small groups, (3) coordination with the social worker, nurse, and public school nurse in working with the family, (4) referral to community agencies for the more serious cases, and (5) research.

Diagnostic evaluation

The diagnostic evaluation should be based upon appropriate testing, behavior, observation, investigation of past records from the parent, the doctor or the school and the observations by staff members.

Treatment

The crux of the treatment program lies in the establishment of play groups where children of like deficiencies come together under a specialized program of instruction. A consultant in Early Childhood Education should be retained to (a) develop curricula and teaching approach for each group; (b) train teachers in small group methods in the use of these specialized curricula; (c) maintain regular teacher conferences to discuss each case systematically. The teacher should supervise aides and coordinate all services for the children in her group and relate these services to the family. Each small group, each teacher, should be assisted by two aides, one male, and one female if possible, who are drawn from the community, who can relate well to children with handicaps and who can work effectively under the guidance of a head teacher. It is visualized that the aides will constitute a miniature family, will be able to give individual attention and will help bridge the gap between the community mores and the professional mores. It is suggested that, where practical, parents who can profit from the experience may be employed either as aides or as special helpers in addition to the above staff.

Group structure and responsibilities

The teacher will be responsible for setting up the day's program and instructing the aides in how to follow through. The teachers and aides should make every effort to assist the family with transportation and should encourage parents to visit the groups whenever it is practical for them to do so. A sample time schedule might be as follows:

10:00—12:00	Visit homes
12:30— 2:00	Planning and coordinating with professional consultants
2:00— 2:30	Teacher meets with aides and plans day
2:30— 2:45	Set up room environment
2:45— 3:00	Greet or pick up children
3:00— 5:00	Play Group meets. All time devoted to children
5:00— 5:15	Children depart or are taken home
5:15— 5:30	Clean up
5:30— 6:00	Evaluation of day's activities. Head teacher writes suggestions for next session. Includes any important anecdotal information in children's files.
	According to her own schedule, head teacher should have regular conferences with other professional personnel and make home visits.

STAFFING OF OTHER PROFESSIONALS

Home school coordinator

A full-time home-school coordinator should be retained to coordinate follow-up services with the public schools. He would visit the public schools to ascertain what they are doing in the way of follow-up for the children. He would visit each teacher to interpret to her the purpose of the project Head Start follow-up program and coordinate with the classroom teacher the treatment suggested by the consultant staff.

Home economist

The follow-up professional staff should include the services of a full-time home economist and assistant. Their duties would be to visit homes upon the request of the head teacher, the home-school coordinator or the social worker, to offer assistance where requested in home management, nutrition, clothing, meal planning and preparation, purchasing, child care or budgeting. The assistant to the home economist should be a person from the community with an interest in what the home economist could offer and the knowledge of how to relate her professional experience to the community by interpreting the community to the professional and the professional to the community.

Social worker or public health nurse

The services of a social worker or a public health nurse should be retained to make home visits in conjunction with the home economist, to coordinate all other existing community agencies who may be working with families concurrently in order to make the most of these services and to assist in locating medical, psychological and other follow-up services for children with extensive pathology. If the enrollment in a follow-up program warrants, both the social worker and public health nurse should be retained. Each family should be visited at least once a week to interpret the Head Start follow-up program as well as to teach the family what they need to know concerning health practices or guidance techniques.

Supporting staff

A full-time office staff should be set up, headed by a full-time *executive secretary* who acts as general coordinator. It would be her responsibility to coordinate the total on-going program, such as maintaining the building, receiving food orders, purchasing of all necessary supplies, supervising routine bookkeeping, arranging transportation of children and personnel as necessary, providing office space for consultants, storage space for teachers, providing transportation not only to and from Head Start but to the doctor, dentist, clinics, and calling substitute personnel when absences occur.

PROFESSIONAL CONSULTANTS ON A PART-TIME BASIS

Speech pathologist

The speech pathologist would be responsible for staffing the speech therapy play group with responsible graduate students, supervision, and development of therapeutic techniques. He would be responsible for speech screening of all entering children, and for a continual reevaluation as the program progressed. He would diagnose and give to the coordinator and teacher copies of his results, be responsible for setting up a Speech Enrichment Program for all play groups, suggest referral agencies for children who need more intensive speech therapy and work with the social worker and teacher in suggesting home programs concerning things parents might do to effect improvement.

Special education consultant

The special education consultant would assist in diagnosis of children who, after screening, appeared to have neurological handicaps. On the basis of diagnosis she would:

1. Suggest special programs of education for each child (a) in the Head Start follow-up through the head teacher; (b) in the public

school through the home-school coordinator; and (c) in the home through the social worker or public health nurse.
2. Make referrals to physicians or community agencies where indicated.
3. Regularly assess the growth of each child and chart educational program for them.
4. Make weekly observations and hold conferences with head teacher of the N. H. group.

Research specialist

The research specialist would be responsible for evaluation of follow-up program through:
1. Initial testing of all children, scoring and recording of all test scores and furnishing copies of results to appropriate personnel.
2. Follow-up testing at 3-month intervals or on the completion of therapy for an individual.
3. Statistical analysis of change for experimental and control groups. Experimental groups will be groups with specially developed curricula. Control groups will be groups taught according to regular nursery school procedures.

Child development consultant

The child development consultant would assist the director of research in initial screening procedures and, on the basis of initial testing, assume responsibility for diagnosis of children and placement of children in play groups. She would give the head teacher a clinical description of each child, develop specialized experimental curricula for each group, and refine the curricula as the year progresses. She would work with the head teacher and social worker in suggesting home programs or parent education programs to facilitate the development of the children and work with the director of research in evaluating the specialized program.

Psychologist

The psychologist would be consulted in developing curriculum and referral services and would supervise all psychological services, including group discussion sessions or group therapy for parents and sensitivity training for the staff.

Summary

The follow-up program as outlined herein is based upon the results found in the research program concerning the needs of Head Start children in psychological, social, intellectual, and speech areas. We suggest that the model follow-up program should be planned for three years with children being dismissed either as they are able to cope with the regular school environment or if the school or other agency undertakes the responsibility for their treatment.

APPENDICES

appendix one

Because research on the effects of a disadvantaged culture on the socialization of children is not readily available, we will present in this section a brief treatise on the impact of social and economic conditions as they apply to the larger social welfare program.

THE IMPACT OF SOCIAL
AND ECONOMIC CONDITIONS
ON HUMAN DEVELOPMENT

by Elizabeth McBroom
Professor, School of Social Work
University of Southern California

Robert Coles, a child psychiatrist who studied how white and Negro children in the South were coping with stresses of desegregation, has reported his conclusions that concern with the complexities of behavior is inseparable from concern about what kind of a world people are living in, that "racism, poverty, and harsh competitive affluence are all related to people's troubles—that trials of the community are part of the life of the mind . . . ," that troubles occur in a climate of social injustice, as well as in private worlds. (Coles, 1965, p. 19)

We don't have to look far from this spot to find children and infants dying of neglect or surviving under conditions that inflict permanent damage. It is only by a backward glance that we can measure some slow and halting progress. In seventeenth century Europe, unwanted infants were discarded in sewers, and the mortality rate from starvation in foundling homes was nearly 100 per cent. Survival, and institutions where physical survival of infants was possible, were achieved in the western world only late in the nineteenth century. Many Oriental communities maintain a seventeenth century outlook even today in this respect. (Brody, 1956).

Effects on physical development

Since mid-nineteenth century, the process of physical growth has accelerated. The causes are not fully understood, but improved nutrition is probably a factor. The faster growth begins at birth. The greatest change occurs between the ages of two and five. Children are growing taller, and increases in height are greater in the middle class than in poor children. Many studies show the same advantage for middle-class children in other measures of size and health. More defective children are born in low socio-economic groups. Factors of maternal age, number and spacing of pregnancies, and maternal health and nutrition are implicated. (Masland, 1961).

A study of a group of Negro children born in New Haven during World War II showed that, contrary to previous reports, their growth curves and adaptive behavior-development progressed according to the best available white rates, and continued to the age of 8 years when the children were last examined. The only explanation was that their mothers had received adequate prenatal diets because of wartime rationing and employment opportunities that improved their economic status. (Pasamanick, 1961).

Rates of prematurity and complications of pregnancy among Negroes are markedly higher than those in the lowest white socio-economic group. Investigators have hypothesized that the cause is not some racial characteristic, but rather the exponential increase in rates of pregnancy risk below certain socio-economic thresholds. (Pasamanick, 1961).

Many studies of developmental failure have been reported in recent years under the general rubric of maternal deprivation. The development of deprived children lags in all spheres: physical, intellectual, emotional, and social. They are, of course, closely interrelated.

Two pediatricians, Patton and Gardner, (1963) have recently reported a study of cases in which there was a primary disruption of the physical and emotional bonds between infant and mother, with serious secondary alterations in the environment. These included nutritional deficiencies, exposure, trauma, and isolation. They were particularly interested in the effects of early environment on the basic biological process of growth. These investigators noted the wide range of susceptibility or vulnerability to effects of deprivation. Some strong babies do survive, even in dreadful institutions. The explanatory variables include inherited constitutional differences, duration and intensity of the experience, age at onset, and previous experience.

Some basic questions about the ability to grow remain unanswered:

Is it primarily a function of constitution which can be modfied by prenatal and infant experience?

Is ability to grow a property only of young cells, or does growth potential remain in the organism until it is exercised? (The infant is most sensitive to earliest nutritional deprivation, and its effects are most persistent.)

Are maximum growth and optimum growth identical? (Undernutrition in animals has prolonged the life span, delayed degenerative changes, and the appearance of tumors.)

The most important index of normal and deviant growth patterns since discoveries early in this century has been the bone age or maturation at skeletal centers: the observed rates of changes in size, shape and fusion. The development of the skeleton of hand and wrist has been most carefully documented. Many recognized genetic and environmental factors produce severe deviations from normal. Scars of interrupted growth have been found at ends of long bones following illness, malnutrition (populations of children in India and Africa) and bombing (Japan). Patton and Gardner described a syndrome of growth retardation, delayed skeletal maturation, and retarded psychomotor development associated with disturbed mothers and disorganized families in which a child was isolated and neglected. Some were physically abused and malnourished. The children were withdrawn, retarded, and showed rhythmic motor activity. There was no endocrine disorder and no organic disease. Their investigations of effects of early environment on the basic biological process of growth led them to classify growth retardation and delayed development associated with environmental factors as a psychosomatic disorder. Their study of response and residual defects suggested critical periods in body growth and neural organization when unfavorable environment causes irreversible reduction of the human potential. (Patton, 1963).

In addition to these studies of growth retardation, there is extensive evidence of development damaged by faulty nutrition, by infectious diseases against which the child has not been immunized, and by trauma and abuse associated with unfavorable social and economic conditions.

Effects on intellectual development

Patton and Gardner also reported that intelligence is profoundly affected by early deprivation. They postulated critical periods of cerebral development in early childhood, during which the absence of cultural stimulation may cause permanent defects. More detailed studies have indicated that the function of speech is a reliable indicator. We have known for a long time that a high percentage of institutionalized children show defective speech. Ainsworth, in a review of research on this subject, acknowledged that the study of deprived children has led to acceptance of the fact that intelligence, as measured by tests, is effected by environment, as well as by constitutional factors. A "grossly depriving environment" affects functions measured by tests given in infancy, and those administered to school children and adults as well. (Ainsworth, 1962). Many psychologists favor the theory of the "sensitive phase" in development. This theory recognizes the possibility that there are certain life periods during which certain kinds of development proceed normally if adequate environmental conditions are present, but if these conditions are inadequate during the sensitive phase for the function in question, development will not only be arrested with respect to the function, but it will either be impossible or very difficult for subsequent stimulation to rectify matters. (Ainsworth, 1962, p. 46.)

In settings of extreme deprivation (usually children's institutions), intellectual development can be grossly retarded, with individual variation related to length of institutionalization and the age of the child at entrance. The fact of institutional life most damaging to intelligence is thought to be lack of interaction between infant and caretaker. There is less serious retardation when an attempt is made to approximate a maternal relationship, as was done in Anna Freud's war nurseries.

The experiences of the first year of life are of utmost importance for development of intelligence, and there is a vulnerable or sensitive phase from six to 12 months. Normally, something crucial happens, and it can still happen in the second year, but probably not later. This is the crucial time for development of the language function. The human speech sounds the baby hears act as "releasers" (environmental stimuli) for the human speech sounds he produces in response. One of the things lacking in an institution with inadequate staff is adults who talk to babies. The more routine the care, the less the talk. Mothers' talk to babies is an important stimulus to development. It is now assumed, but not proved, that early deprivation in hearing human speech creates a lasting handicap not completely reversible by later learning.

The child who is socially or economically deprived thus gets a poor start in intellectual development. His handicaps are likely to be cumulative.

There is much recent work on the learning difficulties of culturally deprived preschool and school children. The whole preschool period is now viewed as critical; i.e., as another growth stage at which inadequate sensory and intellectual stimulation can produce irreversible damage to capacity, which will be diagnosed as retarded development, be reflected in low scores on intelligence tests, and form the base for cumulative school failures, dislike of school, lowered self-esteem and defensive attitudes.

Consider the contrasting stimuli available to the middle-class preschool child whose parents have professional or managerial status and who is additionally the object of attention and gifts by doting grandparents and possibly unmarried or childless young aunts and uncles, and the child of migrant farm laborers who lives in barren temporary housing and from an early age during most of his waking hours has minimal interactions with interested adults. Concept development grows out of sensory contact with and manipulation of objects in the environment. Play and exploration with his toys gives the young middle-class child the basis for beginning to classify and categorize sizes, shapes, colors, weights, textures, flexibility, sounds and spatial relations. He identifies actions of rolling, swinging, and pouring. Conversations with his parents as he eats help him to attach verbal labels to odors, flavors, and temperatures. All these stimuli are lacking in the physical environment of the deprived child. His is a confined world, and the middle-class teacher's assumption that all children have had certain first-hand experiences may only add to his confusion. These failures of stimulation in physical environment make him less ready to learn to read. He lacks clues from experience which will aid his interpretation. Researches in educational psychology suggest a close relationship between a child's experience, the information he acquires, and the skills he can develop in concept formation.

A report by Science Research Associates supplies many additional details about the learning handicaps which accompany social and economic disadvantage. Because all children imitate available speech models in learning their native tongue, those who hear only imprecise language and mispronunciation are set back in their efforts to learn to read. Mastery of printed symbols is dependent on familiarity with the audible sounds they represent, and the child who has lacked opportunity to develop auditory discrimination is penalizea in all learning which proceeds by listening. A child needs an adequate vocabulary for clear, effective communication and success in school, not only for reception (comprehension by reading and listening) but also for expression (speaking and writing). The preschool period is now considered strategic for acquiring word-meanings as a base on which all effective linguistic skills are later elaborated. For optimal use, language must be automatic and fluent, not the occasion for search and struggle. The pre-school child is eager to communicate, and this is the best time to help him acquire the verbal facility that is a means to effective social participation—not after he has come through an experience of failure and humiliation because he has not acquired speech skills before he came to school.

For competence in school, work, and family roles, children need to develop reasoning ability, which is itself stimulated by verbal interaction, and the ability to understand through listening, which is highly supportive to interest and motivaton. Children who grow up in noisy, crowded conditions where most of the interaction is non-verbal and focused to immediate demands are those who have a very short attention span. Meager environments and lack of objects to manipulate also interfere with the formation of quantitative concepts of counting, putting with, taking away, dividing in half, bigger, smaller, more and less.

The child whose lifespace is constricted and who has nothing to play with fails to develop spatial concepts of arrangement, interrelationship and motion, and the vocabulary terms necessary to express these concepts. He also fails to develop the time concepts by which our culture orders its activities and develops some feeling of potency with regard to future time. The deprived child does not acquire habits of punctuality; he doesn't even learn to tell time, or relate time of day to his activities. He does not learn the names of days or months, or learn to distinguish past, present and future time. The child whose environmental stimuli are adequate develops, through play and manipulation of toys, visual discrimination for small details which is the basis for letter and word recognition, prerequisite to reading. The child who has been read to acquires (in addition to the information and stimulus to imagination that he hears) the knowledge that a book reads from front to back and that the printed page (in Western languages) proceeds from left to right.

The deprived child not only brings handicaps to school, but he may meet discrimination at the hands of some teachers, even if he is a bright and striving child. Children are aware of their teachers' rejection, and the net result of such a school experience is a loss of self-confidence, with lowered achievement and additional behavior problems. These children are at a marked disadvantage in taking intelligence tests. They lack experience and motivation and are likely to be afraid of the person administering the test, who may appear as a threatening authority figure. Their I.Q. scores fall with age, because I.Q. tests are based on a progression of experience and vocabulary presumed normal for the culture. The disadvantaged child's lacks have a cumulative effect. (Reisman, 1962).

Effects on Psychosocial Development

In addition to retarded growth and intellectual development, we are aware of disasters in psychosocial development associated with gross disturbances in the environment. In the growth of the human infant, social and emotional factors are complementary to, or on a continuum with, biological factors.

It has long been know that isolation of an infant from a human partner is harmful. There is a report that a thirteenth century emperor carried out an experiment to find out what language or tongue infants would develop spontaneously if no one spoke to them. But he labored in vain, the report concludes, for the children all died. (Reisman, 1962).

Renee Spitz's observations confirmed that extreme forms of emotional starvation in the first year of life are as destructive as physical starvation. Both lead to irreversible damage and to death. Anna Freud emphasized the infant's susceptibility to sensations of pleasure and pain as the basis for the first step in mental growth: the infant who has repeated satisfactory experiences at the hands of his mother develops a strong capacity to distinguish the boundaries of self within the environment. The converse of this is not true: that inevitably frustrating maternal activities produce infantile neurosis. It does mean, however, that the infant's earliest responses to stimuli are effected by the way in which care and attention relieve his bodily discomforts and tensions.

Severely restricted children are thought to become socially conforming, compliant and dependent. These traits are valued in some cultures. However, a compliant response as the limit of development does not represent the achievement of full human potential.

The critical period of infant relationship to mother is now thought to be from three months to two years. This is based on the theory that ego and superego development result from satisfaction with a clearly identified person: the mother. This, then, is one of the periods of development in which external events may have irreversible effects which reduce the potential of the organism. Brody points out that the most sophisticated studies of infants produced to date link development to maternal care: the mother's emotional response to the infant and the way she meets his needs affect his subsequent identification and the susceptibility or resistance he may develop to later mental illness and other forms of disturbance. The father supports the mother in her role and very early has a direct influence on the child. There is growing concern today over the "fatherless subculture" (most children in AFDC families, many of them illegitimate) where children fail early and experience moral and intellectual as well as economic deprivation.

The employment outside the home of mothers of small children is increasing. We know very little about the effects of this. Most studies have been carried out in association with other factors recognized as unfavorable to development: broken homes, poverty, and racial discrimination. There is no evidence that mother's employment *per se* creates disturbance in children. It is necessary to take into consideration the amount of work the mother does, the age and sex of the child, the mother's personality and her attitude toward her roles as woman, employee, and mother, as well as the quality of substitute care provided. We have clinical impressions that a dissatisfied mother does poorly—whether she resents the necessity of working outside the home, or is frustrated because child care interferes with her career opportunities. (Yarrow, 1964).

Many recent studies relate child-rearing practices to socio-economic class of families. For example, in discipline patterns, middle-class parents put strong values on mildness and permissiveness. Permissiveness with children may be a luxury which middle-class parents can afford because they have enough room in the house, have a few, carefully spaced children, and live in a "safe" neighborhood of known values. Class differences are probably narrowing, because so much space in the mass media is devoted to child rearing and it receives increasing consideration in most child health plans. The possible exception is at the lowest levels where there is little motivation because of hopelessness about chances for upward mobility. Hope is a powerful motivation for change in many working class families and is reflected in aspirations that mold their child-rearing practices. (Caldwell, 1964).

Of great significance for social workers is the question of what kind of performance in parental roles the environment permits. Brim, in his study of parent education, contrasted the mother who copes with physical crowding and continuous exposure, who lacks a marital partner and labor saving devices, and who is below par physically, with the mother who has adequate resources to help her be creative and attentive in her maternal role, and who can withdraw to remobilize her energy and emotional stamina. (Brim, 1959).

These class differences have social outcomes for children. Harrington, for example, has suggested that there is a grim process at work to make the children of the poor the likely parents of the next generation in the culture of poverty. (Harrington, 1962). The child-rearing criterion in the most deviant families (those who are illiterate, disorganized, crowded and fatherless) tends to become what is convenient for mother. Depressed and helpless, she punishes only aggression toward herself, prepares her children for social rejection, and perpetuates the lower class role. (Wortis, 1963). From these families emerge children who consider themselves worthless and expect failure. They experience exclusion from friendship cliques of children with a different orientation. The impact of this kind of social experience is increasingly irreversible.

Most of our available studies are on child-rearing practices in middle and working class families. One interesting English study, however, found basic similarities at the extremes of society: the children were described in these terms: insecure, rigid (but not always efficient) impulse control, the effort to see the world whole, extroverted ways, superficial relationships, periodic tendency to be depressed. (Spindley, 1953).

Correctives

The vulnerability of infants and children to social and economic conditions unfavorable to their development reads like a catalog of evils. It must be followed by some effort to answer the question, "What can they do to be saved?"

We know many things that can be done. I would like to preface everything I say about treatment with the reminder that *our ultimate goal is prevention.* Prevention is always better than treatment: it is more efficient, more humane, and more successful.

Patton and Gardner, (1963), who studied growth failure of infants deprived in their own families, reported growth acceleration when the children were hospitalized or placed in other more favorable environments. The initial improvement was rapid; the long time response was variable. Residual damage to personality and intellect were considered probable. The treatment was primarily social. It consisted of education and social action to break a cycle in families where the pattern was self-perpetuating. An important factor was the nature of stimulation the children received during recovery.

There are mass efforts to reverse the effects of deprivation at the crucial preschool level. This is the goal of Operation Head Start, a crash federal program, part of the "War on Poverty" which brought about 700,000 deprived children into prekindergarten classes in its first summer of operation. U.S.C. was one of the 118 colleges and universities which conducted training programs for teachers. The teachers were taught about the culture of poverty and its handicapping effects on the development of a child's potential. They were taught about threats to children's physical well-being. They had the opportunity to discuss needs and problems of the children in small groups. Their classes were small, and had help from aides, parents, and volunteers. They visited the children's homes. The teachers felt professionally enriched by their increased understanding of children, and many of them related that the opportunity and encouragement was such that for the first time individual children became "visible" to them and responded to their interest and concern.

Teachers reported that the attitude of children had been positive. They were eager to come on time, or even early. Those who accompanied them on the bus reported that the fighting, crying, and sickness of the first few days gave way to smiling and singing. They found that teacher was their friend, not their enemy. They were happy enough to begin to talk, to learn to count, to share, and play in groups. Some of the children saw themselves in a mirror for the first time. Fearful, they refused to look, then peeked and ran. With teacher's praise of their physical qualities, they became fascinated and made initial moves toward developing an adequate image of and attitude toward their own bodies, as part of the essential self-concept. The increased maturity and readiness for school has been evident in kindergarten this month by the absence of "first week tears."

The identification with teachers was expressed by one little girl who said, "I want to be a teacher just like you, Mrs. Jones, and wear a red dress just like yours." This is good in itself, but obviously suggests the urgent necessity for more men teachers in pre-school and elementary programs. I saw some young fathers and big brothers volunteering in Head Start classes this summer. The children were invariably swarming about them, and I got the impression that many of these kids are almost literally "man hungry."

Head Start, then, represented a massive effort to reverse the effects of deprivation at the crucial preschool age. Teachers tried to arouse the children's curiosity, promote their independence, success strivings, and language skills, and channel impulses into constructive activities. This was done by direct teaching, but also by creating an atmosphere in which the individual child's relationship with his teacher promoted his confidence and sense of personal worth. Head Start was a beginning on the part of politicians, social workers, educators, and physicians to apply knowledge about the effects of social and cultural conditions on child development in a preventive program.

It should be noted that some investigators have complained that programs for deprived children seek only to create replicas of middle-class children. For example, Frank Reisman (1962) advocates more pluralistic and broader goals of education which will stress visual and active physical techniques, rather than being word-bound and limited to linguistic skills. He also stresses that the school culture is overly polite, prissy, and puritanical and stands in great need of being "masculinized"—in staff, in textbook content, in values.

CONCLUSION

How many children are suffering in their development from the deprivations I have described? Operation Head Start was set up for the one million children born in the U.S.A. in the year 1960 who were considered to be so deprived. A recent administration report finds that half the preschool children in developing countries are seriously undernourished, with 10 to 25 per cent mentally and physically retarded from this cause. Another writer, Barbara Ward (1965), the British economist, has described a widening gap between a white, complacent, wealthy, numerically small North Atlantic elite and everybody else in the world.

Social workers have always been highly conscious of these kinds of problems in the environment, and have observed many of their damaging effects on development. Social work got started out of concern over such conditions. These are the problems we work with, and for which we try to find better solutions.

An eloquent eulogy to Adlai Stevenson, who had devoted his excellence of mind and spirit to a life of public service, was,

> Every great leader in our history has possessed faith in a principle of moral and intellectual development analogous to the biological process, not as the endowment of an elite, but as a potential of all mankind. (*New Republic,* 1965)

Social workers, too, share that faith in the potential of all mankind. We work toward the goal of helping them to achieve that potential.

REFERENCES

"Adlai Stevenson," editorial in *The New Republic,* 7-24-65.

Ainsworth, Mary. "Reversible and Irreversible Effects of Maternal Deprivation on Intellectual Development," in *Maternal Deprivation,* Child Welfare League of America, New York, 1962, 42-62.

Benedek, Therese. "Personality Development," in *Dynamic Psychiatry,* edited by Franz Alexander and Helen Ross, University of Chicago Press, Chicago, 1952, 63-113.

Brim, Orville G., Jr. *Education for Child Rearing,* Russell Sage Foundation, New York, 1959.

Brody, Sylvia. *Patterns of Mothering.* International Universities Press, New York, 1956.

Caldwell, Bettye M. "The Effects of Infant Care," in *Review of Child Development Research,* edited by Martin L. and Lois W. Hoffman, Russell Sage Foundation, New York, 1964, 9-87.

Coles, Robert. "Treating the Mentally Ill," *The New Republic,* 7-20-65, pp. 17-20.

"Fewer Births Essential," editorial in *The New Republic,* 9-18-65.

Harrington, Michael. *The Other America,* The Macmillan Company, New York, 1962.

Masland, Richard L. "Researches into the Prenatal Factors that Lead to Neuropsychiatric Sequelae in Childhood," in *Prevention of Mental Disorders in Children,* edited by Gerald Caplan. Basic Books, New York, 1961, 52-73.

Passamanick, Benjamin and Hilda Knobloch. "Epidemiologic Studies on the Complications of Pregnancy and the Birth Process," in *Prevention of Mental Disorders in Children,* edited by Gerald Caplan. Basic Books, New York, 1961, 74-94.

Patton, Robert G. and Lytt I. Gardner. *Growth Failure in Maternal Deprivation,* Charles C. Thomas, Springfield, Ill., 1963.

Riessman, Frank. *The Culturally Deprived Child,* Harper & Row, New York, 1962.

Science Research Associates. *Program Proposal for Culturally Disadvantaged Pre-School Children,* Chicago, n.d.

Spindley, B. M. *The Deprived and the Privileged, Personality Development in English Society.* Routledge & Kegan Paul, London, 1953.

Tyler, Edward R. "The Process of Humanizing Physiological Man," *Family Process,* Vol. 3 (1964), 280-301.

Wortis, H., et al. "Child-Rearing Practices in a Low Socio-economic group," *Pediatrics,* Vol. 32 (1963), 298-307.

Yarrow, Leon J. "Separation from Parents during Early Childhood," in *Review of Child Development Research,* edited by Martin L. and Lois W. Hoffman, Russell Sage Foundation, New York, 1964, 89-136.

appendix two

THE ROLE OF THE PEDIATRICIAN IN
OPERATION HEAD START

by
Milton Arnold, M.D.
Chairman, Los Angeles County Project Head Start,
American Academy of Pediatrics

Head Start must offer opportunity for the child's growth and development, not simply custodial care. The program should deal with the entire child's health, social service, and educational activities. The programs may be sponsored by community action agencies, local government organizations, schools, volunteer groups, and so forth. They will need widespread community support. Currently, finances are from the Office of Economic Opportunity in Washington, together with local sponsorship. Ninety per cent of the funds are from the federal government, the 10 per cent—local money—may be given by means of service. As an example of service in the past summer, over three hundred pediatricians in the Los Angeles County area, members of the Los Angeles Pediatric Society, volunteered their services, on a no-fee basis to go into Head Start areas and examine the children taking part in this program. This service provided some of the local funds expected of the community.

Problems

There are many problems attendant on such a program as Head Start. To those of us in the various pediatric societies, such as the Academy of Pediatrics, the California Federation of Pediatric Societies, and the Los Angeles Pediatric Society, fell the task of implementing a program with high philosophical and social intent without losing its purpose. It became necessary to design a medical service that could be practical and smooth-running.

One of the problems that immediately became evident was that of reaching that group of people who were truly in need. The parents had to be made aware of the importance of Head Start. Those who heard of Head Start and immediately brought their children under its services were not always the ones who could most benefit by the program. The very fact that the parent is eager to see that her child gets all that is possible to elevate him out of his particular segment of society implies that this parent is a powerful stimulus to her own child's development. We are not trying to discourage these kinds of parents. On the contrary, we are happy to learn that they are trying to help themselves. However, we must also reach those parents who, because of lack of knowledge, fear, apathy or finances, have failed to provide adequately for their own children.

Diligent efforts have been made by social workers to reach this most needy group—even to the point of door-to-door canvassing in areas of high poverty. We cannot assume, however, that if an area is declared a poverty area by geographical borders that *all* within this zoning are poverty stricken, and therefore, would benefit by the program. Each family certainly should be individually assessed on its own merits and needs.

Many of the pediatricians who took part in Head Start this summer found that they frequently saw patients who had their own private physician or were currently receiving services under some group health plan or county hospital or non-profit community hospital. In these cases, any examination performed by the Head Start physician would seem repetitious and not equal in quality to the kind of care that the child would be receiving if his own physician had been seeing him sequentially over several months or years.

It is the feeling of all of us that each child has the *right to individualized care* by a physician who will take a complete and thorough history and make a careful medical evaluation and then selectively perform certain laboratory tests that are designed for this child. All preschool children, whether they are rich, middle-class, or poor should have well-trained medical supervision and guidance, not just mass screening inspections.

I believe we are justly critical of the mass screening examination. Although such an examination may pick up pathology that has not been previously noted, in general they give a feeling to the parent of false security that is not merited. All children with problems should have competent medical care with supervised follow-up and follow-through guidance. In the Head Start program, we were concerned that in some cases the follow-up and follow-through guidance was not under the supervision of the original examiner. This was certainly true for the results of the laboratory work, which in many cases were delayed. (Note: Such was *not* the case in the Delta program.) Had these children been examined in suitable medical facilities, such as a private physician's office, hospital facility, or mobile unit prepared for such a purpose, the laboratory work would have been available probably at the time of the examination or certainly within a day or two thereafter; and suitable follow-up remedial measures could be started promptly.

Physician Recruitment

Now, I would like to discuss *physician recruitment,* which brings up a problem of logistics. Historically, the physician has cared for the indigent. We have done this because we feel that it is part of our community service. Throughout the United States, the county hospital, the non-profit community hospital clinic, the medical school teaching programs, and so forth, are handled to a large extent on a voluntary, no-pay basis, by physicians in private practice.

In the past few years, there has been increasing government participation in the practice of medicine, and the physician has found himself in a position whereby, in volunteering his services, he is being spread pretty thin. He can no longer continue to support his medical school teaching activities, county hospital, and other hospital clinic services and still manage to take care of those children in various community programs, such as Head Start, on a voluntary basis. We are resistant to giving up our support of the medical centers. We will, however, have to change some of our previous attitudes toward voluntary programs. As far as Head Start is concerned, the program started as an eight-week session and is now extended throughout the year. The Office of Economic Opportunity wants doctors to man this program on a full-time basis. This is good, since the program requires a full-time cadre.

Most areas simply do not have enough physicians to handle this type of program. Therefore, the men in private and academic practice must act as a supplementary force. Because of the disparity between the number of physicians and nurses and other trained ancillary personnel needed and the requirements of the program, we feel that one approach would be to *examine these children in the physician's office*. This would eliminate the problems of hiring extra nursing and laboratory personnel. By using such methods, we would be combining physicians and other technical personnel who are accustomed to working together plus a simple method for providing follow-up care. In other areas, comparable medical facilities, such as *mobile units* and *local hospitals* might be used. There should be flexibility in our approach to this problem. If several programs are developed that would require medical examinations, the same resources could provide any one of the several agencies with a copy of the history and physical examination already performed. It should be noted that there are many governmental programs that are being conducted by the private physician on a fee for service basis: Bureau of Public Assistance, Aid to Dependent Children, Crippled Children's Services, and others.

Timing was another problem. The time permitted for each examination was quite limited. On the average, fifteen children were scheduled between 9 and 12 o'clock—this is approximately twelve minutes per child. During this period of time, the physician was expected to perform a hemoglobin on each child, review his audiometric and visual examinations, perform a careful history and physical examination, give a tuberculin, catch up on the child's immunizations, and make proper recommendations for future care. This left no time for the establishment of rapport with the child and the parent, nor did it permit the physician to serve his role as medical educator to these families. Privately, twelve to fifteen minutes are usually allowed for re-examinations of a child who has been previously examined and now has come in to check an ear or throat infection. Medicine simply cannot be practiced with a stop-watch in hand. Each patient requires an individual examination with individual selective testing and variable lengths of time to perform these studies. We are most concerned that *quality control* be established in Head Start or in any other program.

Under present regulations, the grant goes from the federal government to the local recipient. There is no center that is responsible for minimum standards of medical care of each child. *We, as physicians, would like to see quality control established by an appropriate pediatric society before the money funded for these programs is distributed to each center.* We do not feel that the people in the individual participating organizations necessarily have sufficient medical knowledge to assess the quality of the medical program they are sponsoring. We certainly do not feel that as physicians we have sufficient training to decide on the merits of the teaching program associated with Head Start; we would want our colleagues in the teaching profession to set suitable standards in this regard.

Of course, the pediatrician recognizes that Head Start is a program of topmost priority. We realize that the preschool years are crucial in the development of intelligence and general learning patterns and that home environments can make a vital difference in the young child's readiness to learn. We also recognize the need for a program that is custom fitted to each child, not just placing any child into a program that is already existing.

I strongly suggest that in planning medical services for any future program, a suitable medical, in this case a pediatric society, be consulted. *Failure to utilize experts in the field, seems to me poor economy, especially when these very same experts will be necessary for the implementation of such a program.*

Based on the previous report, I have moved that the following resolution be adopted by the Los Angeles Pediatric Society:

> The Los Angeles Pediatric Society has a genuine concern for the welfare of all children and recognizes the need to correct the deficiencies in the educational, social, and health requirements of the underprivileged preschool child. We feel strongly that no child should be deprived of a complete medical evaluation and suitable follow-up care and guidance.

Problems

In reviewing the experiences of the volunteer pediatricians, the following correctable problems were noted:
  a. Deficient physical facilities for the performance of an adequate medical examination.
  b. Insufficient time allotted per child.
  c. Medical forms were confusing and incomplete as to history, physical, and recommending care.
  d. Poor preparation on the part of some of the centers as far as immunization material, TB testing, laboratory, and audio-visual studies.
  e. Lack of Project medical officers to provide vital overall coordination and quality control, including adequacy of follow-up.
  f. Frequent duplication of prior services provided by the family physician or other medical agency.
  g. The medical examinations were mass screening studies rather than individualized evaluations of each child.

Meeting the problems

We, therefore, strongly advise:
  1. The establishment of *standards of quality* for both the medical examination and the physicians participating before funds are approved. Such standards should be assessed by an appropriate pediatric society.
  2. Each child deserves *individualized medical care*. The logical setting for a health evaluation is in a physician's office or comparable medical facility.
  3. A *fee* commensurate with this service should be received.
  4. Suitable *forms* should be designed which are in keeping with the classical standards.
  5. Careful social *screening* to reach a true need group and avoid duplication of services.

6. *Orientation of physicians* participating in the program to simplify standard operating procedures.

7. *Orientation of parent and child,* teacher and social worker, so that each will understand his role in the project.

We believe that these recommendations can readily be achieved, as some centers now participating in the Project have demonstrated. We further believe that they will set a high standard of quality to Project Head Start, and therefore, directly benefit the child and the community.

appendix three

U. S. Census Bureau

information sheets

OPERATION HEAD START WORKER'S ATTITUDE SCALE

BUDGET BUREAU NO. 116-6504
APPROVAL EXPIRES 3-31-66

WORKER'S IDENTIFICATION NUMBER

```
0 === 1 === 2 === 3 === 4 ===   | 5 === 6 === 7 === 8 === 9 ===
0 === 1 === 2 === 3 === 4 ===   | 5 === 6 === 7 === 8 === 9 ===
0 === 1 === 2 === 3 === 4 ===   | 5 === 6 === 7 === 8 === 9 ===
0 === 1 === 2 === 3 === 4 ===   | 5 === 6 === 7 === 8 === 9 ===
0 === 1 === 2 === 3 === 4 ===   | 5 === 6 === 7 === 8 === 9 ===
0 === 1 === 2 === 3 === 4 ===   | 5 === 6 === 7 === 8 === 9 ===
```

CENTER IDENTIFICATION NUMBER

```
0 === 1 === 2 === 3 === 4 ===   | 5 === 6 === 7 === 8 === 9 ===
0 === 1 === 2 === 3 === 4 ===   | 5 === 6 === 7 === 8 === 9 ===
0 === 1 === 2 === 3 === 4 ===   | 5 === 6 === 7 === 8 === 9 ===
0 === 1 === 2 === 3 === 4 ===   | 5 === 6 === 7 === 8 === 9 ===
0 === 1 === 2 === 3 === 4 ===   | 5 === 6 === 7 === 8 === 9 ===
0 === 1 === 2 === 3 === 4 ===   | 5 === 6 === 7 === 8 === 9 ===
```

PLEASE USE A NO. 2 LEAD PENCIL

PART I

THE FOLLOWING STATEMENTS HAVE NO RIGHT OR WRONG ANSWERS. ALL THAT IS REQUIRED IS THAT YOU GIVE YOUR HONEST REACTION TO EACH QUESTION. AFTER READING EACH STATEMENT, SIMPLY MARK, WITH A NO. 2 LEAD PENCIL, THE ALTERNATIVE THAT INDICATES YOUR OWN OPINION. AFTER READING EACH STATEMENT, MAKE ONE OF THE FOLLOWING FIVE CHOICES:

STRONGLY AGREE, AGREE, NOT SURE, DISAGREE, STRONGLY DISAGREE

	STR AGR	AGR	NOT SURE	DISA	STR DISA
1. I WOULD ENJOY WORKING WITH POOR PEOPLE TO HELP THEM BETTER THEIR LIVES.	===	===	===	===	===
2. POOR PEOPLE TEND TO BEHAVE IN CHILDISH WAYS.	===	===	===	===	===
3. POVERTY IS LARGELY A FUNCTION OF BAD LUCK, INJUSTICE, OR DISCRIMINATION.	===	===	===	===	===
4. I WOULD BE EMBARRASSED TO INTRODUCE A POOR PERSON TO MY FRIENDS.	===	===	===	===	===
5. POOR PEOPLE ARE LESS TRUSTWORTHY THAN PEOPLE WITH MORE MONEY.	===	===	===	===	===
6. IN GENERAL, POOR PEOPLE LACK INTELLIGENCE.	===	===	===	===	===
7. THE CITY, STATE, AND FEDERAL GOVERNMENT SHOULD DO ALL IT CAN IN TRYING TO HELP POOR PEOPLE BETTER THEIR LIVES.	===	===	===	===	===
8. POOR PEOPLE TEND TO BE AS INTERESTED IN THEIR CHILDREN AS ARE PEOPLE WITH MORE MONEY.	===	===	===	===	===
9. VIOLENT BEHAVIOR CHARACTERIZES THE POOR.	STR AGR	AGR	NOT SURE	DISA	STR DISA
10. MOST POOR PEOPLE DO NOT KNOW WHAT THEY WANT OUT OF LIFE.	===	===	===	===	===
11. POOR PEOPLE DESERVE AS MUCH RESPECT AND CONSIDERATION AS ANYONE ELSE.	===	===	===	===	===
12. MOST POOR PEOPLE ARE POOR BECAUSE THEY ARE LAZY.	===	===	===	===	===
13. IT'S HARD FOR AN ABLE-BODIED MAN TO RESPECT HIMSELF IF HE DOESN'T WORK.	===	===	===	===	===
14. IMMORAL PRACTICES ARE MUCH MORE COMMON AMONG THE POOR.	===	===	===	===	===
15. WE SHOULD TRY TO HELP ONLY THOSE WHO APPRECIATE OUR HELP.	===	===	===	===	===
16. JUST ABOUT EVERY TYPE OF PERSONALITY CAN BE FOUND AMONG THE POOR.	===	===	===	===	===
17. POVERTY IS A SIGN OF FAILURE IN LIFE.	===	===	===	===	===
18. POVERTY IS QUITE OFTEN DUE TO LACK OF SELF CONTROL, WILL-POWER, OR THE DESIRE TO GET AHEAD.	===	===	===	===	===
19. POOR PEOPLE WOULD IMPROVE THEMSELVES IF THEY WERE GIVEN ADDITIONAL OPPORTUNITIES.	STR AGR	AGR	NOT SURE	DISA	STR DISA
20. HOW MUCH MONEY A PERSON MAKES IS USUALLY A GOOD INDICATOR OF HIS CHARACTER.	===	===	===	===	===
21. THERE IS LITTLE THAT CAN BE DONE TO HELP THE POOR TO BETTER THEMSELVES SHORT OF TAKING CARE OF THEM OR GIVING THEM MONEY.	===	===	===	===	===
22. MOST POOR PEOPLE ARE WILLING TO WORK HARD IF GIVEN THE OPPORTUNITY.	===	===	===	===	===
23. IN GENERAL, THE BEHAVIOR OF POOR PEOPLE TENDS TO BE ERRATIC AND UNPREDICTABLE.	===	===	===	===	===
24. POOR PEOPLE DON'T CARE HOW THEY LOOK.	===	===	===	===	===
25. IT IS THE RESPONSIBILITY OF PEOPLE WHO ARE WELL OFF TO HELP POOR PEOPLE BETTER THEMSELVES.	===	===	===	===	===
26. POOR PEOPLE TEND TO BE LOUD, VULGAR, AND IMPOLITE.	===	===	===	===	===
27. POOR PEOPLE WILL TAKE ADVANTAGE OF YOU IF YOU GIVE THEM THE OPPORTUNITY.	===	===	===	===	===
28. IT WOULD BE ALL RIGHT WITH ME TO HAVE A POOR PERSON AS A CLOSE FRIEND.	===	===	===	===	===
29. POOR PEOPLE ARE INHERENTLY DIFFERENT FROM PEOPLE WHO HAVE MORE MONEY.	===	===	===	===	===
30. POOR PEOPLE SHOULD HAVE SOMETHING TO SAY ABOUT HOW THE GOVERNMENT SPENDS MONEY TO HELP THEM.	===	===	===	===	===

PRESENT WEEK OF CENTER'S OPERATION

```
=1=  =2=  =3=  =4=  =5=      =6=  =7=  =8=  =9=
```

DO NOT MARK IN THIS SPACE

OVER

OPERATION HEAD START WORKER'S ATTITUDE SCALE

PART II

AGAIN THERE ARE NO RIGHT OR WRONG ANSWERS TO THE FOLLOWING ITEMS. WE ARE INTERESTED IN FINDING OUT WHAT YOU FEEL CHARACTERIZES OR DOES NOT CHARACTERIZE YOUNG CHILDREN. FOR EACH OF THE ADJECTIVES BELOW, SIMPLY MARK WHETHER OR NOT YOU FEEL THE DESCRIPTION IS CHARACTERISTIC OR NOT CHARACTERISTIC OF MOST CHILDREN OF THIS AGE, AND THEN DO THE SAME FOR THE CHILDREN IN THE OPERATION HEADSTART PROGRAM. SINCE WE ARE INTERESTED IN YOUR FIRST OVERALL IMPRESSIONS, IT IS ALL RIGHT TO GO THROUGH THE ITEMS RELATIVELY QUICKLY.

	MOST CHILDREN OF THIS AGE ARE:		OPERATION HEADSTART CHILDREN ARE:	
	CHARACTERISTIC	NOT CHARACTERISTIC	CHARACTERISTIC	NOT CHARACTERISTIC
1. ALERT				
2. AMBITIOUS				
3. ANNOYING				
4. ANXIOUS				
5. CALM				
6. COMPETITIVE				
7. CONFIDENT				
8. CONSIDERATE				
9. CREATIVE				
10. CRUEL				
11. DEFIANT				
12. DEMANDING				
13. DEPENDABLE				
14. DESTRUCTIVE				
15. FEARFUL				
16. FRIENDLY				
17. HAPPY				
18. HOSTILE				
19. INQUISITIVE				
20. JEALOUS				
21. MEDDLESOME				
22. NAGGING				
23. PATIENT				
24. POSSESSIVE				
25. SELFISH				
26. SELF-SUFFICIENT				
27. SPOILED				
28. STABLE				
29. WELL-MANNERED				
30. WITHDRAWN				

DO NOT MARK IN THIS SPACE

PAID AND VOLUNTARY WORKER'S EVALUATION OF OPERATION HEAD START

IBMH9221B

CENTER IDENTIFICATION NUMBER

PLEASE USE A NO. 2 LEAD PENCIL TO MARK THIS SHEET.

WORKER'S IDENTIFICATION NUMBER

BUDGET BUREAU NO. 116-6505
APPROVAL EXPIRES 6-30-66

	VERY GOOD	GOOD	FAIR	POOR	CAN'T EVAL.
1. THE GENERAL MORALE OF TEACHER, TEACHER'S AIDES, AND VOLUNTEERS WAS:					
2. HOW REALISTIC WAS YOUR DAILY SCHEDULE?					
3. WERE THERE ENOUGH WORKERS TO CARRY OUT GOALS OF THE PROGRAM?					
4. WAS THE CURRICULUM WITH WHICH YOU WORKED RELEVANT TO THIS AGE CHILD?					
5. COOPERATION FROM THE PARENTS WAS:					
6. THE FACILITIES (SUCH AS LIGHTING, SPACE WATER, STORAGE, BATHROOMS, ETC.) OF THE PRESCHOOL AREA WERE:					
7. THE AMOUNT OF AVAILABLE PLAY MATERIALS WAS:					
8. THE QUALITY OF AVAILABLE PLAY MATERIALS WAS:					
9. HOW ADEQUATE WAS THE PHYSICAL MAINTENANCE OF THE PRESCHOOL AREA?					
10. THE QUALITY OF THE TEACHING SUPERVISION WAS:					
11. HOW HELPFUL TO YOUR TEACHING WERE THE PSYCHOLOGICAL MEASURES AND RATINGS YOU COMPLETED?					
12. HOW ADEQUATE WERE THE TRANSPORTATION ARRANGEMENTS, WHERE NEEDED, FOR CHILDREN AND PARENTS?					
13. HOW AVAILABLE WERE MEDICAL AND/OR DENTAL SERVICES?					
14. HOW AVAILABLE WERE SPECIAL-EDUCATION FACILITIES?					
15. HOW AVAILABLE WERE PSYCHOLOGICAL AND/OR PSYCHIATRIC SERVICES?					
16. HOW AVAILABLE WERE SOCIAL SERVICE AGENCIES?					
17. HOW ADEQUATE WAS THE AMOUNT OF TIME SET ASIDE FOR PARENT-TEACHER CONFERENCES?					

18. IN RESPECT TO THE PHYSICAL AND PSYCHOLOGICAL HEALTH OF THE CHILD AND HIS EDUCATIONAL DEVELOPMENT, MY ATTITUDES TOWARD THE FOLLOWING ARE:

	VERY MUCH WORTHWHILE	WORTHWHILE	OCCASIONALLY WORTHWHILE	WASTE OF TIME	NOT APPLICABLE
1. MEDICAL EXAMINATION					
2. DENTAL EXAMINATION					
3. OPPORTUNITY TO ATTEND SCHOOL AT AN EARLY AGE					
4. INCREASED EXPERIENCE WITH A VARIETY OF TOYS AND GAMES					
5. INCREASED EXPERIENCE WITH A VARIETY OF BOOKS, STORIES, AND MUSIC					
6. TRIPS INTO THE COMMUNITY					
7. INDIVIDUAL ATTENTION GIVEN TO EACH CHILD BY TEACHER AND AIDES					
8. OPPORTUNITY TO PARTICIPATE IN GROUP ACTIVITIES WITH OTHER CHILDREN					

DO NOT MARK IN THIS SPACE

OVER

© by Edward Zigler, 1965   CAP-HS FORM 38 JUN. '65

IBM.H92219

PAID AND VOLUNTARY WORKER'S EVALUATION OF OPERATION HEAD START

19. I FEEL THAT, IN GENERAL, CHILDREN ATTENDING THE OPERATION HEAD START PROGRAM WERE CHANGED IN THE FOLLOWING WAYS:

	MUCH BETTER	BETTER	NO CHANGE	WORSE	MUCH WORSE
1. GETTING ALONG WITH OTHER CHILDREN					
2. SELF-CONFIDENCE					
3. SPEAKING ABILITY					
4. EVERYDAY MANNERS					
5. FINISHING WHAT HE STARTS					
6. DOING WHAT HE'S TOLD					
7. INTERESTED IN NEW THINGS					
8. CAN DO THINGS ON HIS OWN					
9. CHANCES OF SUCCESS IN KINDERGARTEN ARE					

20. AS A RESULT OF THEIR CONTACT WITH OPERATION HEAD START, THE PARENTS ARE:

	MUCH BETTER	BETTER	NO CHANGE	WORSE	MUCH WORSE
1. INVOLVED WITH CHILD'S EDUCATION					
2. CONCERNED ABOUT OWN APPEARANCE					
3. PARTICIPATING IN COMMUNITY ACTIVITIES					
4. AWARE OF ENLIGHTENED CHILD-REARING PRACTICES					
5. EFFECTIVE IN INTERPERSONAL RELATIONS					
6. KNOWLEDGEABLE ABOUT COMMUNITY RESOURCES					

21. AS A RESULT OF MY CONTACT WITH OPERATION HEAD START,

	MUCH MORE	MORE	A LITTLE	NOT AT ALL
1. I AM KNOWLEDGEABLE ABOUT TEACHING CHILDREN OF THIS AGE.				
2. I AM AWARE OF THE ENVIRONMENT THESE CHILDREN EXPERIENCE				
3. I HAVE ACQUIRED NEW TECHNIQUES TO INTERACT EFFECTIVELY WITH THESE CHILDREN				
4. I AM KNOWLEDGEABLE ABOUT AND HAVE THE ABILITY TO DEAL WITH OTHER PROFESSIONAL WORKERS CONCERNED WITH THE CHILD'S PHYSICAL, PSYCHOLOGICAL, AND SOCIAL DEVELOPMENT				

	A GREAT DEAL	SOME-WHAT	A LITTLE	NOT AT ALL
22. HOW MUCH DID YOU ENJOY YOUR DUTIES WITH OPERATION HEAD START?				
23. WOULD YOU LOOK FORWARD TO PARTICIPATING IN OPERATION HEAD START NEXT YEAR?				

24. ADD HERE ANY COMMENTS THAT YOU WOULD LIKE TO MAKE:

DO NOT MARK IN THIS SPACE

OPERATION HEAD START STAFF MEMBER INFORMATION SHEET

BUDGET BUREAU NO. 116-R026
APPROVAL EXPIRES 6-1-66

CENTER IDENTIFICATION NUMBER

0 == 1 == 2 == 3 == 4 ==   5 == 6 == 7 == 8 == 9 ==
0 == 1 == 2 == 3 == 4 ==   5 == 6 == 7 == 8 == 9 ==
0 == 1 == 2 == 3 == 4 ==   5 == 6 == 7 == 8 == 9 ==
0 == 1 == 2 == 3 == 4 ==   5 == 6 == 7 == 8 == 9 ==
0 == 1 == 2 == 3 == 4 ==   5 == 6 == 7 == 8 == 9 ==
0 == 1 == 2 == 3 == 4 ==   5 == 6 == 7 == 8 == 9 ==
0 == 1 == 2 == 3 == 4 ==   5 == 6 == 7 == 8 == 9 ==

STAFF IDENTIFICATION NUMBER

0 == 1 == 2 == 3 == 4 ==   5 == 6 == 7 == 8 == 9 ==
0 == 1 == 2 == 3 == 4 ==   5 == 6 == 7 == 8 == 9 ==
0 == 1 == 2 == 3 == 4 ==   5 == 6 == 7 == 8 == 9 ==
0 == 1 == 2 == 3 == 4 ==   5 == 6 == 7 == 8 == 9 ==
0 == 1 == 2 == 3 == 4 ==   5 == 6 == 7 == 8 == 9 ==
0 == 1 == 2 == 3 == 4 ==   5 == 6 == 7 == 8 == 9 ==

PLEASE USE A NO. 2 PENCIL TO MARK THIS FORM

1. AGE   UNDER 16   16-21   21-30   31-45   46-60   OVER 60

2. RACE CULTURAL BACKGROUND   NEGRO   WHITE   ORIENTAL   AMERICAN INDIAN   MEXICAN   PUERTO RICAN   FRENCH CREOLE   ESKIMO   OTHER

3. SEX   MALE   FEMALE

4. HIGHEST LEVEL OF EDUCATION COMPLETED

NUMBER OF YEARS COMPLETED   GRADUATED

	1-4 / 5-7	YES	NO
ELEMENTARY SCHOOL	1-4 5-7		
HIGH SCHOOL	1-2 3-4		
COLLEGE	1-2 3-4		
GRADUATE SCHOOL		MA.	
		Ph.D	

5. YOUR POSITION IN THE CHILD DEVELOPMENT CENTER
PROFESSIONAL (TEACHER, NURSE, PSYCHOLOGIST, ETC.)   NEIGHBORHOOD RESIDENT   PAID   VOLUNTEER   OTHER VOLUNTEER

6. WHAT IS YOUR USUAL FAMILY INCOME PER YEAR?
UNDER $1000 $1000 TO $1999 $2000 TO $2999 $3000 TO $3999 $4000 TO $4999 $5000 TO $5999 $6000 TO $7999 $8000 TO $9999 $10,000 PLUS

7. PREVIOUS TO HEAD START, HOW LONG HAD YOU WORKED WITH GROUPS OF CHILDREN FROM CONDITIONS OF POVERTY?
NOT AT ALL   1-3 YEARS   3-5 YEARS   OVER 5 YEARS

8. PREVIOUS TO HEAD START, HOW MUCH EXPERIENCE HAD YOU HAD WITH PRESCHOOLERS?
NONE   1-3 YEARS   3-5 YEARS   OVER 5 YEARS

9. DO YOU SPEAK FLUENTLY ANY LANGUAGE OTHER THAN ENGLISH?   YES   NO

10. IS THIS LANGUAGE USED WITH THE CHILDREN IN THE PROGRAM?   YES   NO

11. DID YOU ATTEND AN NUEA TRAINING SESSION?   YES   NO

CAP-HS FORM 41 JUN. '65   IBM H92224

IBMH92221

PSYCHOLOGICAL SCREENING PROCEDURE

II. CHILD DESCRIPTION CHECKLIST READ EACH DESCRIPTION CAREFULLY AND PUT A MARK BESIDE ANY THAT FIT THIS CHILD REASONABLY WELL. IT IS RECOGNIZED THAT DESCRIPTIONS OF THIS SORT DO NOT DO JUSTICE TO THE WHOLE CHILD AND THAT NO CHILD WILL FIT ANY DESCRIPTION EXACTLY. JUST PLACE A MARK BESIDE THE DESCRIPTIONS THAT FIT THIS CHILD REASONABLY WELL. THESE DESCRIPTIONS ARE NOT MUTUALLY EXCLUSIVE. IT IS POSSIBLE THAT SOME CHILDREN WILL FIT TWO OR MORE OF THEM. ALSO, THERE WILL BE MANY CHILDREN WHO DO NOT FIT ANY OF THESE DESCRIPTIONS. IT IS POSSIBLE THAT IN SOME CLASSES THERE WILL BE NO CHILD TO FIT ANY OF THE DESCRIPTIONS. FEW PROFESSIONAL PEOPLE, NO MATTER HOW WELL TRAINED, CAN MAKE THIS KIND OF RATING WITH ABSOLUTE CERTAINTY AND COMPLETE COMFORT. DON'T SPEND TOO MUCH TIME WORRYING WHETHER A PARTICULAR CHILD REALLY DOES OR DOESN'T FIT THE DESCRIPTIONS. MAKE YOUR BEST JUDGEMENT FOR EACH CHILD ON EACH DESCRIPTION AND THEN GO ON TO THE NEXT.

1. **THE DISRUPTIVE CHILD** THE DISRUPTIVE CHILD IS ONE WHO DISTURBS THE ACTIVITIES AND PLAY OF OTHER CHILDREN. HE MAY DO THIS BY PUSHING OR TEASING CHILDREN WHO ARE ENGAGED IN ACTIVITIES OR BY SNATCHING OR OTHERWISE DISTURBING THE MATERIALS WITH WHICH OTHER CHILDREN ARE PLAYING.

2. **THE PROVOCATIVE CHILD** THE PROVOCATIVE CHILD IS ONE WHO DELIBERATELY TRIES TO IRRITATE THE TEACHER. HE ATTEMPTS TO SECURE THE TEACHER'S ATTENTION BY DOING THINGS WHICH ARE PROHIBITED OR WHICH HE SHOULD KNOW THAT THE TEACHER DISLIKES. HE MAY REFUSE TO GO ALONG WITH GROUP ACTIVITIES, HE MAY CURSE OR OTHERWISE INSULT THE TEACHER, HE MAY DAMAGE OR DESTROY CLASSROOM MATERIALS, ETC. THIS CHILD DOES NOT RESPOND TO PUNISHMENTS BY "BEING BETTER."

3. **THE ISOLATED CHILD** THE ISOLATED CHILD NEVER SEEMS TO PLAY WITH OTHER PUPILS. HE DOESN'T SEEM TO BE ABLE TO INITIATE CONTACT WITH OTHER CHILDREN; THEY SEEM TO IGNORE HIM AND HE THEM. OTHER CHILDREN DO NOT INCLUDE HIM IN GROUP ACTIVITIES AND HE DOES NOT SEEM TO CARE.

4. **THE FEARFUL OR TEARFUL CHILD** THE FEARFUL CHILD IS EXCESSIVELY TIMID. HE CRIES MORE OFTEN THAN THE OTHER CHILDREN. OFTEN HE CRIES FOR NO APPARENT REASON. HE SEEMS TO WANT TO PLAY WITH OTHER CHILDREN AND DO THE THINGS WHICH ARE "FUN", BUT HIS FEARFULNESS GETS IN THE WAY. HE MAY BE SOMETHING OF A "TATTLE TALE," A "WHINER," OR A "MOTHER'S BOY (GIRL)."

5. **THE SILENT CHILD** THE SILENT CHILD NEVER TALKS. HE WILL USE GESTURES OR SIGNS RATHER THAN WORDS. HE SEEMS TO UNDERSTAND WHAT OTHER PEOPLE SAY, BUT HE WON'T RESPOND VERBALLY UNLESS REALLY URGED.

6. **THE CHILD WHO DOESN'T LEARN** THE CHILD WHO DOESN'T LEARN NEVER SEEMS TO GET ANY BETTER AT WHAT HE IS BEING TAUGHT. HE MAY TRY HARD, BUT HE DOESN'T SEEM TO IMPROVE. HE MAY HAVE DIFFICULTY UNDERSTANDING WHAT HE IS TOLD, AND MAY HAVE TO HAVE THINGS REPEATED A NUMBER OF TIMES. HE DOESN'T SEEM TO BE AS QUICK OR ALERT AS THE OTHER CHILDREN. OFTEN, HE SEEMS IMMATURE FOR HIS AGE.

7. **THE CHILD WITH SEPARATION PROBLEMS** THE CHILD WITH SEPARATION PROBLEMS SEEMS TO GET ALONG WELL MOST OF THE TIME, BUT HE HAS GREAT DIFFICULTY EARLY IN THE SCHOOL DAY. HIS DIFFICULTIES MAY BE MOST MARKED DURING THE FIRST DAYS OF NURSERY SCHOOL AND AFTER WEEKENDS OR VACATIONS. EARLY IN THE DAY, HE MAY SAY THAT HE DOESN'T WANT TO LEAVE HIS MOTHER OR THAT HE WANTS TO GO HOME TO HIS MOTHER. LATER ON, HE SETTLES DOWN AND SEEMS TO DO FINE. THIS CHILD'S MOTHER MAY COME TO THE CLASSROOM WITH THE CHILD MORE FREQUENTLY THAN OTHERS MOTHERS AND MAY TALK TO THE TEACHER QUITE OFTEN ABOUT HOW DIFFICULT THINGS ARE FOR HER CHILD.

8. **THE UNHAPPY CHILD** THE UNHAPPY CHILD IS ALWAYS "DOWN-AT-THE-MOUTH." HE DOESN'T SMILE VERY OFTEN AND SEEMS TO LACK A "JOY FOR LIFE." HE MIGHT NOT CRY VERY OFTEN, BUT HE DOESN'T APPEAR TO ENJOY HIMSELF OR THE THINGS THAT ARE GOING ON AROUND HIM.

9. **THE HYPERACTIVE CHILD** THIS IS A CHILD WHO JUST CAN'T SIT STILL. HE MAY ROAM AIMLESSLY ABOUT THE ROOM. IF HE IS DISRUPTIVE OF OTHER CHILDREN'S ACTIVITIES IT IS MORE AN ACCIDENTAL RESULT OF HIS RUNNING ABOUT, THAN A DELIBERATE AGGRESSIVENESS. SOME HYPERACTIVE CHILDREN DON'T ROAM AROUND A GREAT DEAL. RATHER, THEY OCCUPY THEMSELVES WITH STRANGE MOTOR ACTIVITIES SUCH AS SHAKING THEIR HANDS OR WAVING THEIR FINGERS BEFORE THEIR EYES, PULLING AT THEIR EARS OR OTHER BODY PARTS, ROCKING BACK AND FORTH. THIS TYPE OF CHILD IS OFTEN EXTREMELY DISTRACTIBLE.

III. REFERRAL OR TREATMENT REPORT ON THE BASIS OF THE BEHAVIORS NOTED ABOVE OR ANY OTHER FACTORS, WAS THIS CHILD REFERRED TO, TREATED AT, OR PLACED INTO ANY OF THE FOLLOWING:

	YES	NO		YES	NO
1. CHILD GUIDANCE CLINIC			8. HOME FOR DEPENDENT CHILDREN		
2. MENTAL HEALTH CENTER			9. OTHER (SEE BELOW)		
3. PUBLIC HEALTH NURSE OR PHYSICIAN			10. IF REFERRAL WAS MADE, WAS THE CHILD DIAGNOSED AS ABNORMAL?		
4. HOSPITAL OR MEDICAL CLINIC			11. IF REFERRAL WAS MADE, WAS TREATMENT INITIATED?		
5. STATE SCHOOL FOR THE MENTALLY RETARDED			DO NOT MARK IN THIS SPACE		
6. HOSPITAL FOR THE EMOTIONALLY DISTURBED					
7. FOSTER HOME					

PLEASE SPECIFY "OTHER", REFERRAL OR TREATMENT

IBMH92220   PSYCHOLOGICAL SCREENING PROCEDURE   BUDGET BUREAU NO. 116-6506
                                                                           APPROVAL EXPIRES 6-30-66

CHILD'S NAME:

CHILD'S IDENTIFICATION NUMBER	EXAMINER'S IDENTIFICATION NUMBER
0 1 2 3 4 [ ] 5 6 7 8 9	0 1 2 3 4 [ ] 5 6 7 8 9
0 1 2 3 4 [ ] 5 6 7 8 9	0 1 2 3 4 [ ] 5 6 7 8 9
0 1 2 3 4 [ ] 5 6 7 8 9	0 1 2 3 4 [ ] 5 6 7 8 9
0 1 2 3 4 [ ] 5 6 7 8 9	0 1 2 3 4 [ ] 5 6 7 8 9
0 1 2 3 4 [ ] 5 6 7 8 9	0 1 2 3 4 [ ] 5 6 7 8 9
0 1 2 3 4 [ ] 5 6 7 8 9	0 1 2 3 4 [ ] 5 6 7 8 9

CENTER IDENTIFICATION NUMBER

0 1 2 3 4 [ ] 5 6 7 8 9	**PRESENT WEEK OF CENTER'S OPERATION**
0 1 2 3 4 [ ] 5 6 7 8 9	1 2 3 4 5 6 7 8 9
0 1 2 3 4 [ ] 5 6 7 8 9	**PLEASE USE A NO. 2 LEAD PENCIL TO MARK THIS FORM**
0 1 2 3 4 [ ] 5 6 7 8 9	PSYCHOLOGICAL SCREENING PROCEDURES ARE MUCH LIKE GENERAL PHYSICAL
0 1 2 3 4 [ ] 5 6 7 8 9	EXAMINATIONS, EXCEPT THAT THEY ARE INTENDED TO REVEAL MENTAL RATHER THAN
0 1 2 3 4 [ ] 5 6 7 8 9	PHYSICAL SYMPTOMS. TWO SUCH PROCEDURES HAVE BEEN INCORPORATED INTO
0 1 2 3 4 [ ] 5 6 7 8 9	OPERATION HEAD START, A SYMPTOM CHECKLIST AND A CHILD DESCRIPTION
0 1 2 3 4 [ ] 5 6 7 8 9	CHECKLIST. BOTH SHOULD BE COMPLETED BY THE HEAD TEACHER AFTER SHE HAS BEEN
	ACQUAINTED WITH HER PUPILS FOR AT LEAST FOUR WEEKS.

1. SYMPTOM CHECKLIST   MARK EACH OF THE BEHAVIORS LISTED IN THIS SECTION WHICH HAVE <u>CHARACTERIZED</u> THIS CHILD'S BEHAVIOR THROUGHOUT HIS ATTENDANCE IN YOUR CLASS. IF A BEHAVIOR OCCURRED ONLY ONCE OR TWICE DO NOT MARK IT.

1. SELFISH OR GREEDY HOARDING OF OWN AND OTHER CHILDREN'S PLAYTHINGS OR CLASSROOM MATERIALS.
2. REFUSES TO EAT OR DRINK.
3. HOLDS BREATH UNTIL LOSES TYPICAL COLORING OR UNTIL DIZZY OR FAINT.
4. TEMPER TANTRUM IN WHICH THROWS SELF ABOUT OR DOWN, CRIES, SCREAMS, HITS FLOOR, ETC.
5. TEMPER TANTRUM IN WHICH VIOLENTLY ATTACKS OTHER CHILDREN OR ADULTS OR DESTROYS PROPERTY.
6. BANGS HEAD AGAINST HARD OBJECT, BITES HIMSELF, SCRATCHES HIMSELF, PULLS OUT OWN HAIR, OR OTHERWISE ABUSES SELF.
7. BITES OTHER CHILDREN OR ADULTS IN ANGER.
8. PLACES FOREIGN OBJECTS IN SOME BODY OPENING OTHER THAN THE MOUTH; FOR EXAMPLE, ROCKS IN EARS, PENCIL IN NOSE.
9. STUTTERS OR STAMMERS TO POINT THAT IT IS DIFFICULT TO UNDERSTAND HIM.
10. FAINTS OR PASSES OUT.
11. COMPLAINS OF PAINS IN HEAD OR STOMACH.
12. INTERESTED IN ONLY ONE OR TWO OBJECTS OR ACTIVITIES. REFUSES TO PARTICIPATE OR SEEMS DISINTERESTED IN OTHER THINGS OR ACTIVITIES.
13. CRIES EXCESSIVELY OR BECOMES VERY ANXIOUS OR WITHDRAWN WHEN MILDLY REPRIMANDED.
14. FREQUENTLY WANDERS OR RUNS AWAY FROM NURSERY.
15. WILL NOT FEED SELF.
16. ALMOST CONSTANT THUMB-SUCKING.
17. EXCESSIVE CLINGING TO SOME OBJECT(BLANKET, CLOTH, SOFT ANIMAL, OR OTHER TOY).
18. ASKS TO BE CALLED BY SOME NAME OTHER THAN OWN AND REFUSES TO ANSWER TO OWN NAME.
19. NEEDS EXCESSIVE PROMPTING AND CONSTANT REASSURANCE TO TRY SOMETHING NEW; BECOMES VERY ANXIOUS IN NEW SITUATIONS.
20. CONSTANTLY CRITICIZES SELF AND OWN PRODUCTIONS.
21. OFTEN CRIES OR LAUGHS SUDDENLY FOR NO APPARENT REASON.
22. SHOWS NO INTEREST IN PLAYING WITH OR BEING ACCEPTED BY OTHER CHILDREN.
23. CANNOT COMMUNICATE WITH SPOKEN LANGUAGE.
24. OFTEN SITS ROCKING BACK AND FORTH.
25. SAD OR FRIGHTENED FOR MOST OF THE DAY.
26. AUDIBLE CLAMPING OR GRINDING OF TEETH.
27. FEAR OF URINATING OR MOVING BOWELS.
28. COMPLETE INABILITY TO INTERACT WITH STRANGERS.

DO NOT MARK IN THIS SPACE

29. UNABLE TO REMAIN SEATED FOR MORE THAN FIVE MINUTES AT
    A TIME (AS WHEN EATING OR BEING READ TO).   **OVER**

30. SEVERAL WEEKS AFTER INITIAL PARTICIPATION IN OPERATION
    HEAD START, STILL CRIES OR BECOMES DEPRESSED WHEN MOTHER LEAVES.
                          CAP-HS FORM 40 JUN. '65

OPERATION HEAD START BEHAVIOR INVENTORY

CHILD'S NAME: _____ SCHOOL: _____

CHILD'S IDENTIFICATION NUMBER

0 ==== 1 ==== 2 ==== 3 ==== 4 ==== 5 ==== 6 ==== 7 ==== 8 ==== 9 ====
0 - ·· 1 ==== 2 ==== 3 ==== 4 ==== 5 ==== 6 ==== 7 ==== 8 ==== 9 ====
0 ==== 1 ==== 2 ==== 3 ==== 4 ==== 5 ==== 6 ==== 7 ==== 8 ==== 9 ====
0 ==. 1 ==== 2 ==== 3 ==== 4 ==== 5 ==== 6 ==== 7 ==== 8 ==== 9 ====
0 ==== 1 ==== 2 ==== 3 ==== 4 ==== 5 ==== 6 ==== 7 ==== 8 ==== 9 ====
0 ==== 1 ==== 2 ==== 3 ==== 4 ==== 5 ==== 6 ==== 7 ==== 8 ==== 9 ====

EXAMINER IDENTIFICATION NUMBER

0 ==== 1 ==== 2 ==== 3 ==== 4 ==== 5 ==== 6 ==== 7 ==== 8 ==== 9 ====
0 ==== 1 ==== 2 ==== 3 ==== 4 ==== 5 ==== 6 ==== 7 ==== 8 ==== 9 ====
0 ==== 1 ==== 2 ==== 3 ==== 4 ==== 5 ==== 6 ==== 7 ==== 8 ==== 9 ====
0 ==== 1 ==== 2 ==== 3 ==== 4 ==== 5 ==== 6 ==== 7 ==== 8 ==== 9 ====
0 ==== 1 ==== 2 ==== 3 ==== 4 ==== 5 ==== 6 ==== 7 ==== 8 ==== 9 ====
0 ==== 1 ==== 2 ==== 3 ==== 4 ==== 5 ==== 6 ==== 7 ==== 8 ==== 9 ====

CENTER IDENTIFICATION NUMBER

0 ==== 1 ==== 2 ==== 3 ==== 4 ==== 5 ==== 6 ==== 7 ==== 8 ==== 9 ====
0 ==== 1 ==== 2 ==== 3 ==== 4 ==== 5 ==== 6 ==== 7 ==== 8 ==== 9 ====
0 ==== 1 ==== 2 ==== 3 ==== 4 ==== 5 ==== 6 ==== 7 ==== 8 ==== 9 ====
0 ==== 1 ==== 2 ==== 3 ==== 4 ==== 5 ==== 6 ==== 7 ==== 8 ==== 9 ====
0 ==== 1 ==== 2 ==== 3 ==== 4 ==== 5 ==== 6 ==== 7 ==== 8 ==== 9 ====
0 ==== 1 ==== 2 ==== 3 ==== 4 ==== 5 ==== 6 ==== 7 ==== 8 ==== 9 ====
0 ==== 1 ==== 2 ==== 3 ==== 4 ==== 5 ==== 6 ==== 7 ==== 8 ==== 9 ====

BUDGET BUREAU NO. 116—6504
APPROVAL EXPIRES 3—31—66

INSTRUCTIONS

PLEASE DESCRIBE AS ACCURATELY AS POSSIBLE HOW THIS CHILD BEHAVES BY MARKING, WITH A NO. 2 LEAD PENCIL, ONE OF THE FOUR RESPONSES TO EACH QUESTION:

VERY MUCH LIKE   SOMEWHAT LIKE   VERY LITTLE LIKE   NOT AT ALL LIKE

PLEASE GIVE A RESPONSE TO EVERY ITEM AND BASE YOUR RESPONSE UPON YOUR PERSONAL OBSERVATION AND EXPERIENCE WITH THE CHILD.

	VERY MUCH LIKE	SOME-WHAT LIKE	VERY LITTLE LIKE	NOT AT ALL LIKE
1. IS USUALLY CAREFREE; RARELY BECOMES FRIGHTENED OR APPREHENSIVE.				
2. IS SYMPATHETIC, CONSIDERATE, AND THOUGHTFUL TOWARD OTHERS.	====	====	====	====
3. IS EASILY DISTRACTED BY THINGS GOING ON AROUND HIM.	====	====	====	====
4. IS VERY SUGGESTIBLE; LETS OTHER CHILDREN BOSS HIM AROUND.	====	====	====	====
5. TALKS EAGERLY TO ADULTS ABOUT HIS OWN EXPERIENCES AND WHAT HE THINKS.	====	====	====	====
6. IS UNDULY UPSET OR DISCOURAGED IF HE MAKES A MISTAKE OR DOES NOT PERFORM WELL.	====	====	====	====
7. OFTEN KEEPS ALOOF FROM OTHERS BECAUSE HE IS UNINTERESTED, SUSPICIOUS, OR BASHFUL.	====	====	====	====
8. DEFENDS OR PRAISES HIS OWN EFFORTS.	====	====	====	====
9. IS CONFIDENT THAT HE CAN DO WHAT IS EXPECTED OF HIM.	====	====	====	====
10. IS JEALOUS; QUICK TO NOTICE AND REACT NEGATIVELY TO KINDNESS AND ATTENTION BESTOWED UPON OTHER CHILDREN.	====	====	====	====

	VERY MUCH LIKE	SOME-WHAT LIKE	VERY LITTLE LIKE	NOT AT ALL LIKE
11. IS METHODICAL AND CAREFUL IN THE TASKS THAT HE UNDERTAKES.				
12. IS RARELY ABLE TO INFLUENCE OTHER CHILDREN BY HIS ACTIVITIES OR INTERESTS.	====	====	====	====
13. TRIES TO FIGURE OUT THINGS FOR HIMSELF BEFORE ASKING ADULTS OR OTHER CHILDREN FOR HELP.	====	====	====	====
14. GREATLY PREFERS THE HABITUAL AND FAMILIAR TO THE NOVEL AND THE UNFAMILIAR.	====	====	====	====
15. APPEARS TO TRUST IN HIS OWN ABILITIES.	====	====	====	====
16. HAS LITTLE RESPECT FOR THE RIGHTS OF OTHER CHILDREN; REFUSES TO WAIT HIS TURN, USURPS TOYS OTHER CHILDREN ARE PLAYING WITH, ETC.	====	====	====	====
17. SEEMS DISINTERESTED IN THE GENERAL QUALITY OF HIS PERFORMANCE.	====	====	====	====
18. RESPONDS TO FRUSTRATION OR DISAPPOINTMENT BY BECOMING AGGRESSIVE OR ENRAGED.	====	====	====	====
19. IS EXCESSIVE IN SEEKING THE ATTENTION OF ADULTS.	====	====	====	====
20. STICKS WITH A JOB UNTIL IT IS FINISHED.	====	====	====	====

PRESENT WEEK OF CENTER'S OPERATION

==1== ==2== ==3== ==4== ==5==   ==6== ==7== ==8== ==9==

DO NOT MARK IN THIS SPACE

OVER

© by Edward Zigler, 1965   CAP-HS FORM 37, JUN. '65

OPERATION HEAD START BEHAVIOR INVENTORY

18MH92217

	VERY MUCH LIKE	SOME-WHAT LIKE	VERY LITTLE LIKE	NOT AT ALL LIKE
21. GOES ABOUT HIS ACTIVITIES WITH A MINIMUM OF ASSISTANCE FROM OTHERS.				
22. IS CONSTRICTED , INHIBITED , OR TIMID; NEEDS TO BE URGED BEFORE ENGAGING IN ACTIVITIES.	=====	=====	=====	=====
23. IS EVEN-TEMPERED, IMPERTURBABLE; IS RARELY ANNOYED OR CROSS.	=====	=====	=====	=====
24. IS RELUCTANT TO TALK TO ADULTS; RESPONDS VERBALLY ONLY WHEN URGED.	=====	=====	=====	=====
25. WORKS EARNESTLY AT HIS CLASSWORK OR PLAY; DOESN'T TAKE IT LIGHTLY.	=====	=====	=====	=====
26. IS OFTEN QUARRELSOME WITH CLASSMATES FOR MINOR REASONS.	=====	=====	=====	=====
27. DOES NOT NEED ATTENTION OR APPROVAL FROM ADULTS TO SUSTAIN HIM IN HIS WORK OR PLAY.	=====	=====	=====	=====
28. WHEN FACED WITH A DIFFICULT TASK, HE EITHER DOES NOT ATTEMPT IT OR GIVES UP VERY QUICKLY.	=====	=====	=====	=====
29. DOESN'T LIKE TO BE INTERRUPTED WHEN ENGAGED IN DEMANDING ACTIVITIES, E. G., PUZZLES, PAINTING, CONSTRUCTING THINGS.	=====	=====	=====	=====
30. WELCOMES CHANGES AND NEW SITUATIONS; IS VENTURESOME, EXPLORES, AND GENERALLY ENJOYS NOVELTY.	=====	=====	=====	=====

	VERY MUCH LIKE	SOME-WHAT LIKE	VERY LITTLE LIKE	NOT AT ALL LIKE
31. CALMLY SETTLES DIFFICULTIES THAT ARISE WITHOUT APPEAL TO ADULTS OR OTHERS.				
32. IS RELUCTANT TO USE IMAGINATION; TENDS NOT TO ENJOY "MAKE-BELIEVE" GAMES.	=====	=====	=====	=====
33. LIKES TO TALK WITH OR SOCIALIZE WITH TEACHER.	=====	=====	=====	=====
34. OFTEN WILL NOT ENGAGE IN ACTIVITIES UNLESS STRONGLY ENCOURAGED.	=====	=====	=====	=====
35. IS EAGER TO INFORM OTHER CHILDREN OF THE EXPERIENCES HE HAS HAD.	=====	=====	=====	=====
36. EMOTIONAL RESPONSE IS CUSTOMARILY VERY STRONG; OVER-RESPONDS TO USUAL CLASSROOM PROBLEMS, FRUSTRATIONS, AND DIFFICULTIES.	=====	=====	=====	=====
37. IS UNCOOPERATIVE IN GROUP ACTIVITIES.	=====	=====	=====	=====
38. IS USUALLY POLITE TO ADULTS; SAYS "PLEASE," "THANK YOU," ETC.	=====	=====	=====	=====
39. ASKS MANY QUESTIONS FOR INFORMATION ABOUT THINGS, PERSONS, ETC. (EMPHASIS HERE SHOULD BE ON QUESTIONS PROMPTED BY GENUINE CURIOSITY RATHER THAN BIDS FOR ATTENTION.)	=====	=====	=====	=====
40. USUALLY DOES WHAT ADULTS ASK HIM TO DO.	=====	=====	=====	=====

	VERY MUCH LIKE	SOME-WHAT LIKE	VERY LITTLE LIKE	NOT AT ALL LIKE
41. REQUIRES THE COMPANY OF OTHER CHILDREN; FINDS IT DIFFICULT TO WORK OR PLAY BY HIMSELF.				
42. RESPONDS TO FRUSTRATION OR DISAPPOINTMENT BY BECOMING SULLEN, WITHDRAWN, OR SULKY.	=====	=====	=====	=====
43. DEMONSTRATES IMAGINATIVENESS AND CREATIVITY IN HIS USE OF TOYS AND PLAY MATERIALS.	=====	=====	=====	=====
44. INSISTS ON MAINTAINING HIS RIGHTS, E. G., WILL NOT YIELD HIS PLACE AT PAINTING, OR AT THE CARPENTRY BENCH, ETC.; INSISTS ON GETTING HIS TURN ON THE SLIDE OR IN GROUP GAMES, ETC.	=====	=====	=====	=====
45. IS WANTED AS A PLAYMATE BY OTHER CHILDREN.	=====	=====	=====	=====
46. IS LETHARGIC OR APATHETIC; HAS LITTLE ENERGY OR DRIVE.	=====	=====	=====	=====
47. HAS A TENDENCY TO DISCONTINUE ACTIVITIES AFTER EXERTING A MINIMUM OF EFFORT.	=====	=====	=====	=====
48. IS GENERALLY A HAPPY CHILD.	=====	=====	=====	=====
49. APPROACHES NEW TASKS TIMIDLY AND WITHOUT ASSURANCE; SHRINKS FROM TRYING NEW THINGS.	=====	=====	=====	=====
50. WHAT HE DOES IS OFTEN IMITATED BY OTHER CHILDREN.	=====	=====	=====	=====

DO NOT MARK IN THIS SPACE

PARENT EVALUATION OF OPERATION HEAD START

BUDGET BUREAU NO. 116-6510
APPROVAL EXPIRES 6-1-66

CENTER IDENTIFICATION NUMBER

0	1	2	3	4		5	6	7	8	9
0	1	2	3	4		5	6	7	8	9
0	1	2	3	4		5	6	7	8	9
0	1	2	3	4		5	6	7	8	9
0	1	2	3	4		5	6	7	8	9
0	1	2	3	4		5	6	7	8	9
0	1	2	3	4		5	6	7	8	9

TO THE PARENTS: WE WOULD LIKE TO KNOW WHETHER YOU FEEL THAT YOU AND YOUR CHILD HAVE PROFITED FROM PROJECT HEAD START. WE ARE PARTICULARLY INTERESTED IN KNOWING WHAT THINGS YOU LIKED AND WHAT THINGS YOU DID NOT LIKE. THE INFORMATION FROM THIS FORM WILL BE USED TO MAKE FUTURE HEAD START PROGRAMS MORE EFFECTIVE.

THIS EVALUATION IS TO BE DONE WITHOUT PERSONAL IDENTIFICATION. PLEASE DO NOT WRITE YOUR NAME ON THE FORM. THE ONLY IDENTIFYING MARK SHOULD BE THE CHILD DEVELOPMENT CENTER NUMBER, WHICH THE HEAD START CENTER STAFF WILL PROVIDE.

PLEASE USE A NO. 2 PENCIL TO MARK THIS SHEET
COMPLETE BOTH SIDES OF THIS FORM

I. FORMAL CONTACT AND PARTICIPATION

MY REACTIONS TO THE FOLLOWING WERE:

	VERY MUCH WORTHWHILE	WORTHWHILE	OCCASIONALLY WORTHWHILE	WASTE OF TIME	NOT IN THE PROGRAM
1. TALKING WITH CHILD'S TEACHERS.					
2. MEETING WITH OTHER PARENTS.					
3. SPEAKING WITH PARENT-COUNSELOR OR SOCIAL WORKERS.					
4. SPECIAL EVENTS:					
DISCUSSION ABOUT a. CHILD CARE					
b. HOMEMAKING SKILLS					
c. HOUSING CONDITIONS					
d. EMPLOYMENT OPPORTUNITIES					
e. PERSONAL PROBLEMS					
5. GROUP TRIPS IN THE COMMUNITY					
6. FILMS SHOWN IN CONNECTION WITH THE PROGRAM					
7. OTHER (PLEASE SPECIFY ACTIVITY IN LOWER LEFT CORNER OF FORM)					

II. THE CHILD

MY REACTIONS TO THE EXPERIENCES MY CHILD HAS HAD IN THE OPERATION HEAD START PROGRAM ARE:

	VERY MUCH WORTHWHILE	WORTHWHILE	OCCASIONALLY WORTHWHILE	WASTE OF TIME	NOT IN THE PROGRAM
1. MEDICAL EXAMINATION					
2. DENTAL EXAMINATION					
3. OPPORTUNITY TO ATTEND SCHOOL AT AN EARLY AGE.					
4. INCREASED EXPERIENCE WITH A VARIETY OF TOYS AND GAMES.					
5. INCREASED EXPERIENCE WITH A VARIETY OF BOOKS, STORIES, AND MUSIC.					
6. TRIPS INTO THE COMMUNITY.					
7. INDIVIDUAL ATTENTION GIVEN TO EACH CHILD BY TEACHER AND AIDES.					
8. OPPORTUNITY TO PARTICIPATE IN GROUP ACTIVITIES WITH OTHER CHILDREN.					

AS A RESULT OF ATTENDING THE OPERATION HEAD START PROGRAM, MY CHILD WAS AFFECTED IN THE FOLLOWING WAYS:

	MUCH BETTER	BETTER	NO CHANGE	WORSE	MUCH WORSE
1. GETTING ALONG WITH OTHER CHILDREN					
2. SELF-CONFIDENCE					
3. SPEAKING ABILITY					
4. EVERYDAY MANNERS					
5. FINISHING WHAT HE STARTS					
6. DOING WHAT HE IS TOLD					
7. INTERESTED IN NEW THINGS					
8. CAN DO THINGS ON HIS OWN					

OVER

PLEASE SPECIFY OTHER FORMAL CONTACTS AND PARTICIPATIONS

_____
_____
_____
_____

DO NOT MARK IN THIS SPACE

© by Edward Zigler, 1965   IBMH92222   CAP-HS FORM 41 JUN. '65

PARENT EVALUATION OF OPERATION HEAD START

111. THE HOME (a)

CHECK ANY OF THE FOLLOWING WHICH APPLY AS A RESULT OF YOUR CONTACT WITH
OPERATION HEAD START:

1. MY HUSBAND OR I HAVE BEEN HELPED BY SOME SOCIAL AGENCY.

2. MY HUSBAND OR I RECEIVED MEDICAL AND/OR DENTAL ATTENTION.

3. A CHILD (OTHER THAN THE ONE(S) ENROLLED IN OPERATION HEAD START) RECEIVED MEDICAL AND/OR DENTAL ATTENTION.

4. MOVED TO BETTER LIVING QUARTERS.

5. REPAIRED OR ADDED THINGS, e.g., FURNITURE, NEW CURTAINS, ETC., TO MY PRESENT LIVING QUARTERS.

6. A FAMILY MEMBER GOT A JOB OR SWITCHED TO A BETTER JOB.

7. MY HUSBAND OR I PLAN TO CONTINUE OUR OWN EDUCATION.

8. MY HUSBAND OR I HAVE SOUGHT LEGAL AID AND/OR FINANCIAL ASSISTANCE.

111. THE HOME (b)	MUCH MORE	MORE	A LITTLE MORE	NOT AT ALL
1. AM AWARE OF NEW THINGS THAT MY FAMILY AND I CAN DO IN THE COMMUNITY.				
2. FEEL THAT THE COMMUNITY CARES ABOUT ME AND MY PROBLEMS.				
3. HAVE LEARNED NEW THINGS ABOUT RAISING CHILDREN.				
4. HAVE BEEN GIVEN NEW IDEAS ABOUT HOW TO TAKE CARE OF MY FAMILY.				
5. FEEL HOPEFUL ABOUT MY CHILDREN'S FUTURE.				
6. FEEL BETTER ABLE TO HANDLE FAMILY ARGUMENTS THAT ARISE.				
7. MADE NEW FRIENDS.				

DO NOT MARK IN THIS SPACE

IBMH92223

appendix four

SELECTED BIBLIOGRAPHY

I. Essential books for the coordinator

Baruch, Dorothy. *Parents and Children Go to School,* Chicago: Scott Foresman and Co., 1939.

Gesell, A. *Child Development,* N.Y.: Harper and Row, 1949.

Hammond, Sarah Lou, and others. *Good Schools for Young Children,* N.Y.: McMillan, 1963.

II. Education of the disadvantaged child

Bloom, Benjamin S., Allison Davis, and Robert Hess. *Compensatory Education for Cultural Deprivation.* New York: Holt, Rinehart and Winston, 1965.

Davis, W. A. and John Dollard. *Children of Bondage: The Personality Development of Negro Youth in the Urban South.* New York: American Council on Education, 1941.

Greene, Shirley. *The Education of Migrant Children.* Washington, D.C.: National Education Association, The Department of Rural Education, 1954.

Havighurst, Robert J. et al. *Growing Up in River City.* New York: John Wiley & Sons, 1962.

Hunt, J. McV. "The Psychological Basis for Using Preschool enrichment as an Antidote for Cultural Deprivation," *Merrill-Palmer Quarterly,* Vol. 10 (July, 1964), 209–248.

Information Retrieval Center on the Disadvantaged. Vol. I, Number 2 Issue March, 1965, "Preschool Educational Programs," New York: Ferkauf Graduate School of Education.

John, Vera P. "The Intellectual Development of Slum Children: Some Preliminary Findings," *American Journal of Orthopsychiatry,* Vol. 33 (1963), 813-822.

Journal of Negro Education. "Educational Planning for Socially Disadvantaged Children and Youth." Vol. XXXIII (Summer, 1964).

Montague, D. O. "Arithmetic Concepts of Kindergarten Children in Contrasting Socio-Economic Areas," *Elementary School Journal,* Vol. 64 (1964), 393–397.

Passow, A. Harry, Editor. *Education in Depressed Areas.* New York: Teachers College, Columbia University, 1963. [359 pp.]

Sutton, Elizabeth. *Knowing and Teaching the Migrant Child.* Washington, D.C.: National Education Association, Department of Rural Education, 1962.

III. Child development

A. *Language Development*

Bellugi, Ursula and Roger Brown. *The Acquisition of Language.* Monographs of the Society for Research in Child Development. Vol. 29, No. 1. Serial No. 92, 1964.

Bernstein, Basil. "Language and Social Class," *British Journal of Sociology,* Vol. 11 (1960), 271-276.

Bingham, Alma. *Improving Children's Facility in Problem Solving.* New York: Teachers College, Columbia University, 1958.

Bruner, Jerome, Jacqueline Goodnow, and George Austin. *A Study of Thinking.* 5th printing. New York: John Wiley & Sons Inc. 1961.

Church, Joseph. *Language and the Discovery of Reality.* New York: Random House, 1961.

Ervin, Susan M. and Wick R. Miller. "Language Development," *Child Psychology.* Sixty-second Yearbook, National Society for the Study of Education. Chicago: University of Chicago Press, 1963. Chapter 3.

Flavell, John H. *The Developmental Psychology of Jean Piaget.* Princeton, New Jersey: D. Van Nostrand Co., Inc., 1963.

Fowler, William. "Cognitive Learning in Infancy and Early Childhood," *Psychological Bulletin,* Vol. 59 (1962), 116-52.

Herrick, V. & Jacobs, L. *Children and the Language Arts.* Englewood Cliffs: Prentice-Hall, 1955.

Inhelder, Barbara and B. Matalon. "The Study of Problem Solving and Thinking," in Paul Mussen, editor, *Handbook of Research in Child Development.* New York: Wiley, 1960. pp. 421-455.

Irwin, O. C. "Language and Communication," pp. 487-516, in *Handbook of Research Methods in Child Development,* edited by Paul H. Mussen. New York: John Wiley & Sons, 1960.

Isaacs, Susan. *Intellectual Growth in Young Children.* New York: Harcourt, Brace & Co., 1930.

John, Vera P. and Leo S. Goldstein. "The Social Context of Language Acquisition," *Merrill-Palmer Quarterly,* Vol. 10 (July, 1964), 266-275.

Jones, Harold E. "Environmental Influences on Mental Development," pp. 582-632 in *Manual of Child Psychology,* edited by Leonard Carmichael. New York: John Wiley and Sons, Inc., 1946.

Lewis, M. M. *Language, Thought and Personality in Infancy and Childhood.* New York: Basic Books, Inc., Publishers, 1963.

McCarthy, Dorothea, "Language Development in Children," pp. 476-581, in *Manual of Child Psychology,* edited by Leonard Carmichael. New York: John Wiley & Sons, Inc., 1946.

Noel, Doris. "A Comparative Study of the Relationship Between the Quality of a Child's Language Usage and the Quality and Types of Language Used in the Home," *Journal of Educational Research.* Vol. 47: March, 1953, 161-67.

Russell, David H. *Children's Thinking.* Boston: Ginn and Company, 1956.

Wann, Kenneth D., Miriam S. Dorn, and Elizabeth Ann Liddle. *Fostering Intellectual Development in Young Children*. New York: Bureau of Publications, Teachers College, Columbia University, 1962.

Watts, A. F. *The Language and Mental Development of Children*. Boston: D. C. Heath and Company, 1948.

Wright, John C. and Jerome Kagan. *Basic Cognitive Processes in Children*. Monograph of the Society for Research in Child Development. Serial No. 68, 1963. Vol. 28, Number 2.

B. *Research and Theory*

Almy, Millie. *Ways of Studying Children*. New York: Bureau of Publications, Teachers College, Columbia University, 1959.

Erikson, Erik H. *Childhood and Society*. 2nd edition. Revised and enlarged. New York: Norton, 1963.

Freud, Anna and Dorothy Burlingham. *Infants Without Families*. New York: International Universities Press, 1944.

Gabriel, John. *Children Growing Up*. London: University of London Press Ltd. 1964.

Hoffman, Martin L. and Lois V. Hoffman. *Review of Child Development Research*. Vol. I. New York: Russell Sage Foundation, 1964.

Isaacs, Susan. *Social Development in Young Children*. New York: Harcourt, Brace & Co., 1933.

Jersild, Arthur T. *Child Psychology*. Fifth Edition. Englewood Cliffs, New Jersey: Prentice-Hall, Inc., 1960.

Josselyn, Irene M. *Psychosocial Development of Children*. New York, New York: Family Service Association of America. No date.

National Society for the Study of Education. *Child Psychology*. Sixty-second Yearbook. Chicago, Illinois: University of Chicago Press, 1963, Ch. II "Sociological Correlates of Child Behavior;" Ch. III "Language Development;" Ch. IV "Research on Children's Thinking;" Ch. VII "Moral Development and Identification;" and Ch. XII "Developmental Theory in Transition."

Palermo, David S. and Lewis P. Lipsitt. *Research Readings in Child Psychology*. New York: Holt, Rinehart and Winston, Inc., 1963.

Schaffer, Rudolph H. and Peggy E. Emerson. *The Development of Social Attachments in Infancy*. Monographs of the Society for Research in Child Development. Serial No. 94, 1964. Vol. No. 29, No. 3.

Sears, Robert R. "Relation of Early Socialization Experiences to Aggression in Middle Childhood," *Journal of Abnormal Social Psychology*. LXXXX (1961), 466–92.

Seidman, Jerome, editor. *The Child: A Book of Readings*. New York: Holt, Rinehart and Winston, 1958.

C. *Self-concept and Learning*

ASCD. *Perceiving, Behaving, Becoming*. Yearbook. Washington, D.C. ASCD. 1962.

Bledsoe, J. C., and Garrison. *The Self-Concepts of Elementary School Children in Relation to Academic Achievement, Intelligence, Interest and Manifest Anxiety*. University of Georgia. Athens, 1962.

Cattell, R. R., Radcliff, J., and Sweeney, A. B. "The Nature and Measurement of the Components of Motivation," *Genetic Psychology Monographs*. 68: 49–211. 1963.

Combs, Charles Franklin. *A Study of the Relationship Between Certain Perceptions of Self and Scholastic Underachievement in Academically Capable High School Boys.* Doctoral Dissertation. Syracuse University. Dissertation Abstract. 63–5034. 1963, pp. 620-21.

Foote, N., and Cottrell, L. *Identity and Interpersonal Competence.* Chicago: University of Chicago Press, 1955.

Havighurst, R. J., Robinson, Myra, and Dorr, Mildred. "The Development of the Ideal Self in Childhood Adolescence," *Journal Educational Research.* 40, 1946, 241-57.

Jersild, A. *Child Psychology.* Prentice-Hall, Englewood Cliffs, New Jersey. 1964.

Lamy, Mary W. *Relationship of Self-Perceptions of Early Primary Children to Achievement in Reading.* Doctoral Dissertation. University of Florida. Dissertation Abstracts. 63–5796. 1962, p. 628.

Staines, J. W. "The Self Picture as a Factor in the Classroom," *British Journal of Educational Psychology.* 28:97-111. June, 1958.

Trager, Helen, and Yarrow, Marion. *They Learn What They Live: Prejudice in Young Children.* New York: Harper and Brothers, 1952.

Wylie, Ruth. *The Self-Concept. A Control Survey of Pertinent Literature.* University of Nebraska Press. Lincoln, 1961.

D. *Sociology of Child Development*

Davis, W. A. and Havighurst, R. J. *Father of the Man.* Boston: Houghton, Mifflin Co., 1947.

Elkin, Frederick. *The Child and Society.* New York: Random House, 1961.

Kneller, George F. *Educational Anthropology.* New York: John Wiley and Sons, Inc., 1965.

Ritchie, Oscar and Marion R. Koller. *Sociology of Childhood.* New York: Appleton-Century-Crofts, 1964.

Schiller, Johannes A. and Robert K. Leik. "Symbolic Interaction and Family Role Adjustment," *Pacific Sociological Review.* Vol. 6 (Spring, 1963), 30–36.

Shibutani, Tamotsu. *Society and Personality.* Englewood Cliffs, New Jersey: Prentice-Hall, Inc. 1961.

Thomas, Alexander et al. *Behavioral Individuality in Early Childhood.* New York: New York University Press, 1963.

IV. Early childhood education

A. *Teacher Certification and Professionalization*

ACEI Teacher Education Committee. "Standards for Teachers in Early Childhood Education," *Child Education 35,* 2. 1958, 65–66.

Bliss, Leora. "Certification of Teachers in Nursery Schools and Day Care Centers," *Child Education 34*: 6, 1958, 275–78.

Council of Chief State School Officers: *Responsibilities of State Department of Education for Nursery School and Kindergarten, A Policy Statement,* NEA, Washington, D.C., 1961.

Moustakas, C., and Berson, Minnie. *A Directory of Nursery Schools and Child Care Centers in the U. S.,* Detroit: Merrill-Palmer, 1951.

B. *Physical Facilities, Equipment, and Supplies*

Association for Childhood Education International:
Equipment and supplies, ACEI, Washington, D.C., 1957. *Creating with materials for work and play, Leaflet 5.* ACEI, Washington, D.C., 1957.

Recommended Equipment and Supplies for Nursery, Kindergarten, Primary, and Intermediate Schools, General Service Bulletin No. 39. Washington, D.C.: ACEI. (no date)

Bureau of Child Development and Parent Education, *Suggested Equipment for Four- and Five-Year-Old Kindergarten Children.* Albany, New York, 1948.

Franklin, Adele. "Blocks—A Tool of Learning," *Child Education 26,* 5, 1950, 209–13.

Heffernan, Helen, in *Nursery—Kindergarten Education,* edited by Leavitt, J., New York: McGraw-Hill, 1958.

McConkie, Gwen, and Hughes, Marie. "Quality of Classroom Living Related to Size of Kindergarten Group," *Child Education,* 32: 9, 1956, 428–32.

Todd, Vivian, and Heffernan, Helen. *The Years Before School.* New York: MacMillan, 1964.

C. *General References*

Baruch, Dorothy, *Parents and Children Go to School.* Chicago: Scott-Foresman, 1939.

Burgess, Evangeline. *Values in Early Childhood Education.* Second edition. Washington, D.C.: Department of Elementary - Kindergarten - Nursery Education, 1965.

California State Department of Education. *Teachers Guide to Education in Early Childhood.* Sacramento: California State Department of Education, 1956.

Christianson, Helen M., Mary M. Rogers, and Blanche Ludlum. *The Nursery School.* Boston: Houghton Mifflin Company, 1961.

Fuller, Elizabeth Mechem. *Values in Early Childhood Education.* Washington, D.C.: Department of Kindergarten - Primary Education, National Education Association, 1960.

Heffernan, Helen and Vivian Edmiston Todd. *The Kindergarten Teacher.* Boston: D. C. Heath and Company, 1960.

Hammond, Sarah Lou, and others, *Good Schools for Young Children.* New York: The Macmillan Company, 1963.

Isaacs, Susan. *The Nursery Years.* New York: Vanguard Press, 1929.

Lambert, Hazel. *Teaching the Kindergarten Child.* New York: Harcourt, Brace and Company, 1958.

Logan, Lillian M. *Teaching the Young Child.* Boston: Houghton Mifflin Company, 1960.

Moore, Elenora Haegele. *Fives at School.* New York: G. P. Putnam's Sons, 1959.

Moore, Sally Beth, and Phyllis Richards. *Teaching in the Nursery School.* New York: Harper & Row, 1959.

Moustakas, Clark E. and Minnie Berson. *The Young Child in School.* New York: William Morrow and Company, 1956.

Pitcher, Evelyn Goodenough and Louise Bates Ames. *The Guidance Nursery School.* New York: Harper & Row, Publishers, 1964.

Read, Katherine H. *The Nursery School.* Philadelphia: W. B. Saunders Company, 1960.

Sears, Pauline S. and Edith Dowley. "Research on Teaching in the Nursery School," *Handbook of Research on Teaching,* edited by Nathaniel L. Gage. Chicago: Rand McNally & Co., 1963.

Todd, Vivian, and Heffernan, Helen. *The Years Before School: Guiding Pre-school Children.* New York: McMillan, 1964.

V. Parent education

Baruch, Dorothy. *New Ways in Discipline.* New York: Appleton - Century - Crofts; 1949.

Baruch, Dorothy. *Parents and Children Go to School.* Chicago: Scott-Foresman, 1939.

Bigelow, H. *Family Finance.* Philadelphia: Lippencott, 1953.

Duvall, Evelyn. *Family Development.* Philadelphia: Lippincott, 1962.

Green, Marjorie, and Woods, Elizabeth. *A Nursery School Handbook for Teachers and Parents.* Sierra Madre, California: Sierra Madre Community Nursery School Assn., 1955.

Gruenberg, Sidone. *The Wonderful Story of How You Were Born.* Garden City, New York: Hanover House, 1952.

Guttmacher, A. *Babies by Choice or by Chance,* Garden City, New York: Doubleday, 1959.

Hereford, Carl F. *Changing Parental Attitudes through Group Discussion.* Austin, Texas: University of Texas Press, 1963.

Kohn, Melvin. "Social Class and Parental Values," *American Journal of Sociology.* LXIV (Jan. 1959), 337–51.

Newton, Niles. *Family Book of Child Care.* New York: Harpers, 1957.

Smart, Mollie and Russell, *Living and Learning with Children.* Boston: Houghton-Mifflin, 1956.

Spock, B. *The Pocketbook of Baby and Child Care,* New York: Pocket Books, Inc., 1946.

Rainwater, L. *And the Poor Get Children.* Chicago: Quadrangle Books, 1960.

POVERTY IN THE UNITED STATES

Selected Bibliography

Compiled by Donna Levine
Education and Public Welfare Division
The Library of Congress
Legislative Reference Service

A. Books

Bagdikian, Ben H. *In the Midst of Plenty; the Poor in America*. Boston: Beacon, 1964.

Bremner, Robert H. *From the Depths: the Discovery of Poverty in the United States*. New York: New York University Press, 1956.

Caplovitz, David. *The Poor Pay More: Consumer Practices of Low-income Families*. New York: Free Press of Glencoe, 1963.

Clark, Henry. *The Christian Case Against Poverty*. New York: Association Press, 1965.

Dunne, George H., *ed. Poverty in Plenty*. New York: P. J. Kennedy, 1964.

Galbraith, John Kenneth. *The Affluent Society*. Boston: Houghton Mifflin, 1958.

Harrington, Michael. *The Other America*. New York: Macmillan, 1962.

Humphrey, Hubert H. *War on Poverty*. Toronto, New York: McGraw-Hill, 1964.

Hunter, David H. *The Slums: Challenge and Response*. New York: Free Press of Glencoe, 1964.

Kolko, Gabriel. *Wealth and Power in America*. New York: Praeger, 1962.

May, Edgar. *The Wasted Americans*. New York: Harper and Row, 1963.

Miller, Herman P. *Income of the American People*. Published for the Social Science Research Council in cooperation with the Bureau of the Census, U. S. Department of Commerce. New York: Wiley, 1955.
——. *Rich Man, Poor Man: A Study of Income Distribution in America*. New York: T. Y. Crowell, 1964.

Morgan, James N. [et al.] *Income and Welfare in the United States*. New York: McGraw-Hill, 1962.

Myrdal, Gunnar. *Challenge to Affluence*. New York: Pantheon, 1962.

Riessman, Frank, *et al., eds. Mental Health of the Poor: New Treatment Approaches for Low-Income People*. London: Free Press of Glencoe, 1964.

Sexton, Patricia Cayo. *Spanish Harlem: Anatomy of Poverty*. New York: Harper and Row, 1965.

Shostak, Arthur B. and William Gombert, *eds. New Perspectives on Poverty*. Englewood Cliffs, N. J.: Prentice-Hall, 1965.

Will, Robert H. and Harold G. Vatter, *eds. Poverty in Affluence: The Social, Political, and Economic Dimensions of Poverty in the United States*. New York: Harcourt, Brace, and World, 1965.

B. Pamphlets, monographs, government prints

American Enterprise Institute. Legislative Analysis: The revised "War on Poverty" bill. Washington, 1964. (88th Cong., 2d sess. Report no. 7, June 22, 1964)

American Public Welfare Association. "Poverty"—Selected reading references. Chicago, 1964.

Bird, Alan R. Poverty in rural areas of the United States. Washington, U. S. Department of Agriculture, Economic Research Service, Resource Development Economics Division, 1964. (Agricultural economic report no. 63)

California. *State Office of Planning*. Poverty in California, a staff memorandum. Sacramento, 1964.

Chamber of Commerce of the United State of America. *Task Force on Economic Growth and Opportunity*. The concept of poverty. Washington: The Chamber, 1965.

Community Council of Greater New York. *Research Department*. Poverty in New York City: selected facts for planning community action. New York, 1964.

Keyserling, Leon H. Poverty and deprivation in the United States: The plight of two-fifths of a nation. Washington, Conference on Economic Progress, 1962.

———. Progress or poverty: The U.S. at the crossroads. Washington, Conference on Economic Progress, 1964.

MacIntyre, Duncan M. Public assistance: too much or too little? Ithaca, N.Y.: New York State Schools of Industrial and Labor Relations, Cornell University, 1964. (Bulletin 53-1, December 1964: The dimensions of poverty and its remedies, 1)

Massachusetts. *Governor's Conference on State-local Relations, 1964*. Massachusetts surveys its poverty: proceedings of the Sixteenth Governor's Conference on State-local Relations, June 1964. Amherst, Mass.; Bureau of Government Research, University of Massachusetts, 1964.

Oppenheim, Micha F. The culturally deprived; a bibliography. New York, National Conference of Christians and Jews, Lazrus Library of Intergroup Relations, 1964.

Radomski, Alexander L. and Anita U. Mills. Family income and related characteristics among low-income counties and States. Washington: U.S. Department of Health, Education and Welfare, Welfare Administration, Division of Research, 1964. (Welfare research report no. 1)

Shriver, R. Sargent. *Poverty*. New York: Americana Corporation, 1965.

Stewart, Maxwell S. *The Poor Among Us—Challenge and Opportunity*. New York: Public Affairs Pamphlets, 1964. (Pamphlet no. 362)

U.S. *Attorney General's Committee on Poverty and the Administration of Criminal Justice*. Report . . . submitted to the Hon. Robert F. Kennedy, Attorney General of the United States, February 1963. Washington, 1963.

U.S. *Congress. House. Committee on Education and Labor*. Economic

Opportunity Act of 1964 . . . 88th Cong, 2d sess. Washington: U.S. Govt. Print. Off., 1964.

——. ——. ——. Economic Opportunity Act of 1964. Hearings before the Subcommittee on the War on Poverty Program . . . 88th Cong., 2d sess., on H.R. 10440 . . . 3 parts. Washington: U.S. Govt. Print. Off., 1964.

——. ——. ——. Economic Opportunity Act of 1964; report to accompany H.R. 11377. Washington: U.S. Govt. Print. Off., 1964. (88th Cong., 2d sess. House. Report no. 1458)

——. ——. ——. Economic Opportunity Amendments of 1965; report to accompany H.R. 8283. Washington: U.S. Govt. Print. Off., 1965. (89th Cong., 1st sess. House. Report no. 428)

——. ——. ——. Subcommittee on the War on Poverty. Examination of the war on poverty program. Hearings. 89th Cong., 1st sess. on examination of the facts which have developed under the Administration of the act. Washington: U.S. Govt. Print. Off., 1965.

——. ——. ——. Poverty in the United States . . . 88th Cong., 2d sess. Washington: U.S. Govt. Print. Off., 1964. (Committee print)

——. Joint Committee on the Economic Report. Characteristics of the low-income population and related Federal programs. Staff report. Washington: U.S. Govt. Print. Off., 1955.

——. ——. Low-income families. Hearings before the Subcommittee on Low-Income Families; 84th Cong., 1st sess. Washington: U.S. Govt. Print. Off., 1955.

——. Joint Economic Committee. Low-income population and economic growth, by Robert J. Lampman, and the adequacy of resources for economic growth in the United States, by Joseph L. Fisher. Washington: U.S. Govt. Print. Off., 1959. (Its study papers no. 12 and 13)

——. ——. The distribution of personal income. A study of statistics on the size distribution of personal income in the Unted States, prepared for use of the Subcommittee on Economic Statistics by T. Paul Schultz. Washington: U.S. Govt. Print. Off., 1965.

——. Senate. Committee on Labor and Public Welfare. Economic Opportunity Act of 1964. Hearings before the Select Subcommittee on Poverty . . . 88th Cong., 2d sess. on S. 2642 . . . Washington: U.S. Govt. Print. Off., 1964.

——. ——. ——. Economic Opportunity Act of 1964. Report . . . to accompany S. 2642. Washington: U.S. Govt. Print. Off., 1964. (88th Cong., 2d sess. Senate. Report no. 1218)

——. ——. ——. The war on poverty: The Economic Opportunity Act of 1964; a compilation of materials relevant to S. 2642, prepared for the Select Subcommittee on Poverty . . . Washington: U.S. Govt. Print. Off., 1964. (Committee print)

U.S. Department of Commerce. Bureau of the Census. Low-income families, 1960. Washington: U.S. Govt. Print. Off., 1964. (Its Supplementary reports no. PC(S.1) - 43)

U.S. Department of Health, Education, and Welfare. Welfare Administration. A constructive public welfare program; a report . . . on recent Federal legislation to aid States and communities in dealing with poverty and other social problems. Washington, 1965.

——. ——. Office of Juvenile Delinquency and Youth Development.

Conference proceedings: the extension of legal services to the poor, November 12-14, 1964. Washington, 1965.

U.S. *Laws, statutes, etc.* Public Law 88-452, 88th Cong., S. 2642, August 20, 1964. Washington: U.S. Govt. Print. Off., 1964.

U.S. *Office of Economic Opportunity.* Community Action Program guide: instructions for developing, conducting and administering a Community Action Program, as authorized by Sections 204 and 205 of Title II-A, Economic Opportunity Act of 1964. Volume I. Instructions for applicants. Washington: 1965.

————. The first step on a long journey. 2 vols. Congressional presentation, April 1965. Washington, 1965.

————. An invitation to help Project Head Start: a program for preschool children. Washington, 1965.

————. Job Corps facts. Washington, 1964.

————. The war on poverty—a hometown fight. Washington, 1964.

U.S. *President (Johnson).* Poverty, message from the United States relative to poverty, and a draft of a bill to mobilize the human and financial resources of the nation to combat poverty in the United States. Washington: U.S. Govt. Print. Off., 1964. (88th Cong., 2d sess. House. Document no. 243)

————. War against poverty. Communication of the President of the United States, transmitting certain recommendations regarding the war against poverty. Washington: U.S. Govt. Print. Off., 1965. (89th Cong., 1st sess. House. Report no. 90)

U.S. *President's Committee on Consumer Interest.* The most for their money; a report of the Panel on Consumer Education for persons with limited incomes. Washington: U.S. Govt. Print. Off., 1965.

U.S. *President's Task Force on Manpower Conservation.* One-third of a nation. Washington: U.S. Govt. Print. Off., 1964.

Washington Center for Metropolitan Studies. A selective bibliography of writings on poverty in the United States. Washington, 1964.

C. Articles

Chilman, Catherine S. "Child-rearing and Family Relationship Patterns of the Very Poor," *Welfare in Review,* v. 3, (January 1965), 9-19.

Coll, Blanche D. "Deprivation in Childhood: Its Relation to the Cycle of Poverty," *Welfare in Review,* v. 3, (March 1965), 1-10.

Frankel, Marvin E. "Experiments in Serving the Indigent," *American Bar Association Journal,* v. 51, (May 1965), 460-464.

Friedman, Milton. "Poverty: a Direct Approach," *Context,* a University of Chicago magazine, v. 2, (Winter 1964), 1-3.

Froomkin, Joseph. "The Poor Program," *Columbia University Forum,* v. 8, (Spring 1965), 35-38.

Galbraith, John Kenneth. "Let Us Begin: an Invitation to Action on Poverty," *Harper's Magazine,* v. 228, (March 1964), 17-26.

Knoll, Erwin *and* Jules Witcover. "Fighting Poverty—and City Hall," *Reporter,* v. 32, (June 3, 1965), 19-22.

Lees, Hannah. "VISTA: a New Kind of Public Service," *Reporter,* v. 32, (April 22, 1965), 31-32.

Orshansky, Mollie. "Children of the poor," *Social Security Bulletin,* v. 26, (July 1963), 3-13.

Richmond, Charlotte. "The Job Corps: What It is and How It Works," *Occupational outlook quarterly,* v. 9, (February 1965), 7–11.

Riessman, Frank. "The Lessons of Poverty," *American Education,* v. 1, (February 1965), 21–23.

Riessman, Frank *and* Arlene Hannah. "The Poverty Movement," *Columbia University Forum,* v. 6, (Fall 1963), 28–32.

Silberman, Charles E. "Give Slum Children a Chance: a Radical Proposal." *Harper's Magazine,* v. 228, (May 1964), 37-42.

U.S. *Congress. House.* "Economic Opportunity Act of 1964. Debate." *Congressional Record* (daily ed.), v. 110, (August 5, 1964), 17617-17652: (August 6, 1964), 17672-17739; (August 7, 1964), 17972-18025.

———. ———. "Economic Opportunity Amendments of 1965. Debate." *Congressional Record* (daily ed.), v. 111, (July 20, 1965), 16851-16912; (July 21, 1965), 16947-16996; (July 23, 1965), 17270-17321.

———. *Senate.* "Economic Opportunity Act of 1964. Debate." *Congressional Record* (daily ed.), v. 110, (July 22, 1964), 16055-16069, 16072-16091, 16101-16110; (July 23, 1964), 16142-16170, 16178-16197, 16199-16244.

Witmer, Helen L. "Children and poverty," *Children,* v. 2, (November - December 1964), 207-213.

Wolfe, Deborah P. "What the Economic Opportunity Act Means to the Negro," *Journal of Negro Education,* v. 34, (Winter 1965), 88-92.

"World Poverty and the Christian," *Commonweal,* v. 81, (November 13, 1964), 215-237.

appendix five

SUGGESTED FILMS FOR HEAD START WORKERS

A Chance at the Beginning (29 minutes, black and white).
How preschool experience can help compensate the child from the disadvantaged cultural background to help him educationally.
Anti-Defamation League of B'nai B'rith, 315 Lexington Ave., New York, N.Y. 10016 (or regional office nearest you).

Children Without (30 minutes, black and white). National Education Association.
How teachers and counselors help children in Detroit public Schools who are without parental love, care, and basic needs.
Modern Talking Picture Services, Inc., Concourse Shop #7, 10 Rockefeller Plaza, New York, N.Y. 10020.

The Dropout (29 minutes, black and white). ABC.
What are the real causes of dropouts? What can be done?
International Film Bureau, 332 South Michigan Avenue, Chicago 4, Illinois.

The Hard Way (60 minutes, black and white). NETV.
The one-fifth of the U. S. population who can not reach the ladder of mobility and opportunity.
NET Film Service, Audio-Visual Center, Indiana University, Bloomington, Indiana 47405.

Harvest of Shame (54 minutes, black and white). CBS.
The tragedy of the migrant workers.
Audio-Visual Center, Florida State University, Tallahassee, Fla.; University of California, Berkeley, Calif., and others.

Incident on Wilson Street (50 minutes, black and white). NBC.
A case history approach to helping the underprivileged child which shows much promise.

A Morning for Jimmy. (28 minutes, black and white). National Urban League.
A true story of a young Negro boy who encounters racial discrimination and is caught in the conflict of "not trying" because it won't do any good to try to study and make something of himself. Shows actual on-the-spot jobs.

Association Films, 347 Madison Avenue, New York, N.Y. 10017.
California State Department of Mental Hygiene.

The Pine School (27 minutes, black and white).
The Portrayal of a research and demonstration project working with low-income families and their mentally retarded children.
University of Iowa, Extension Division, Ames, Iowa.

The Road Ahead (28 minutes, black and white). National Urban League.
The story of thousands of young people all over the country who find that they lack the training and skills needed to maintain a responsible job.
Association Films, 347 Madison Avenue, New York, N.Y. 10017.

Small Miracles (15 minutes, black and white).
A VISTA film showing the work of volunteers involving the poor in poverty programs.
VISTA, Washington, D. C. 20506.

Superfluous People (54 minutes, black and white).
A CBS documentary telling the story of modern urban poverty, its major causes and effects.
Audio-Visual Center, Penn State University, University Park, Penna.; University of Illinois, Champagne, Ill.; Florida State University, Tallahassee, Fla., and others.

Teaching of the Culturally Disadvantaged Child Film Series (18 minutes, black and white). McGraw-Hill.
Portrait of a Disadvantaged Child: Tommy Knight introduces viewer to special needs and special strengths of the inner city child.
Portrait of the Inner City shows streets, schools, and living quarters in the inner city of a large, but nameless, urban community in the United States, and suggests techniques of communication between the school and the community.
Portrait of the Inner City School: "A Place to Learn" shows how school can be a place for the inner city child to learn and grow toward maturity, or a place of confinement where the child is forced into failure and frustrations.
Audio-Visual Center, Florida State Univ., Tallahassee, Fla.; New York University, New York, N.Y.; University of Michigan, Ann Arbor, Mich.

Walk in My Shoes (42 minutes, black and white). ABC.
Many Negroes from all walks of life speak as individuals and in groups about how racial prejudice looks to them.
Anti-Defamation League of B'nai B'rith, 315 Lexington Ave., New York, N.Y. 10016.

When I'm Old Enough, Goodbye (25 minutes, black and white).
A film portraying with sensitivity and depth, some of the behavioral dynamics associated with the needs of some adolescents to leave school and find work.
State Employment Services, everywhere in the U.S.A. Free.

Films on Head Start: Procedure, Program and Promise
A film catalog illustrating film strips and movies based on the contents of this book may be obtained from: The Film Centre, 189 N. Wheeler, Orange, California.

AUDIO VISUAL MATERIALS BASED ON HEAD START IN ACTION

Head Start in Action (Color.)

A film strip in color depicting the outstanding sequences from this book. Accompanying record with narration based on text. Excellent for public relations, parents, community groups, clubs, and training classes.

For sale only from The Film Center, 189 North Wheeler, Orange, California.

Parent Education (Color.)

Series of film strips based on Chapter 10 of *Head Start in Action,* "Parent Education." Narration based on text with illustrative slides of actual Head Start children, personnel and events. For parents, teachers personnel, students and volunteers.

TOPICS: 1. How Children Grow and Learn
               2. Helping Your Child Talk Better
               3. Health Education for Preschoolers
               4. Good Nutrition for Preschoolers
               5. Creative Experiences for Children

For sale only from The Film Centre, 189 North Wheeler, Orange, California. *FILM*

From Inner-City to Mountain Ranch. (Color, 20 minutes.)

A full length feature film of Head Start children and their families on a visit to a ranch-like summer camp which creates a farm experience for campers.

Delta Sigma Theta's Head Start innovated by taking Head Start children *and their* families to the country. In the film, we see them arrive via bus, somberly inspect farm animals, romp through open fields, picnic under gnarled oak trees, ride horseback, boat on a calm lake, splash in a pool, and gaze at an open fire, expanding their senses and their world.

Filmed to depict the expanding sensory experiences the city child enjoys on the farm, this movie is excellent for both children and adults, either in the Head Start Center or in any educational setting.

For sale only from The Film Centre, 189 North Wheeler, Orange, California.

index